MEMOIRS OF AN ARABIAN PRINCESS.

MEMOIRS OF AN ARABIAN PRINCESS FROM ZANZIBAR

BY
EMILY RUETE

Born Salme, Princess of Oman and Zanzibar

with a new introduction by
Patricia W. Romero

 **Markus Wiener Publishers**
Princeton

Third Printing 2000

© 1989 by Patricia W. Romero for the introduction
© 1989 by Markus Wiener Publishers for the modernized and corrected translation.

For information write to:
Markus Wiener Publishers
231 Nasssau Street, Princeton, NJ 08542

Library of Congress Cataloging-in-Publication Data

Ruete, Emilie, 1844-1924.
    Memoirs of an Arabian Princess from Zanzibar.
    (Topics in World History)
    Translation of: Memoirs einer arabischen Prinzessin.
    Originally published: Memoirs of an Arabian princess.
  New York: D. Appleton, 1888.
  ISBN 1-55876-011-3 (hc)   ISBN 1-55876-007-5 (pb)
    1. Ruete, Emilie, 1844-1924. 2. Zanzibar—History—to 1890.
  3. Zanzibar—Princes and princesses—Biography.
  I. Title.   II. Series
DT449.Z275R83713   1989   89-9064
967.8'103'092 [B]   CIP

Cover Design: Cheryl Mirkin
Cover Photos: The Palace of Syed Said at Mtony (in background);
and Salme, Princess of Zanzibar and Oman

Printed in The United States of America on acid-free paper

INTRODUCTION
BY PATRICIA W. ROMERO

This is a remarkable memoir. It was written in German in the 1880s after Salme Saīd (Emily Ruete), raised as a Muslim princess in Zanzibar, had converted to Christianity, married a German merchant-trader, and lived a long life of unhappy widowhood in exile in Germany, raising her three children on her own.

Salme wrote her autobiography because, as she says in her preface, she wanted her children to know something about the Eastern civilization from which she came. What she did not add is that she also needed the money. Her limited income was provided by the German government. Some of it may have come from trusts established after her husband's death, and doled out to her under a guardianship established for the purpose. As a woman in nineteenth century Europe, Salme had less control over her financial affairs than she had enjoyed in the Muslim world of Zanzibar.

Although it is necessary to elaborate on and at times correct Seyyida Salme's recollections, it is also imperative to recognize that *Memoirs of an Arabian Princess* is a document without parallel in nineteenth-century Indian Ocean/East African history. Few people in Zanzibar could read or write Arabic or Swahili, the languages of the island. For a Zanzibar woman to be educated was unusual indeed; Salme, in an amusing passage, speaks of her sisters who hired scribes and induced friends to write their letters to Oman. Salme may have been the only woman of her generation on that island who could both read and write,[1] and is certainly the only one to have left a personal memoir, providing us with a fascinating glimpse into the world of the harem.

While she was not her father's favorite daughter, Salme enjoyed a close relationship with him— as did all of her sisters. This, too, was unusual for the Arab world of her time. The girls, and Salme especially, engaged in hearty outdoor activities that are not in keeping with the stereotypes of housebound and veiled Muslim women. They learned to ride horseback and made excursions to the small agricultural plots in the center of Zanzibar island. They played games and seemed to have moved freely within the context of palace life in the houses by the sea, as well as those they occupied in Zanzibar town.

In her memoir, Salme tells us about the lives of women in her class, giving the impression that women had much more power over their lives than is commonly assumed about Middle Eastern women. Perhaps some of the liberated lifestyle can be attributed to the frontier situation of Zanzibar, as opposed to Muscat in Oman, from which the royal family moved before Salme was born. Seyyid Saīd's official wife, the heavy-handed stepmother to whom Salme refers in the early portion of her memoir, exercised authority not only over her own home, but seemingly over

[1] Neither Oman nor Zanzibar was representative in this respect of the centers of 19th-century Islamic culture, where many women were highly educated.

her husband as well. Then there are the wives
Salme discusses who divorce—not an option open
to most women in the Muslim world. The picture
we get of life in the harem is skewed, no doubt,
through eyes clouded by the passing years; yet, it
seems clear from the examples Salme presents
that the royal women of Zanzibar were not altogether excluded from areas usually reserved for
men in the Muslim world of the Middle East.

The question of the age at which women could
exercise authority is confused in the memoir.
Salme says she received her inheritance at twelve,
and was upgraded to the status of adult so she
could manage her own affairs. This seems quite
unlikely, and in actual fact she was sixteen at the
time. For reasons that are unclear, Salme seems to
have adjusted her age downward by four years
throughout her memoir. Perhaps the best clue to
why is the old admonition that a man is as old as
the number of years since he was born, but a
woman is the age she says she is.

Her father, Seyyid Saīd BuSaīd, was a much
admired ruler during his lifetime. He came to
power by a route all too common among aspirants
to the Sultanate in Oman: he murdered the cousin
who had earlier usurped his throne. While the
political squabbles in Oman are of little relevance
to Salme's life, we need to sketch in the background in order to give her story some perspec-
tive.

Oman had long had ties to the East African
coast, from Mozambique to Somalia, since she
routed the Portuguese from the areas in the late
1600s. From the end of the Portuguese occupation until Saīd's relocation, Omani rule was
mostly maintained by appointed governors, and
by occasional forays from Muscat to put down

uprisings, especially on the northern coastal islands. The old Omani fort was built in 1700—
during a period of rather constant occupation—
and from that time on, soldiers occupied
Zanzibar in the name of Omani rulers.

Mombasa, an island next to the African main-
land, had been held, nominally for Oman, by the
Mazrui family who, by the late eighteenth century, had come to consider themselves an independent dynasty. When Mombasa joined the
island city-state of Pate in a war against its neigh-
bor, Lamu, the Lamu town leaders turned to
Oman for military support. Saīd used the occasion not only to aid Lamu, which then became a
client, but to bring Mombasa back under his
control by overthrowing the Mazrui clan.

Zanzibar, and its neighboring island of Pemba,
also under the suzerainty of Oman, were especially suitable to the production of cloves,
sugar cane, and coconuts. The slave trade
reached its zenith in the early nineteenth century,
bringing increasing numbers of slaves to work the
plantations of Zanzibar and Pemba—and large
sums of money into the Sultan's coffers since he
charged customs fees on each slave who passed
through his ports. The slaves were transported in
caravans from Central Africa overland to East
African harbors, which were under the control of
Omani rulers, and then shipped out to the Red
Sea and Indian Ocean ports.

Trade with the East African coast brought
more than slaves: ivory and hides were profitable
commodities, as were the mangrove poles which
came from the Rufiji delta in present-day Tan-
zania and the northern coastal islands. The slave
trade, which has indirect bearing on Salme's life
and on the history of Zanzibar through the period

of her autobiography, had begun at that time to suffer the consequences of British interference with Omani-Zanzibari politics. Geopolitical considerations in the Omani-Indian Ocean nexus forced Sultan Saīd to submit to one small concession after another. The end result was the gradual elimination of the slave trade. Conscious of how much the profits from the trade enriched his own royal purse, as well as the agents and traders who served him, Saīd submitted to each restriction reluctantly. Some rumors at the time suggested that the British privately paid him a substantial sum of money in order to gain their desired anti-slave trade treaties.

The costs of jewels, silks, expensive weapons, and other luxuries described by Salme in this autobiography seem to substantiate these rumors. A German missionary describes his wife's visit to the harem in 1846—six years after Salme was born:[2]

> I was not allowed. [My wife was] conveyed to a large room upstairs, which, she says, was splendidly furnished with European articles. His daughters were richly dressed according to Arab fashion and behaved very respectfully in the presence of the Sultan. When he stood, they stood, and when he sat down, they sat down. They were masked from the forehead to the mouth. . . The room was furnished with large mirrors, couches and chairs of all kinds: and tables covered with various articles of luxury of European extraction.

The luxury in which they lived did not exhaust the Sultan's resources; he left a huge estate, which his son, Madjid, distributed among the surviving

[2]Mr. Krapf quoted in Sir John Grey, *The History of Zanzibar* (London, 1962), p. 190.

sons and daughters according to the dictates of
Islam (less for the daughters than the sons). In
fact, since the private and public purses were
intermingled in the Sultan's finances, British
sources of the time reported that Madjid was hard
pressed to pay the inheritances and still keep the
Zanzibar economy afloat—this means, of course,
that the inheritances were very large.

At the time Salme was born, Zanzibar was already under considerable British influence. The
British government, in this period, ran its Indian
Ocean operations from Bombay. As time passed,
however, they opened a consular office in Aden,
and later spread their operations to East Africa
from the consulate established in Zanzibar. But
the British were not the only foreigners on the
island. German traders representing Hamburg
merchants lived in the foreign quarter of the city
alongside American and French traders and even,
briefly, a Russian merchant (representing a
French trading company).

As a frontier town, Zanzibar was primitive by
comparison with the European cities from which
the merchants came. Stone houses linked to one
another along narrow dirt roadways provided
housing, but sanitary was sadly lacking. Salme
herself tells us that in the royal palaces an area of
the courtyard was set aside as a slaughterhouse so
that all animals could be killed in accordance
with the Muslim faith (throats slit and blood
drained before cutting them up).

James Christie, who visited Zanzibar in mid–
century, described the rubbish and "filth swept to
the sea by . . . torrents [with] animal droppings
everywhere. After streets were laid out, there
were only superficial efforts to sweep, and cows
and sheep penned near houses [with] no attempts

to remove the accumulated manure." Garbage
and rubbish piled up among the ruins of the old
houses with "myriads of ants and beetles, millions
of rats and armies of wild dogs."[3] Early in her
book, Salme talks about the dread diseases of
smallpox and cholera.

By 1842, although the numbers of stone houses
had multiplied, no efforts were made to connect
the island internally. The state carriage sent that
year by Queen Victoria went unused. There were
no roads to drive it on. In order to move about
the island, inhabitants traveled by boat. Salme,
as well of speaking of inland travel by horseback
and donkey, makes mention of the use of boats—
yet she never explains their necessity to her European readers.

In the opening of her memoir, Salme describes
the palace she and her mother occupied during
the earliest period of her life. According to former Zanzibari residents now living in coastal East
Africa, there were many large old stone houses
scattered around the island, almost all built near
the sea. The houses seem to have preceded Seyyid
Saīd's move to Zanzibar, but one Salme mentions,
The House of Wonders in Zanzibar town, was
possibly built for his use, or perhaps comman-
deered from local wealthy families as need arose.

Salme and her mother moved several times during her youth, always to homes described as palaces, though one suspects the title was assigned to
any large house the royal family occupied. Some
were small, as she describes them; others, especially those occupied by her father, quite spacious.

[3] James Christie, *Cholera Epidemics in East Africa*
(London, 1876), p. 154.

Although Salme presents harem life as generally harmonious, she reverses herself on occasion—especially in the passages dealing with her brother, Madjid and his wife and sister, Khadudj. Salme and her mother moved from their seafront home to Madjid's, enjoying the patronage not only of Madjid himself, but a favorite sister with whom he lived. Salme mentions in several instances that Madjid was not well, but never tells us he suffered from epilepsy. When he married and the marriage proved unhappy, Salme assigns the blame to the jealous controlling Khadudj, rather than the more obvious problem of his frequent fits. However, Arab sisters are notorious for acting as troublemakers between their brothers and their wives, so Salme's memories may not be entirely incorrect.[4]

Jealousies were also rampant among concubines (after giving birth called sarari, which meant they had equal status with legal wives). Saintly though Salme's mother is made to appear, she could not have been unaware that the move first to town, and later to the Sultan's residence, presented better opportunities for herself and her daughter.

In 1854, when Salme was fourteen, her father was called back to Oman. The return trip was not initially motivated by problems with the Persians (as she contends) but was the result of the unrest of a religious group in Oman. Seyyid Saïd returned to aid his regent son, Tuēni. Later, having settled the local dispute, Saïd did engage in combat with the Persians, and so was away from Zanzibar much longer than originally intended. The years of his absence are remembered by

[4] Rula Ghani, in a personal communication, Baltimore, March 10, 1989.

Salme as times of loneliness and preparations for her father's return. While these memories are no doubt true as far as they go, surely the death of her brother, Khalid, the Zanzibari regent, must have been more distressing than the mere mention of his demise suggests. This is but another example of selective memory—and the need to glorify her father, the Sultan, at the expense of others.

Again, if we accept 1840 as her birth year, Salme was sixteen when her father died on the way home from Oman. At sixteen, she would have been considered adult—in fact, by that age most girls of her class were married. It is possible she expected Saīd to bring someone from Oman for her to marry; or perhaps she was unwed due to his absence and inability to arrange a marriage for her in Zanzibar. She tells us how she managed her considerable inheritance, but she does not tell us that she sold off large portions of it at the time of her departure from Zanzibar. At the end of her memoir, she refers to her property having been confiscated during her absence, and describes attempts to regain it for her children.

When her father died in 1856, he was succeeded by Madjid, the next son in line. The sultanship was also divided between Zanzibar and Oman with Tuēni, the Omani descendants retaining undivided income and control over the Gulf country; and the Zanzibari family dividing the spoils there. Tuēni's reactions to his father's death were not as dispassionate and remote as Salme would have us believe in her autobiography. Realizing that Zanzibar was more profitable than Oman, Tuēni led a force from Oman with the idea of invading and taking over Zanzibar. Before he reached Zanzibar, the British again intervened, working out a financial settlement which provided a yearly subsidy from Zanzibar to Oman, and further crippling the economic situation in Zanzibar.

Prior to Tuēni's threat, however, Madjid was forced to deal with rebellion from within the ranks of his own Zanzibari family. Bargash, the next in line for the throne, had been with Saīd in Oman and was on board ship when his father died. Bargash knew Madjid was subject to epileptic fits, and no doubt had, in addition, his share of the Saīd greed for the throne. Soon after his return, Bargash hatched a plot with several Zanzibari families and gained the support of some members of his own family—including his sister Khole, who was also close to Salme. Salme describes the intrigue, the discovery, and the eventual intercession of the British, which resulted in Madjid successfully hanging on to the throne while Bargash and a younger brother went into exile in India. As a traitor to Madjid, Salme's role is amply described in the text.

Ironically, although Madjid was forced to turn to the British consul for aid in putting down both Bargash's attempted revolution and the potential invasion from Oman, he also managed to play a game of cat and mouse with the British regarding the slave trade. Though handicapped by illness, Madjid was clever. Through circumlocution and deviousness, he and his family continued to benefit from the trade—mainly working through the French and Madjid's Indian agents. On a further note of irony, it was Bargash who finally succumbed to British pressure and in 1873 signed a treaty totally prohibiting the slave trade, incidentally bringing Zanzibar further into British orbit.

Perhaps, as she suggests, the gentle Madjid did forgive Salme for betraying him, but the fact remains that by the mid-1860s, now in her twenties, she was still unmarried. Either there were other problems she doesn't tell us about, or Madjid refused to find her a suitable husband, revenge for her collaboration with Bargash in the attempted coup. Salme took matters into her own hands by beginning a covert courtship with a German merchant, Heinrich Ruete, whose Zanzibar residence was located close to hers; from their houses they were said to have talked regularly.

Her memoirs are so sketchy about her romance with Ruete that for information we are confined to the rumors which emanated from the European community resident in Zanzibar at the time. Salme seems to have established more than a passing flirtation with Ruete if, as rumor suggested, she did indeed become pregnant. According to reports, after realizing she was pregnant, Salme quickly sold off her possessions, and arranged through the British consul for a berth on a steamship sailing to Aden. One of her slaves accompanied Ruete and Salme to the ship, and then after her departure gossiped about her "delicate condition"—thus providing a plausible reason for her hasty departure by stealth.

Salme tells us that Madjid allowed Ruete to tie up his affairs and leave Zanzibar as soon as the monsoon winds made sailing east possible. In the meantime, Salme converted to Christiantity and was baptized while still in Aden—in the Anglican faith, and not the Lutheran or Catholic church to which the German Ruete must have belonged.

Ruete joined her, and they were married on the spot—giving further credence to the rumors. She gave birth to a child every year, beginning soon after her marriage. Her two daughters and one son were raised as Christians in Germany. Unfortunately, Heinrich Ruete died soon after the last child was born, leaving Salme alone and widowed in a strange land. One can empathize with her increasing nostalgia for her family back in Zanzibar. And one can appreciate the BuSaīd family memories of the "disgrace" she brought on them by, first, her illegitimate pregnancy (a crime punishable by death in some Arab societies), and then her marriage to a Christian.

Her German years appear to have been for the most part unhappy, although she does not provide much detail. Whatever relations she enjoyed with her in-laws go undiscussed, but she did not stay long in Hamburg. It is when her brother, Bargash, now Sultan of Zanzibar, comes to England to ratify the slave trade treaty, in 1873, that Salme delves once more into detail.

Bargash's trip to England coincides with Europe's awakening to other possibilities for Africa. Germany had been unified in 1870 under the able leadership of Otto von Bismarck, and, while not yet conquest-minded, merchants were aware of potential trading possibilities in areas like East Africa. England and France were vying for territories, and their armies were marching against African foes in various parts of the continent. Salme is sketchy about how Bargash's English trip might have been regarded by the Germans and about her role, if any, as a German agent.

It seems likely that she saw her brother's trip to Europe as an opportunity to reestablish relations with him, and indirectly with the family from whom all ties had been cut since she left Zanzibar in the mid-1860s. Salme would have been opposed to the slave trade treaty. The fear that "Emily Ruete" might try to exercise undue influence on

Bargash to reject the treaty was no doubt the reason Sir Bartle Frere, a staunch anti-slavery man, intervened to cut her off from all contact with her brother. Whether to keep out foreign influence (if in fact she was acting as a German agent), or to be assured the treaty was ratified without interference, the British government played a shabby role in this affair.

On the other hand, Bargash himself offered no hospitality to his sister on her return to Zanzibar. That voyage, made by German warship, may have been regarded as political; it is difficult to know just how much influence the British exercised over Bargash in Zanzibar at the time of her visit. Her experience as pariah to the family was somewhat mitigated when she was able to speak with a few friends; and the sympathy displayed by family and former slaves alike provided a bit of comfort. Her children, who accompanied her, never got to know their Eastern family—and thus the original reason for her memoir.

The final pages of her autobiography were written in the aftermath of the painful return from Zanzibar, and in equally painful recognition that the rest of her life would be spent in Germany. Now she cares less about the "faithful picture of a foreign nation" she attempted to paint after years of separation and longing. Seyyida Salme, a tragic figure at this point, requests her readers to "bear a friendly memory for one whose life has already gathered so rich a store of changes and vicissitudes." Having read her story, we can not but do as we are bid.

Patricia W. Romero
Towson State University
Baltimore, March 1989

AUTHOR'S PREFACE

Nine years ago I made up my mind to write down some sketches of my life for my children, who at that time knew little more about my origin than that I was an Arabian and a native of Zanzibar. Tired out in body and in mind, I did not then expect to live to be able to tell them, when they had grown up, of the many changes in my life, and of the recollections of my youth. I therefore resolved to write my memoirs for them, and this I have done for love and devotion to my children, whose affection has been my only solace for many long and anxious years, and whose tender sympathy has kept me from despair in my heaviest troubles.

Originally, therefore, my memoirs were not intended for the general public, but for my dear children alone, to whom I desired to bequeath the same, in token of a fond mother's love, and I only yielded to the repeatedly expressed wishes of many friends in having them published now.

These pages were concluded years ago—with the exception of the last chapter, which was added recently, after a voyage I was permitted to undertake, with my children, to my old home, Zanzibar, in the course of last year.

May this book, then, go out into the world and gain as many friends as it has been my good fortune to make for myself!

Berlin, May 1886
Emily Ruete

PUBLISHER'S NOTE

Memoirs of an Arabian Princess is a unique and fascinating historical document which reflects the remarkable cultural and linguistic environment in which Salme Saīd lived. Zanzibar, famous for its spices and its slave trade, had for nearly a thousand years lured adventurers, conquerors and merchants from Persia, Arabia, India, East Africa, and Europe. Its language and culture were an ever-changing amalgam of Persian, Indian, Arabic, Swahili and, finally, British and German influences. Salme was brought up and educated in this complicated milieu, which is reflected in her multi-lingual work.

It is extremely lucky from our point of view that Salme, unlike the other female members of her household, learned how to write as well as read, and was able to provide us with this invaluable account of her life. Her education, however, was relatively rudimentary, and she left Zanzibar in early adulthood. Writing in German for a German audience many years later, and cut off from an Arabian milieu, she seems no longer able infallibly and consistently to record Arabic, Swahili and other words in the pronunciation of the local Zanzibari dialect of her youth.

The original book was printed in German Gothic type. The contemporary English translation— now only available in one Rare Book Department—mentioned no translator. In any case, the translator seems to have been unfamiliar with the German Gothic type, as well as with the Arabic language.

Since the memoir is an important historical text, as well as an exciting story, the editors have tried to make as few changes in the original version as possible. Transliterations from the Arabic have been Anglicized and modernized where the originals were misleading or inconsistent, while others have been left as they appear in the first translation in order to retain the flavor of Salme's dialect. For clarity and correctness, a small number of grammatical and syntactical changes have been made in the English text.

We would like to thank the translator Rula Ghani, for her help in emending and clarifying transliterations from the Arabic.

CONTENTS

Chapter I

BET IL MTONI

In Bet il Mtoni, the oldest of our palaces in the island of Zanzibar, I was born, and there I lived until the age of seven.

Bet il Mtoni, distant about five miles from the city of Zanzibar, lies on the sea coast, surrounded by most beautiful scenery, and quite hidden in a grove of palm and mango trees, and other gigantic specimens of tropical vegetation. The house of my birth is called "Mtoni house," after the little river Mtoni, which rises only a few miles inland, runs through the whole palace into numerous fountains, and flows directly behind the palace walls into the splendid and animated inlet which severs the island from the African continent.

Only one large-sized courtyard divides the numerous buildings of Bet il Mtoni, which, on account of their heterogeneous styles, invented as occasion required, with their numberless and puzzling passages, must be called, on the whole, ugly rather than beautiful.

I do not distinctly remember now the arrangement of the vast number of rooms these buildings contained, but I can well recall to my mind the large bathing accommodation at Bet il Mtoni. There were a dozen baths in one row at the extreme end of the courtyard, and in rainy weather these popular resorts could only be reached under the shelter of an umbrella. Apart from them lay what was called the "Persian" bath, a Turkish steam bath, whose ingenious and tasteful architecture was unequalled in Zanzibar.

Each bathing house contained two baths, five yards long by four yards wide, and just deep enough to let the water come up to the breast of a grown-up person.

These refreshing baths were a favourite resort with all people in the house; most of them stayed in them for many hours every day, to pray, sleep, work, and read there, even to take their meals; and from four o'clock in the morning till midnight they were never once empty.

On entering these bath-houses, which are all alike, two raised resting-places may be observed to the right and left for prayer and repose, which are covered with the finest coloured mats. Every other article of luxury, such as carpets, was banished from these rooms. Every Muslim (Mahometan) requires a separate and perfectly clean dress for prayers, intended only for this purpose, and which ought to be quite white. Of course this rather inconvenient religious precept is only followed by extremely devout persons.

The places of repose are separated by narrow arcades from the bath-rooms, which are all in the open air; two arched bridges of stone, with steps gradually rising, lead again to other rooms lying apart.

Each bath-room was allotted to a special set of occupants; woe to the person who did not keep within her proper bounds! A very rigorous spirit of caste ruled at Bet il Mtoni, which was observed by high and low alike.

Tall orange trees, as high as the largest cherry

trees in these parts, throve in dense rows in front of the bath-houses; their branches often sheltered us while young, when we were afraid of punishment from our excessively strict teacher.

Man and beast lived amicably together in the large courtyard, without being in the least inconvenienced by each other's presence—peacocks, gazelles, guinea-fowls, flamingoes, geese, ducks, and ostriches roamed about in perfect liberty, and were petted and fed by old and young. We children vastly enjoyed hunting out the many eggs that lay about here and there, especially the large ostrich eggs, and to hand them over to the head cook, who would reward us with presents of sweetmeats.

Twice a day, early in the morning and in the evening, all children above five years of age had riding lessons in this court from one of the eunuchs, during which the members of our little zoological garden roamed about as freely as ever. When we had made sufficient progress in this art, our father helped us mount. The boys got permission to choose a horse from the royal stud, while we girls received large white donkeys from Mesket,* which are often much more expensive than horses. Of course we were provided with a complete harness for these handsome beasts at the same time.

Our chief amusement in these family houses consisted in taking long rides, as we had neither theatricals nor concerts to entertain us. We frequently had races in the country, which as frequently ended in an accident. Once I nearly lost my life in such a race. Afraid of being overtaken by my brother Hamdān, I had paid no attention to a very large crooked cocoa tree right in my way,

*Muscat

and my forehead had almost come in contact with its stem before I had even noticed it. Quick as thought I threw myself back, and in this way mercifully escaped a horrid death.

Among the peculiarities of Bet il Mtoni were the numerous flights of stairs, which were unusually steep, and had huge steps, apparently made for a race of giants. Straight up they went, without a turning or a landing place; one's only assistance a very primitive kind of railing, which, being in constant use, needed as constant repair. I remember even now how all the people living in our wing of the house were frightened one morning when both railings of our stone staircase were found to be missing, and I am yet surprised that of the many persons passing up and down no one came to grief.

Statistics being a thing quite unknown in Zanzibar, nobody of course could tell how many people actually lived in our house. I think I do not exaggerate, however, in estimating the total number of inhabitants at Bet il Mtoni at one thousand. To understand this it must be remembered that great numbers of servants are employed in the East by all people of quality and by those who want to appear rich. At least an equal number of persons were lodged in my father's city palace, Bet il Sahel, or "Coastal House."

In the wing nearest to the sea at Bet il Mtoni were the apartments of my father, Seyyid Saîd, Imam of Mesket and Sultan of Zanzibar, and those of his principal wife, who was a distant relation of his. He resided, however, only four days a week in the country with us, and the remainder he spent in his city palace, Bet il Sahel. The title "Imam" is a religious dignity, which is but rarely conferred on a sovereign. Originally we owe this distinction to our great-grandfather Ahmed; the title has since that time been hereditary in our family, and every member of it is authorized to append it to his signature.

Being one of his younger children I only remember my father with his venerable, snow-white beard. He was above middle height, his features had a very fascinating and engaging expression, and his whole appearance commanded respect. In spite of his war-like propensities and his delight in conquest, he was a model father and sovereign. Justice he valued as the highest of all things, and in this respect he knew no difference of person, not even between one of his own sons and the lowest slave. He humbled himself before God; nor was he self-conceited and proud like so many high-born people. It happened, and not rarely either, that he would ride over by himself to the wedding of a simple slave, who had gained his regard by many years of loyal service, to offer his congratulations to the young couple in person. He always used to call me, "Old woman," as I was very fond of cold milk soup (Arabic, "farni"), which is the favourite meal of all our old and toothless people.

My mother was a Circassian* by birth, who in early youth had been torn away from her home. Her father had been a farmer, and she had always lived peacefully with her parents and her little brother and sister. War broke out suddenly, and the country was overrun by marauding bands; on their approach the family fled into an underground place, as my mother called it—she probably meant a cellar, which is not known in

*From a region in the southern part of Russia bordering on the Black Sea. Circassian women were noted for their beauty.

Zanzibar. Their place of refuge was, however, invaded by a merciless horde, the parents were slain, and the children carried off by three mounted Arnauts. One of these, with her elder brother, soon disappeared out of sight; the other two, with my mother and her little sister, three years old, crying bitterly for her mother, kept together until evening, when they too parted, and my mother never heard any more of the lost ones as long as she lived.

She came into my father's possession when quite a child, probably at the tender age of seven or eight years, as she cast her first tooth in our house. She was at once adopted as playmate by two of my sisters, her own age, with whom she was educated and brought up. Together with them she learnt to read, which raised her a good deal above her equals, who, as a rule, became members of our family at the age of sixteen or eighteen years, or older still, when they had outgrown whatever taste they might once have had for schooling. She could scarcely be called pretty, but she was tall and shapely, had black eyes, and hair down to her knees. Of a very gentle disposition, her greatest pleasure consisted in assisting other people, in looking after and nursing any sick person in the house; and I well remember her going about with her books from one patient to another, reading prayers to them.

She was in great favour with my father, who never refused her anything, though she interceded mostly for others, and, when she came to see him, he always rose to meet her half-way—a distinction he conferred but very rarely. She was as kind and pious as she was modest, and in all her dealings frank and open. She had had another daughter besides myself, who had died quite young. Her mental powers were not great, but she was very clever at needlework. She has always been a tender and loving mother to me, but this did not hinder her from punishing me severely when she deemed it necessary.

She had many friends at Bet il Mtoni, a circumstance rarely to be met with in an Arab harem. She had the most unshaken and firmest trust in God. When I was about five years old I remember a fire breaking out in the stables close by, one night while my father was at his city residence. A false alarm spread over the house that we, too, were in imminent danger; upon which the good woman hastened to take me on one arm, and her big Kurān (we pronounce the word thus) on the other, and hurried into the open air. On the rest of her possessions she set no value in this hour of danger.

My father had only one Horme (plural Harīno), or legitimate wife, at my time, as far as I recollect; his other wives, or Sarari (singular Surīe), numbering seventy-five at his death, had all been purchased by him gradually, and the former, his first wife, Azze bint Sēf, a princess of Oman by birth, reigned as absolute mistress over the household. In spite of her very small size, and of her plain exterior, she possessed an immense power over my father, who willingly submitted to all her arrangements. She treated all the other wives and their children in a very imperious, haughty, and pretentious manner; happily for us she had no children of her own, since they not have failed to be as disagreeable in their way! All my father's children, thirty-six in number, when he died, were by his Sarari, and there was consequently no difference between us.

Bibi (mistress, lady) Azze, who had to be addressed as "Highness" (Seyyīde),* was feared by old and young, by high and low, and liked by no one. Even now I remember her well, and how stiffly she used to pass by without a kind word to any one. How different was my dear old father! He talked kindly to everybody, no matter what rank the person addressed might be. My exalted stepmother knew very well how to keep her station, nor did any one dare to approach her without her own invitation or encouragement. I never saw her walk about without a retinue, except when she went with my father to the bath-house, which was set apart for their special use. All who met her in the house were as deferential to her as a recruit to his officer.

Though her imperiousness was felt very acutely by all, it had not sufficient power to deprive the residents at Bet il Mtoni of all charms of life. My brothers and sisters, of all ages, were supposed to go every day and wish her good morning; but rarely were her vanity and pride gratified by more than one visitor at the appointed time—before her breakfast hour—so greatly was she disliked by us all.

My older brothers and sisters lived at Bet il Mtoni; some of them, Shēkhe and Zuēne,* for instance, were old enough to have been my grandmothers. The latter had a son, Ali bin Sūd, whose beard had turned grey already when I knew him first; she was a widow, and had found a shelter in her paternal home after the death of her husband.

*Bibi is Swahili; Seyyīde, Arabian. Both words mean "Highness." The old spellings have mostly been retained in the text to reflect the 1880s.

*Saīd must have sired these children during his periodic visits to Zanzibar. He did not move there permanently until 1840, the year before Salme was born.

It is generally believed by Europeans that with us the sons are greatly preferred to the daughters; but such was not the case in our family. I know not a single instance in which the son was more liked by father or mother, merely because he happened to be a son. Though the law in some cases favours sons more than daughters, and grants them larger privileges—as, for instance, in the division of inheritances—yet the children are everywhere loved and treated alike. It is, of course, but natural, and only human, that in the South, as well as all over the world, one child, whether boy or girl, is secretly more beloved by his parents than the other, but this is never shown openly. It was thus with our father also; for the two of his children he loved best were not sons, but daughters, Scharīfe and Khole. When I was nine years old I was once wounded in the side by an arrow, by my wild brother Hamdām, who was about my own age; fortunately the hurt was not a severe one. As soon as my father heard of this affair, he said to me: "Salme, go and call Hamdām." And the boy was so terribly scolded for his misbehaviour, that he remembered it for a long time after. This instance proves how greatly people are often misinformed on foreign matters. It stands to reason that a good deal depends everywhere upon the children themselves, and it would wrong good children to treat them in the same way as bad ones.

The Bendjle was the prettiest spot at Bet il Mtoni. It was an immense round tower in front of the main building, and close to the sea, large enough for a ball, had such a thing been known in our country. It looked very much like a gigantic merry-go-round, with a vaulted ceiling in the same style as the building. The entire framework,

the floor, railing, and the tent-like ceiling were
constructed of painted wood. My dear father used
to walk up and down in this place for hours and
hours together, plunged in deep thought, and with
head bent down. A bullet which he received in
battle, and had settled in the hip, caused him
frequent pain, and made him limp a little.

Some dozens of cane chairs were placed all
about this lofty balcony, and a large telescope was
put up for general use. The view from this raised
Bendjle was surpassingly beautiful. Several times
during the day my father, Azze bint Sēf, and all
his grown-up children would take their coffee
here. Any one wishing to speak to my father
privately would be sure of finding him here alone
for several hours in the day.

Il Rahmāni, a man-of-war, was anchored off
the Bendjle all the year round, whence they fired
the signals in the fasting season; the crews required for the many rowing boats had their quarters there. A tall flagstaff was erected on the shore
to signal whenever these boats and crews were
wanted.

Both at Bet il Mtoni and at Bet il Sahel the
meals were cooked in the Arab as well as in the
Persian and Turkish manner. People of all races
lived in these two houses—the races of various
beauty. The slaves were dressed in Swahili style,
but we were permitted to appear in Arab fashion
alone. Any newly-arrived Circassian or Abyssinian woman had to exchange her ample robes and
fantastic attire within three days for the Arab
costume provided for her.

Bonnets and gloves are no less indispensable
articles of toilet to any Western lady or woman of
respectability than jewellery is to us. Trinkets are
considered so necessary, that even beggar-women

may be seen plying their trade decked out in them. My father had special treasure chambers in both his houses at Zanzibar, and in his palace at Mesket, in Oman, amply stocked with sovereigns and gold pieces of Spanish and other coinage; besides these, however, they contained large assortments of feminine adornments, from the simplest article to the diamond-set crown, expressly procured to serve as presents. Each time an increase to the family had taken place, either by the purchase of a Sarari, or by the frequent births of princes or princesses, the doors of these chambers were opened, to take out presents for the new arrival according to its rank and station. On the seventh day after the birth of a child my father used to pay a visit to the infant and its mother to present some article of jewellery to the baby. In the same way a new Surīe received at once the necessary jewels, and had her servants assigned to her by the chief eunuch.

Though himself very simple in all his ways, my father was very particular about all people around him. No one was permitted to appear before him except in full dress, and this was the rule with his children as well as with the youngest eunuch. The little girls used to wear their hair in thin plaits, as many as twenty sometimes, with the ends collected together, and a heavy gold ornament, set with precious stones, suspended from their centre. Sometimes a gold coin was attached to each plait, which looked much prettier. These ornaments were taken off at bedtime, and re-attached in the morning. The girls had their hair dressed in this pony fashion up to the period when they had to go about veiled. Once I ran off to my father without these ornaments in my hair-dress, to get some of the French sweetmeats he

used to give us every morning. Instead of obtaining these, however, I was promptly sent back in
charge of a servant—I had appeared before him
not properly dressed; but I took good care never
again to commit the same offense.

My sister Zejāne and my stepmother Medīne
were my mother's most intimate friends. Zejāne
was the daughter of an Abyssinian*, Medīne, a
Circassian, who came from the same part of the
country as my mother, like Sara, another stepmother of mine. Sara's two children were my
brother Madjid and my sister Khadudj, of whom
the former was the junior by some years. My
mother and Sara had solemnly promised each
other, that whoever survived the other should
replace her with her children. Khadudj and Madjid, however, were nearly full-grown when Sara
died, and they did not need my mother's help as
long as they lived in their paternal home. It was
the custom in our family for boys up to the age of
eighteen or twenty to remain with their mothers in
our father's house, and to submit to the general
house rules. At about this stage of life each prince
was pronounced of age, though this depended
entirely upon his behaviour. When of age he was
numbered amongst the grown-up people—an
honour which was always eagerly coveted. A separate residence was then assigned to him, together
with horses, servants, and everything else he required, also an adequate monthly allowance.

My brother Madjid had now obtained this honour, more on account of his conduct than of his
age. He was very modest, and won all hearts by
his kind and gentle manners. Not a week passed
but he rode over from the city (he lived at Bet il
Sahel with his mother) to see us, and he always

*Ethiopian

liked to play with me, though he was my senior by twelve years.

He came over perfectly delighted one day to tell my mother that he had just been pronounced of age, and that, being his own master now, he had received a house of his own. He insisted at the same time upon our removing to his new place to live with him, and he was joined in this request by Khadudj. My mother begged him to consider that she could not well accede to his wishes without first consulting my father, but promised to inform him of the result as soon as she had done so. On her part she declared herself willing to live with him as long as it suited both himself and his sister. Madjid at once offered to save her all trouble by speaking himself to my father, and next day, indeed, he informed us that the latter had given his consent. Our removal being thus settled, it was arranged, after a long consultation, that we were to take up our new residence with him in the course of a few days, after he had completed all necessary arrangements at his place.

Chapter II

BET IL WATORO

My mother did not find it easy to reconcile herself to the prospect of her impending removal. She was very much attached to Bet il Mtoni, where she had lived from her childhood; she was not fond of any change, and was very much afflicted by the separation from Zejāne and from my stepmother Medīne. She told me, however, afterwards that her own scruples had been outweighed by the consideration of making herself useful to the children of her dear departed friend.

As soon as it became known that she had decided to remove to town, every person she met cried out, "Have you lost all trust in us, Djilfidan, that you are going to leave us for ever?" "Oh, my friends," she replied, "I do not leave you of my own free will, but it is my fate to part from you!"

I am sure a good many people will shake their heads with a feeling of pity on reading the word "fate." Maybe such persons have hitherto shut their eyes and their ears to the will of God, and have spurned to take any notice of it, laying a far greater stress upon what they call chance. It should be borne in mind, however, that I once was a Mahometan, and grew up as such. I am, moreover, speaking of Arab life, of an Arab home, and there are two things above all quite unknown in a

real Arab house, the word "chance" and mate-
rialism. The Mahometan not only believes in God
as his Creator and Preserver, but he is convinced
at all times of His presence, and he feels likewise
sure, that not his own will, but the will of the Lord
is done in little things as well as in great.

It took us some days to complete all our arrangements, and then we waited for the return of
Madjid, who was to arrange about our journey. I
had had one brother and two sisters, all nearly of
my own age, as companions at Bet il Mtoni, and I
was very sorry to leave them, little Ralub in particular, who had been greatly attached to me; on
the other hand, I was right glad of the opportunity of getting away from our excessively severe
teacher.

Our large room looked something like a beehive
during the parting scenes with so many friends
and acquaintances; everybody brought a parting
gift in proportion to his means and affection. This
is a custom very much in use with us, for no Arab
will deny himself the pleasure of presenting a
parting gift to his friend, even if he has nothing to
give but the merest trifle. I remember a case in
point which occurred in my early youth. We had
made an excursion from Bet il Mtoni to one of our
estates, and were just about to step into our boats
to return home, when I felt some one tugging at
my dress from behind. Turning round, I saw a
very old negro woman, who handed me a parcel,
wrapped in plantain leaves, with the words, "This
trifle is my parting gift to you, bibijangu (my
mistress), it is the first ripe fruit of my garden."
Undoing the leaves, I found they enclosed—one
cob of newly-gathered Indian corn. I did not
know the poor old woman at all, but afterwards

she proved to have been an old *protégée* of my mother's.

Madjid arrived at last with the news that the captain of the *Rahmāni* had been ordered to send a cutter for us next evening, and another boat for our luggage and for the servants who were to accompany us to the city.

My father happened to be at Bet il Mtoni at the time, and next day my mother went up with me to bid him good-bye. We found him walking up and down the Bendjle as usual, and he came at once to meet us as soon as he saw us. My parents began talking at once about our journey, and, to stop the many questions with which I continually interrupted them, one of the attending eunuchs was ordered to bring me sweets and sherbet. I was of course very curious to know something about our new home and about life in town. I had only once been there for a very short time, and had not even seen all my brothers and sisters, nor my numerous stepmothers who lived there.

We then went to the apartments of my august stepmother to take leave of her. Azze bint Sēf was graciously pleased to dismiss us standing, which with her was a great honour, as she always remained seated when she received people. We were also permitted to kiss her hand before turning our back upon her for ever.

We had still to run up and downstairs a good many times to shake hands with all our friends, of whom, however, we met but few in their rooms. My mother resolved, therefore, to say good-bye to them after prayers, which all had to attend.

The cutter lay off the Bendjle ready to receive us at 7 p.m.; it was a fine big boat with a crew of fourteen oarsmen, with an awning over the stern, carrying our standard—a plain, blood-red flag. The passenger seats were covered with pretty silk cushions for ten to twelve persons.

Old Djohar, a trusty eunuch, came to report everything ready to my father, who was watching our departure from the Bendjle, and took the helm; he was to convey us to our new destination in company with another eunuch. All our friends in tears accompanied us as far as the house door, and their cries, "Wedā, wedā," (farewell, farewell), ring in my ears to this very day.

There was no landing pier on the flat shore, and we had to get into the boat either by being carried in a chair or by walking through the dry sand and over a plank; my mother got into the cutter in this manner, attended on both sides by some eunuchs, while another carried me in his arms and placed me in the stern sheets. The light of the coloured hanging-lanterns in the boat, together with the glittering stars above, cast a magic brightness over the sea, and the oarsmen pulled away, keeping time by the tune of a melancholy Arab song.

We kept close in shore, and I was soon fast asleep in my mother's lap. I was suddenly and rather roughly roused up by a number of persons calling out my name; very much frightened and half asleep yet, I learned that we had arrived at our journey's end. We were just below the lighted-up windows of Bet il Sahel, which were occupied by crowds of people—they were my stepmothers and sisters with their mothers, most of whom I had never seen before, and who were curious to have a look at me. My mother told me they had commenced crying out my name as soon as the boat had come in sight.

On landing, I was received by my young broth-

ers in a very lively manner. They wanted us to go
with them at once, but my mother had to decline,
as she did not wish to keep Khadudj, who was
watching our arrival from her house, waiting. I
was very sorry that I was not allowed to join my
young relations at once, but my mother remained
firm, and I was consoled by the promise that we
were to spend a day at Bet il Sahel as soon as my
father had returned to it.

We therefore passed on to get to Madjid's residence, Bet il Watoro, which was close by, and
from which there was also a splendid view over
the sea. Khadudj received us at the bottom of the
staircase and bid us heartily welcome: she conducted us to our rooms, and her chief eunuch,
Emān, brought in some refreshments. Madjid was
below in his reception room with his friends, waiting for permission to come up and join us. How
delighted he was, good, noble fellow, to welcome
us in his new home!

Our own room was of but middling size, and
looked out on the mosque close by. It was furnished like all Arab apartments, and there was
nothing wanting for our comfort. As the dresses
worn by day are not taken off at night, and all
Arabs of standing are accustomed to the strictest
cleanliness, there is no need for separate bed-
rooms, and the room allotted to us quite sufficed
for our wants.

Rich and distinguished people generally fur-
nish their houses in the following style: Persian
carpets or very fine and soft matting cover the
floors; the thick, whitewashed walls are divided
from floor to ceiling into several partitions by
deep recesses; these recesses are again subdivided
by shelves of wood, painted green, forming a kind
of open cabinet. Upon these shelves are sym-

metrically ranged the choicest and most expensive objects of glass and china. To an Arab nothing can be too costly to decorate these shelves; a handsome cut glass, a plate beautifully painted, or an elegant and tasteful jug, may cost any price; if they look pretty they are sure to be purchased.

The bare and narrow walls between the recesses are carefully concealed by large mirrors reaching from the low divans to the ceiling; these mirrors are generally expressly ordered from Europe. As a rule, pictures are prohibited to a Mahometan as imitations of Divine creation: of late, however, they are tolerated now and then. Clocks, again, are in great favour everywhere, and some houses contain quite a rich collection of them; they are placed above and in pairs on each side of the mirrors. The walls of the gentlemen's rooms are decorated with costly weapons from Arabia, Persia, and Turkey, and this is done by every Arab according to his means.

A large curtained bed of rosewood, of Indian workmanship, very prettily carved all over, is placed in one corner of the room. Arab beds are very high, and to get into them it is necessary to mount upon a chair or to call in the assistance of a chambermaid. The empty space beneath is often occupied by the children's or sick nurse.

Tables are rarely seen, and only in the houses of people of high station, but there are chairs of all kinds and colours. Wardrobes, chests of drawers, and the like are not in use; we had, however, a chest or trunk with two or three drawers, and a secret drawer to put away money and jewellery.

Windows and doors stand open all the year during the day; they are only shut for a short time during the rainy season. In our country we do not at all understand what "draught" means.

At first I did not like our new residence at all; I missed my young brothers and sisters very much, and Bet il Watoro appeared to me very small compared to gigantic Bet il Mtoni. I was by no means pleased that I was to stay here for ever. I could not sail my boats here, unless I chose to do so in a washtub, as there was no river near, and all water had to be fetched from a well outside the house. My dear mother, whose greatest pleasure was to give away all she possessed, wanted me to send my beautiful sailing boats to my brothers at Bet il Mtoni, but I could not make up my mind to do that at once. For the first time in my life I felt indeed very unhappy and downcast.

My mother, on the other hand, soon reconciled herself to her new duties, and was so busily engaged all day in directing and arranging things in company with Khadudj, that she did not even find time to look after me. Dear Madjid alone took some trouble about me, and showed me over the house from top to bottom; but nothing could please me, I was perfectly indifferent to everything, and I urged my mother incessantly to return at once to Bet il Mtoni and to my dear relations there. This could not be done, of course, and the less so as she really proved a great help to my brother and sister.

Fortunately I soon discovered Madjid to be a great friend of all kinds of live beasts, of which he had quite a collection, amongst others any number of white rabbits, which spoiled the new house completely, much to the annoyance of my mother and sister. He also kept a great many fighting cocks of all countries; I have never again seen such a fine collection together, not even in zoological gardens.

I was soon his constant companion on his visit

to his favourites, and he was kind enough to let
me share in all his amusements. Before long I
owned a number of fighting cocks myself, and I
felt not quite so lonely now at Bet il Watoro.
Nearly every day we inspected our champions,
which were led up and down by servants. A cock-
fight is, indeed, by no means an uninteresting
affair—it is very entertaining, as it takes up the
entire attention of the spectator, and often it is
intensely amusing.

Afterwards he gave me fencing lessons with
swords, daggers, and lances, and taught me to
practise with gun and pistol when we went into the
country. In fact he made quite an amazon of me,
greatly to the distress of my dear mother, who
declined to learn anything about fencing and
shooting. All this, of course, did not improve my
taste for fancy needlework, and I much preferred
handling all kinds of weapons to sitting quietly at
the bobbin-machine for hours together.

The perfect liberty I enjoyed in all these pastimes—for as yet a new teacher had not been
found for me—made me soon feel in better spirits, and my objection to lonely Bet il Watoro soon
vanished. Nor did I neglect riding, and, by Madjid's orders, Mesrur the eunuch improved me in
horsemanship.

My mother being too busily employed in the
house to have much spare time for me, I soon got
attached to a clever Abyssinian woman, who grew
very fond of me, and who taught me her language;
but I have long since forgotten all I learned from
her.

A lively intercourse was kept up with Bet il
Mtoni, and whenever we went there we were always received most affectionately by all our
friends. The communication between the two

places was kept up by slaves carrying verbal messages to and fro. Eastern people are not very fond
of letter-writing, even when able to write. Every
person of note or wealth keeps some slaves who
are only employed as runners. They must travel a
certain number of miles daily, but they are well
treated otherwise, and special care is taken of
them. They are trusted with the most confidential
messages. Upon their honesty and secrecy depends frequently their master's welfare, and even
more! It is by no means a rare occurrence that the
most intimate relations between people have been
severed and destroyed for ever by an act of ven-
geance on the part of these messengers. In spite of
this great drawback, people cannot be induced to
learn to write, and to make themselves independent for life. The saying, "Leave the world to take
its course," is nowhere more true than with us.

My sister Khadudj was very fond of society.
Hardly a day passed without any number of visitors being in the house from six o'clock in the
morning till midnight. Those who arrived very
early were received by the servants, and conducted to a room, where they could rest until
eight or nine o'clock, when they were welcomed
by the lady of the house. Later on I shall have
occasion to say more of these ladies' visits in a
separate chapter.

I did not at all succeed in being on the same
friendly terms with Khadudj as I was with Madjid. She was rather forbidding, and I never got to
love her fondly. There was too great a contrast
between good, noble Madjid and her. Nor was I
the only one who was of this opinion. Everybody
who became more intimately acquainted with
them soon found out who of the two was the more
amiable. Above all, she could be very cold to

strangers, and ungracious, and on this account
she had many enemies. She had the greatest dislike of all novel and foreign things, and nothing
annoyed her more than the call of a European
lady, though it never lasted above half or three-
quarters of an hour.

In other respects she was very circumspect and
of a practical turn, considering her station; she
was never idle, and when she had nothing else to
do she sewed and embroidered dresses for the
children of her married slaves as assiduously as
the fine shirts for her brother. Among these children there were three very pretty boys, whose
father was superintendent of buildings in our service. These boys were called Selim, Abdallah, and
Tani, and, being only a few years younger than
myself, they soon became my daily companions,
as I had no others of my own age in the place, till I
went over more frequently to my brothers and
sisters at Bet il Sahel.

Chapter III

A DAY AT BET IL SAHEL

The long-looked-for day at last arrived on which I was to pay a visit to Bet il Sahel with my mother and Khadudj from early morn till night. It was on a Friday, the Mahometan Sabbath, that we left our house as early as half-past five, wrapped in our big black shawls with gold borders (called Schele). We had not far to go, only some one hundred paces, to get to our destination.

The faithful but rather cross old gatekeeper did not receive us in an over-friendly manner. More crossly even than was his wont, he told us that he had been on his feeble legs for the last hour admitting lady visitors. Saīd il Nubi, as the crusty old fellow was called, was a Nubian slave of my father's, whose beard—I cannot express myself otherwise, as the Arabs wear their heads shaved bare—had grown white in long and loyal service. My father thought much of him, as Saīd had once stayed his master's hand in a moment of great, though righteous, wrath from committing an act of rashness, which he would have deeply regretted all his life.

The little ones, however, did not know much about Said at the time, and it gave us great pleasure to play all sorts of tricks upon the crotchety old fellow. Our designs were chiefly directed

against his enormous keys, and I believe there
was not a spot in all Bet il Sahel where they had
not, at one time or another, been hidden. My
brother Djemschīd above all showed great skill in
making them disappear so completely, that even
we could not find out their hiding-place.

We found the people occupying the first floor all
astir already; only those who were still engaged in
their morning devotions remained as yet invisible.
Nobody would have dared to disturb them, even if
the house had been on fire. We had chosen this
day because my father happened to be there, and
the same reason had caused many others to come
too.

Nor were all the ladies who arrived friends or
acquaintances of ours—many, indeed, were perfect strangers to all of us. Most of them had come
from Oman, our native country, and on purpose
only to obtain some pecuniary aid from my father,
which was rarely denied them. Oman and our
kinsfolk there are very poor, and our own pros-
perity dates from the time of my father's conquest
and occupation of Zanzibar.

Women are as a rule forbidden by law to speak
to a strange man. There is, however, an exception
to this in two cases: they may appear before their
sovereign and before a judge. As hardly any of
these visitors in question were able to write or
send a petition, there was nothing left for them
but to undertake the short voyage from Asia to
Africa, and to prefer their request in person. All
of them received presents according to their position and rank freely, and without the numerous
questions that a poor applicant in Europe is usually subjected to. It is taken for granted in our
country that no respectable person will ask for
assistance merely for the sake of begging, and this
view proves correct in most cases.

I was most affectionately received by all my brothers and sisters, especially by my dearly beloved and never-to-be-forgotten sister Khole. Hitherto my mother had been the only one whom I really and fondly loved, but I now began to adore this "light of our house" from my very soul. She was my only ideal soon, as she had been our father's favourite child before, and she deserved, indeed, to be admired by all. She was admitted to be a girl of rare beauty by all who were unprejudiced and without envy. No one can remain quite insensible to beauty—it was so with her in our house, as there was, indeed, no one to equal her in our whole family, and the fame of her beauty had spread far and wide. Fine eyes are very common in the East, but hers were so eminently beautiful, that she got the name, Nidjm il subh, or "Morning Star." An Arab chief, taking part on a certain feast day in the popular game of sham fighting in front of our house, was observed with his looks fixed upon a certain window, quite unconscious of the blood which gushed from his wounded foot, and of the pain this wound must have caused him. It was my sister Khole whom he had seen at the window by chance; her beauty had so overwhelmed him that he accidentally pierced his foot with his iron-pointed lance, and wounded himself without so much as noticing it, until one of my brothers drew his attention to the fact. For years after poor innocent Khole was teased by my brothers about this affair.

Bet il Sahel, which is a good deal smaller than Bet il Mtoni, lies also close upon the seashore; it is a bright and cheerful-looking place, and a very pleasant house to live in.

There is a splendid view of the sea and the shipping from all its windows, which delighted me much. The doors on the upper floor, which contains many rooms, open upon a long and wide gallery of such grandness as I have never seen equalled. The ceiling is supported by pillars reaching down to the ground, and these pillars are connected by a high parapet, along which chairs are placed. A great many coloured lamps, suspended from the ceiling, throw a magic glow over the whole house after dark.

The gallery looks down upon a courtyard, always full of bustle and noise; I have sometimes been reminded of all this in after years by market scenes on the stage, reproducing something like a picture of it on a small scale.

Two large separate flights of stairs lead from this court to the rooms on the first floor. Crowds of people are continually going up and down these stairs, and the crowding is often so great that it takes some minutes before one can get to the staircase at all.

One corner of the courtyard is taken up by the slaughter-house, according to the Eastern custom of killing one's own meat. In another spot negroes have their heads shaved; tired-out water-carriers stretch themselves rather lazily on the ground, heedless to all calls for water, until they are unceremoniously roused and reminded of their duty by one of the eunuchs; generally they do not wait for the approach of those taskmasters, but get up and run off with their big "Mtungi" (water jars), amid the jeerings of the bystanders. Not far off a dozen or so of nursemaids sit basking in the sun with their little charges, telling them thrilling stories and fairy tales.

The kitchen is put up in the open, near one of the ground-floor pillars; the numberless cooks quarrel and fight continually, until one of the head cooks steps in, dealing blows right and left,

and restoring order for a time. The quantities of
meat boiled here are enormous, the beasts being
always cooked whole. Fish of so large a size were
often brought, as had to be carried by two
negroes; smaller ones were only bought by the
basketfull, and poultry by the dozen. Flour, rice,
and sugar were counted by bags, and butter, imported in a liquid state from the Isle of Socotra,
by jars of about a hundredweight each. Spices
alone were taken by the pound (ratti).

The quantities of fruit consumed were still
more enormous. Thirty to forty porters, and
sometimes as many as fifty, came in daily laden
with fruit, not to count the small boats arriving
from the seashore plantations. I should not over-
estimate the daily supply of fresh fruit at Bet il
Sahel, in putting it down as equal to the load of a
large railway truck. During the mango season
(embe) more than double this quantity was consumed every day. Great carelessness prevailed in
the conveyance of the fruit, and large quantities
were made quite unfit for use owing to the manner
in which the baskets were treated and flung on the
ground by the slaves.

A wall, about six feet deep, ran along the shore
to protect the house against the sea, with a grove
of very fine pomegranates behind. Several of the
best horses were brought out every morning from
the stables, and fastened to this wall with long
ropes, to roam about and wade in the soft sand at
low tide. My father took great delight in his thor-
oughbreds from Oman; he inspected them daily,
and himself tended them when they were sick. It
is well known how tenderly attached an Arab is to
his favourite horse. My brother Madjid had a
splendid brown mare, and he ardently wished to
obtain a foal from her. This wish was at last

fulfilled, and when "il Kehle," the mare, was about to foal, he ordered his head groom to call him, be it night or daytime. We were actually roused from our sleep one morning, between two and three o'clock, and informed that the happy event had taken place. The groom who had brought the glad news received a reward of fifty dollars from his happy master. This is by no means a single instance; the attachment to horses in Arabia proper is said to be carried still farther.

After prayers we went to see my father in his apartments. Fond of joking as he always was, he turned to me after a while, saying: "Well now, Salme, how do you like this place? Would you like to return to Bet il Mtoni? And don't they forget here to give you your—milk soup?"

About ten o'clock all my elder brothers came in from their houses to breakfast with my father. Besides us, his children and grandchildren, who were admitted after the age of seven, no one but his legitimate wife, Azze bint Sēf, and his sister Asche sat down at his table. No Surīe was ever permitted to take meals with him, however high she might stand in his favour. Social distinction in the East never shows itself more than at meals; guests are on the most friendly and intimate footing with their hosts—often more so than would be the case in Europe—but at meal-time this equality ceases, and the strictest observance of rank is adhered to by common consent. Even the Sarari have established a division of rank among themselves. The handsome Circassians, well aware of their better breeding, decline to break bread with the coffee-coloured Abyssinians: thus by tacit understanding they dine apart. I have already mentioned that among us children no distinction of colour was made.

It soon struck me that the occupants of Bet il
Sahel seemed much happier and more cheerful
than those of Bet il Mtoni, and I began to understand the reason for this afterwards. In this latter
place Azze bint Sēf ruled supreme; she ruled over
husband, stepchildren, and their mothers—in
short, over every one and everything within her
reach, while at Bet il Sahel all, my father not
excepted, were more free and at liberty to do as
they liked; there was no one here to give orders
but my dear and gentle father. I think he was
himself so conscious of the great difference between the two houses, that for years he had not
sent any one to live at Bet il Mtoni, except by
desire, although there was plenty of room to spare
in the palace, while Bet il Sahel was always overcrowded. This state grew so bad at last that he
conceived the happy thought of building wooden
pavilions on the large gallery aforementioned. Finally, however, another house was built on the
shore some miles to the north of Bet il Sahel, to
serve as residence to the younger generation,
which was called Bet il Rās (Costal House).

A painter would have found many models for a
picture in our gallery, for a more variegated company could not easily be met with. The faces of
the people showed eight to ten different shades of
complexion at least; and it would, indeed, have
puzzled even a clever artist to make out the many-
tinted garments worn. The noise was truly appalling—quarrelling or romping children in every
corner—loud voices and clapping hands sum-
moning servants, the Eastern equivalent for ring-
ing a bell—the rattle and clatter of the women's
wooden sandals (Kabakīb)—all combined in producing the most distracting din.

Our chief amusement was listening to the babel

of languages spoken in our midst. Arabic was the
only language really sanctioned in my father's
presence. But as soon as he turned his back, a
truly Babylonian confusion of tongues commenced, and Arabian, Persian, Turkish, Circassian, Swahili, Nubian, and Abyssinian were
spoken and mixed up together, not to mention the
various dialects of these tongues. This excitement
seemed, however, to disturb no one, and only sick
people complained of it sometimes. My father,
too, had got quite accustomed to it, and never
interposed.

All my grown-up sisters presented themselves
in festive array on this day, partly because it was
our Sunday, and in honour of our father's presence. Our mothers walked about or stood together in groups, talking, laughing, and jesting
with each other so amicably that a stranger, unaware of the fact, would never have guessed them
to be the wives of one man. The clashing of arms
on the staircase announced the arrival of my
numerous brothers and their sons, most of whom
intended to stay with us all day.

Things were kept up at Bet il Sahel in a much
more sumptuous and extravagant style than at
Bet il Mtoni, and I met there a far greater number
of handsome and pretty faces than at the latter
place, where my mother and her friend Medīne
had been the only Circassian women. But the
majority here were Circassians, who beyond a
question are more distinguished in outward appearance than Abyssinians, though even amongst
the latter great beauties are to be found. This
natural superiority was the cause of a good deal of
ill-will and envy, and one beautiful Circassian in
particular was treated coldly, and even hated by
the Abyssinian women on account of her beauty.

It cannot be a matter of surprise that under these circumstances a kind of ridiculous "hatred of race" had broken out among my brothers and sisters. In spite of many good qualities they have, Abyssinian women are almost always of a spiteful and vindictive disposition, for, their passions once roused, they know no bounds or decency. We, that is, the children of Circassian mothers, were generally called "cats" by those who had Abyssinian blood in their veins, merely because some of us were the unfortunate possessors of blue eyes and a fair complexion, for which they nicknamed us "Highness." My father was never forgiven the fact that he had chosen his two favourite children, Sharīfe and Khole—both by Circassian mothers, the former even blue-eyed— from the hateful "race of cats."

At Bet il Mtoni we had always led a kind of monastic life under the rigid rule of Azze bint Sēf, whilst Bet il Watoro was still more lonely and dull. I was therefore well pleased to join in the merry doings of Bet il Sahel, and soon made friends with the brothers and sisters, and two of my nieces, of my own age, Shembūa and Farschu, the only children of my brother Khalid. They came to Bet il Sahel from their own house every morning, and went back in the evening and took part in the lessons and games of their uncles and aunts. Khalid's mother, Churschīt, was a Circassian, and quite an exceptional woman. She was uncommonly tall, and possessed a great strength of will combined with a high degree of common sense; I have never met any woman like her in all my life. Later on, and during the time that Khalid represented my father in his absence, it was said that it was she who actually governed the country, and that her son was only her tool. Her advice and counsel in all matters concerning our family was considered quite indispensable, and much depended always upon the decision she came to. She took in at a glance as much as if she had owned the hundred eyes of an Argus, and on all momentous occasions gave proof of a wisdom and sagacity truly Solomonic. She was not, however, very much liked by the little folks, and we rather avoided coming near her if we could help it.

When about to return to Bet il Watoro in the evening, I was rather dismayed on hearing my father tell my mother that I was still to go on with my lessons, *i.e.*, reading; and upon her telling him that as yet no other teacher had been found, he decided that I was to come to Bet il Sahel, and return home every night, like my nieces, so as to take part in the general lessons there. I was not very much pleased when I heard this; lessons had never attracted me, the less so as my last teacher had inspired me with a thorough dislike of all learning. I got soon reconciled, however, to the new arrangement in consideration for the companionship of my brothers and sisters, on all days except Fridays, and my charming sister Khole promising my mother to watch over me. She kept her promise faithfully, quite taking the place of a mother.

My own dear mother was very much downcast at my father's decree, which took me away from her six days in the week, but there was no help for it; she made me promise, however, to show myself several times a day at a certain place, from which she could see and nod to me in the distance.

Chapter IV

OUR LIFE AT BET IL WATORO AND
AT BET IL SAHEL

All I can say here of my new teacher is, that I
shall always remain deeply grateful to God for
having given me such a faithful friend in youth.
She was very strict, but also very just. I was often
quite alone with her, as her other pupils did not
much care to enter her darkened sick chamber,
and preferred to keep out of her reach instead,
taking advantage of her helpless state. I could
not, however, bear to hear her ask for me, and
leave her alone in her sufferings. She was highly
pleased at my obedience, it is true, but my refrac-
tory brothers and sisters not only laughed at me
for my pains, but often cuffed me.

In course of time I liked Bet il Sahel very much,
for there was plenty of room for roaming about,
and we played any number of foolish pranks,
which were not left without punishment when
found out; but I had generally the best of it on
such occasions, as Khole was too tender-hearted
to punish me as I deserved.

We had some splendid peacocks at the house;
one of them was rather savage, and could not bear
the sight of children. One day, when we were
walking round the cupola of the Turkish bath,
which was connected by a suspension bridge with

Bet il Sahel and Bet il Tani, this peacock suddenly
and furiously darted at my brother Djemschid.
We threw ourselves on the beast, and conquered
it at last, not feeling inclined, however, to set it
free without punishment. We resolved upon a
very cruel revenge, viz., depriving the animal of
its magnificent plumage; and miserable enough
the pugnacious bird looked after this. My father
was fortunately absent at the time, and when he
returned the affair was hushed up.

Two Circassian women had arrived from Egypt,
and after a time it appeared to us as if one of them
was rather haughty and indifferent to us. We were
rather galled at this, and put our heads together
to find out a punishment equal to the offence; but
we found it very difficult since we rarely had the
opportunity of seeing or meeting her. She was
only a few years older than ourselves, and therefore the affront was the greater. With this grievance in our minds, we were once passing her
apartment, the door of which stood open as
usual. The poor thing was seated at the time on a
very light Swahili bed, which consists of four
posts only held together by ropes and a mat,
merrily singing one of her pretty national songs.
On this occasion my sister Shewāne was our
leader; a sign from her sufficed to make us at once
understand what she proposed to do. In a trice we
took hold of the connecting ropes, and, pulling all
together, we hoisted the matting upon which she
was sitting, and dropped the frightened girl down
again with a jerk. It was a very childish trick
indeed, but a success in so far as it cured her
effectually of her indifference to us—this was all
we had wanted.

Being full of mischief, I used to play tricks
quite by myself sometimes, and soon after our

removal to Bet il Watoro I once nearly broke my
neck. We had gone on a visit to one of our plantations. One morning I managed to escape from my
attendants, and climbed up a high palm-tree as
nimbly as a cat, without using the pingu, a thick
rope to keep the feet together, and without which
the most skilled climber cannot be prevailed upon
to ascend a cocoa-tree. When about half-way up
the tree, I began calling out to the people uncon-
sciously passing below, and wishing them good
morning.

What a fright I caused them all! A crowd collected, begging and entreating me to get down. It
was impossible to send any one up to help me. In
climbing a cocoa-tree both hands must be free,
and therefore the encumbrance of a child of eight
would render the feat an impossible one. I was,
however, quite pleased to remain where I was, and
only made up my mind to slip down when my
mother, who was standing below, wringing her
hands in despair, had promised me all kinds of
delightful things. Everybody spoiled me that day,
and loaded me with presents on account of my
lucky escape, instead of soundly thrashing me as I
deserved.

Such and similar pranks we played daily, and
no punishment could deter us from a new one. We
seven—three boys and four girls—turned the
whole house topsy-turvy, and caused no small
annoyance to our mothers.

Sometimes my dear mother kept me at home on
a week-day, and this was always an opportunity
for Madjid to spoil me thoroughly. On one of
these days he greatly frightened us. He frequently
suffered from severe spasms, and for this reason
he was hardly ever left without an attendant to
render immediate assistance. When he was in his

bath-room, my mother and Khadudj watched alternately at the door, not trusting the slaves, and spoke to him from time to time, and he used to tell them jokingly that he was still alive. While Khadudj was thus walking up and down one day at his door, she suddenly heard the sound of a heavy fall in the room, and when she rushed in frightened to death, she found her beloved brother on the raised platform convulsed by a terrible attack, the worst he had ever had. A messenger on horseback was at once despatched to Bet il Mtoni to fetch my father.

In all cases of sickness and disease we are unfortunately exposed to the most ignorant quacks and mountebanks, and now that I have come to know and to appreciate the natural and reasonable means employed by medical men in Europe, I am induced to think that in the majority of cases our dead have not succumbed to their disease, but have been sacrificed to the barbarous treatment to which they were subjected. I am sure we could not have borne the many cases of death in our family, and among our friends so resignedly, without being sustained by the firm and irrefutable belief in our "destiny."

For many hours poor Madjid was lying on his bed perfectly senseless and in convulsions, inhaling all the time an atmosphere unwholesome even to any person in good health. For in spite of our predilection for fresh and pure air, the patients in our parts are hermetically shut out from the fresh air, but especially so when, as in the present instance, the evil one himself is supposed to have a hand in it, for then the sickroom and the whole house are thoroughly fumigated.

To the great surprise of everybody, my dear father arrived an hour afterwards in a mtumbi, a small fishing-boat holding only one person, and hurried into the house. The old man was deeply affected by the illness of this son, he who had more than forty children alive at the time. The tears ran down into his beard as he stood at Madjid's sick bed. "O Lord! O Lord! preserve the life of my son!" was his incessant prayer. And God granted his prayer, for Madjid was spared to us.

My mother afterwards asked him why he had come in such a miserable vessel. "When the messenger brought the news," he replied "there was not a single boat on shore; it would have had to be signalled for, and I had no time to wait. It would also have taken too long to have a horse saddled. At the very moment I saw a fisherman pass the Bendjle in his mtumbi, so I seized my weapons, called to him to stop and to get out, and jumped into the boat to pull here by myself." I may mention here that a mtumbi is a most primitive kind of boat, made of the hollowed-out trunk of a tree, and holds hardly more than one person, who has to paddle it along. It is narrow, pointed, and comparatively short, in shape somewhat like a whaleboat.

It may be thought strange, according to Western views, that a father so uneasy about the life of his child, and who sets aside all regards of etiquette in his anxiety, should find time to think of his weapons. Here, also, the saying comes true: "So many countries, so many customs." Incomprehensible as this great attachment which the Arab has for his weapons may appear to a European, so incredible are to us some of the Northern habits, as that of excessive drinking in this country, for instance. I continued to go to school daily at Bet il Sahel, and returned at night to my mother at Bet il Watoro. When I had succeeded in learning by heart about the third part of the Kurān, at the age of nine, I was considered too old for school, and after this only went to Bet il Sahel with my mother and Khadudj on Fridays to see my father.

Chapter V

REMOVAL TO BET IL TANI

We lived quietly and peacefully at Bet il Watoro for about two years. Unfortunately good times never last long, and events often arise which have been least foreseen or expected, as it was in our case. Nor is it possible to fancy a creature more lovable and of more gentle disposition than the one who unwittingly disturbed the tranquillity of our domestic life. Asche, a distant relation of ours, had only lately arrived at Zanzibar from our native country, Oman, and shortly after she became Madjid's wife. All of us liked her very much, and rejoiced at the happiness and good fortune of our brother, all except his own sister Khadudj. It grieves me much to have to admit that, from beginning to end, Khadudj greatly wronged Asche. The latter was a truly charming person, and still very young; but, instead of instructing and training her to her new station as she ought to have done, Khadudj behaved to her in a most unsisterly fashion. She was the mistress of the house by right of her marriage, but, disregarding this, Khadudj ruled over her so tyranically, that poor, gentle Asche frequently came to my mother in tears, complaining of her troubles.

My mother now found herself, as it were,

placed between two fires, and her position became
more and more embarrassing. Khadudj could not
be prevailed upon to give up any of her pretended
rights, but continued to treat Asche as a child. My
mother tried to impress Khadudj with a sense of
Asche's position as Madjid's wife, and begged her
to avoid, for Madjid's sake, all that might vex or
cause him annoyance. It was all to no purpose,
and her life at Bet il Watoro, once so agreeable
and happy, grew gradually unbearable. So at last
my mother decided to quit the house which was so
dear to her rather than be a witness any longer to
the continual discord.

But Madjid and his wife would not listen to
this—Asche in particular, who never called my
mother otherwise than Umma ("mamma"), was
quite inconsolable. Khadudj, on the other hand,
remained perfectly indifferent, and this only con-
firmed my mother still more in the resolve she had
taken.

Asche herself could stand the life no longer. She
therefore sued for and obtained a divorce from
Madjid. But after this sad experience of her
young life, her heart turned against Zanzibar and
its inhabitants; therefore, as soon as the favourable south wind set in, which our ships had been
waiting for, she came to bid us good-bye. Being an
orphan, she purposed returning to an old aunt of
hers in Oman, who lived somewhere in the neighbourhood of Mesket.

Our exodus from Bet il Watoro had already
been effected previous to this event, and we had
taken up our residence at Bet il Tani. My sister
Khole was greatly pleased with this, as we now
lived quite close to her, and nearly in the same
place, where she had taken the trouble to select
and arrange our new quarters.

It was really a difficult matter to obtain rooms
in our houses, and for this reason it had gradually become a custom to give a kind of reversion-
ary promise on the death of persons in
possession, as is done in the case of charitable
institutions in Europe. Sometimes it was indeed
revolting to see how people would carefully watch
the slightest attack of coughing, or other alarming
symptoms in their neighbours, and mentally dispose of the coveted rooms. All this was very
wicked, and mainly the consequence of our overcrowded condition. It was due to Khole's intercession that we obtained large and handsome
apartments, without the unpleasant consciousness of being usurpers.

We saw but little of Khadudj now; she was
offended at our removal, and reproached my
mother very unjustly with want of affection. The
latter had, however, too strong a sense of justice
as to suffer quietly such unfair treatment of a
defenceless and inexperienced woman, whose
only offence had been that she had dared to become Madjid's wife. My brother, on the other
hand, came to see us frequently, and he remained
the dear and true friend he had always been.

Bet il Tani lies quite close to Bet il Sahel, and is
connected, as previously mentioned, with the latter by a suspension bridge, which runs over the
roof of the Turkish bath between both houses. It
now retained but the shadow of its former splendour, for in the upper floor of this palace had
lived, many years ago, a second legitimate wife of
my father's, Shesade, a Persian princess of en-
trancing beauty. She is said to have been excessively extravagant, but to have fondly loved her
step-children. Her little retinue was composed of
one hundred and fifty cavaliers, all Persians, who

lived on the ground floor; with them she hunted and rode in the broad day—rather contrary to strict Arab notions. The Persian women are subjected to quite a Spartan training in bodily exercise; they enjoy great liberty, much more so than Arab women, but they are also much more rude in mind and action.

Sehesade is said to have carried on her extravagant style of life beyond bounds; her dresses, cut always after the Persian fashion, were literally covered with embroideries of pearls. A great many of these were picked up nearly every morning by the servants in her rooms, where she had dropped them from her garments, but the princess would never take any of these precious jewels back again. She did not only drain my father's exchequer most wantonly, but violated many of our sacred laws; in fact, she had only married him for his high station and his wealth, and had loved some one else all the time. He was about to protest her conduct one day on her return from one of her excursions, and it was on this occasion that faithful old Nubi had saved him from committing a great crime. Such a scene could, of course, only end in a divorce; fortunately Sehesade had no children of her own. There is a rumour still current amongst us that beautiful Sehesade was observed some years after this event, when my father carried on war in Persia, and had the good fortune of taking the fortress of Bender Abbās, on the Persian Gulf, heading her troops, and taking aim at the members of our family herself.

In the former home of this princess I began to learn to write by myself in a very primitive way. It had to be done secretly, too, as women never receive lessons in writing, and are not even allowed to show their skill therein. Taking the Kurān as guide, I tried to copy the letters as faithfully as I could upon the shoulder-blade of a camel, which we use in place of a slate. My courage rose as I got on, and I only required at last some finishing instructions in calligraphy, for which end I appointed one of our slaves, who was notoriously proficient in the art, to the dignity of writing master.

My friends greatly ridiculed my efforts, but I did not allow my enthusiasm to be damped thereby, nor have I ever had cause to regret the hours I spent in acquiring the art of writing, since it has proved a means of communicating with the few loyal and faithful ones of my far-away home.

Chapter VI

DAILY LIFE IN OUR HOUSE

How many times have I been asked: "Do please tell me how can people in your country manage to live, with nothing to do?" I had the pleasure of answering this question six or eight times over at a large party, and I need not say how amusing and interesting it was to me to give the same reply so many times over. Coming from a person inhabiting a Northern country, the question is quite a natural one I admit, for it is hard for such to fancy a life without work, being firmly convinced, moreover, that women in the East do nothing all day but dream away their time in a shut-up harem, or, for a change, play with some luxurious toy.

The ways of life differ everywhere; all our views, our habits, and customs are shaped to suit our surroundings. Men and women work in the North either for an existence or for enjoyment. It is not so with people in our blessed South. I use the word "blessed" advisedly, as I look upon the contentedness of a people as a great and priceless boon; and because the Arab, so frequently described in books as idle and lazy, is accustomed to an absteminousness in which perhaps only a Chinaman equals him. The climate itself brings it about that the Southerner *may* work if he likes,

while the Northerner is obliged to. Northern people are inclined somewhat to form opinions and
prejudices in their own favour; they are accustomed to look down upon their antipodes
proudly and contemptuously, which, to my taste
at least, is not a very commendable quality to
possess. It is but too often overlooked in this
country how indispensable industry and activity
are to the North to save hundreds of thousands
from starvation. Are Italians, Spaniards, and
Portuguese not a great deal less industrious than
Englishmen or Germans? And for what reason?
Simply because their summer time lasts so much
longer than their winter, and because they have
not to struggle so hard for existence. In the cold
season so many things of the direst necessity are
required, the mere name and existence of which
are beyond the comprehension of people in the
South.

Extravagant habits may be met with in every
country. Those who possess both inclination and
means will never lack the opportunity of gratify-
ing the one and spending the other to the fullest,
wherever they may be. Indeed, I do not intend to
enlarge on this subject, but merely draw comparisons between the respective requirements of
different countries.

Countless objects are needed in this country to
protect the frail life of a newborn child against
the effects of an ever-changing temperature, while
the Southern baby is left almost naked, and
sleeps in a draught of warm air. Here a child of
two years—from the richest to the poorest—cannot do without shoes, stockings, drawers, a dress,
petticoats, gloves, bonnet, ties, gaiters, fur muff,
and muffler—their sole difference being quality;
whilst there, all the clothing the son of a prince

requires consists of two articles—a shirt and the kofije.

Now, I ask, is the Arab mother, who wants so very little for herself and for her child, to work as hard as the European housewife? She has not the slightest idea what is meant by darning stockings or mending gloves, or of any of those numerous trifles that a nursery entails; and as for that important and troublesome domestic item, a washing-day, it is a thing to us unknown; our linen is washed daily, and dried in little more than half an hour, smoothed flat (not ironed), and put away. We do not use, and are therefore spared the anxiety of those useless ornaments called muslin curtains. The garments of an Eastern woman, those of the greatest lady included, require an incredibly small amount of attention and mending: this is easily explained, as women move very little either indoors or out, and have fewer dresses.

All this helps to render life to Eastern women, without distinction of station and rank, much less complicated. But to become properly acquainted with, and to get initiated into all these minor details of household life, it is necessary to have been in the East, and to have lived there for a considerable time. No reliance is to be placed on the reports of travellers, who stop for a short time only, who are unable to gain an insight into all these details, and maybe obtain all their information from hotel waiters. Foreign ladies even, supposing they have actually entered a harem either at Constantinople or Cairo, have never seen the inside of a real harem at all, but only its outside, represented by the state rooms decorated and furnished in European style.

Our climate, moreover, is so splendid and productive that it is hardly necessary to provide for the coming day. I do not deny that our people, taken as a whole, are averse to "flurry"; but it will be easier to realize the effects of a tropical sun, if one only considers how very trying a hot July or August in Europe can be sometimes.

I repeat it—Arabs are by no means inclined to be industrious; they only value two things, the art of war and husbandry, and but very few settle down to a trade. Though they are obliged to do much barter trade, they are poor merchants on the whole, and have but little of the Semitic talent for trading. Very little suffices for their few wants, and the future is left to provide for itself. An Arab never thinks of making plans for the morrow, as he may expect to be called away any day. He never plants but that which he can reap himself; and he considers him who acts otherwise to be "like the rich man who set up greater barns" (Luke xii.).

In this way life in the East is less laborious and more peaceful: it was this that I wanted particularly to point out and to prove before entering on a more minute description of the daily life in an Arab household. Let me, however, state expressly that I am only speaking here of things referring to Omân and Zanzibar, which, in many respects, differ from those in other Eastern countries.

The hours of prayer regulate the daily life of every Mahometan; they are said five times a day, and if this be strictly observed, as is ordained by the holy book, including ablution and changing of dress, they take up three hours at the very least.

Persons of rank are roused between four and half-past five o'clock a.m. for the first prayer, and return to sleep afterwards; devout people wait for sunrise at six o'clock a.m. before doing so; the lower classes begin their daily task immediately after the first prayer. All persons in our house could live just as they pleased, provided they followed the regulations set down for devotions and for attendance at the two principal meals.

The majority slept till eight o'clock, when the women and girls are gently roused by a slave, who begins to rub and knead them all over, which produces a very agreeable sensation. In the meantime the bath has been filled with fresh spring water, and the garments—on which jessamine and orange blossoms have been strewn during the night—are fumigated with amber and musk before they are put on.

About an hour is spent on the toilet, after which everybody has to wish our father good morning before sitting down to breakfast, the first of our two daily meals. Though a very copious and abundant repast, it took us very little time to get it over, as all the dishes had been prepared and placed on the table in readiness.

After breakfast everybody is at liberty to employ his leisure as he likes. The gentlemen get ready to go to the audience-chamber; the women, who have no work on hand, sit down at the windows to look out into the animated streets, or watch for a stealthy glance from the flashing eye of a belated noble hurrying to the *levée*, until alas! the voice of an apprehensive mother or aunt calls the unhappy girl away from the gay scene below.

Two or three hours are thus rapidly passed away. Meanwhile the gentlemen call upon each other and send word to the ladies whom they wish to visit in the evening. The older women, who take no pleasure in all this lively stir, retire to their rooms, alone or in company, to take up some fancy work, to embroider their veils, shirts, or drawers with gold thread, or cambric shirts for their husbands and sons with red and white silk—an art which requires considerable skill. Others, again, read novels, visit the sick in their rooms, or employ themselves with their own private affairs.

At one o'clock the servants announce that it is time for the second prayer. The sun is now in full-blaze, and after prayer all escape gladly to some cool place to dream away an hour or two upon handsomely plaited soft mats, into which sacred mottoes are woven, or to chat and eat cakes and fruit.

The third prayer is said at four o'clock p.m., and then we dress in our more elaborate afternoon costumes. Again we call upon our father, wishing him "good afternoon"—our grown-up brothers and sisters are allowed to call him father, the little children and their mothers only address him as hbābi (sir).

Now followed the liveliest time of the day: we sat down to our principal meal, at which all members of our large family met together for the second time. After the meal the eunuchs placed European chairs on the grand piazza in front of my father's apartments for the grown-up people, whilst we little children remained standing in deference to old age, which is, I believe, nowhere honoured to that degree. The numerous family grouped round our usually grave father, the trim and well-armed eunuchs being ranged at some distance in rank and file along the gallery. Coffee and all kinds of French fruit-syrups were handed round, of which we children partook freely. Conversation was carried on accompanied by the tunes of a mighty barrel-organ (the largest I have ever seen), or, for a change, by some large musical box; sometimes a blind Arab woman, called Amra, who possessed an exquisite voice, was called in to sing.

An hour and a half later we all separated, and employed ourselves as we liked. Some chewed betelnut, which is a Suahely habit, and not liked on that account by Arabs born in Arabia proper. Those, however, among us who had been born on the East coast of Africa, and were brought up together with negroes and mulattoes, rather fancied this habit, notwithstanding the disapproval of our Asiatic relations, though we never indulged in it in our father's presence.

Not long afterwards, gunshots and the beat of drums of the Indian guard announced sunset and the time for the fourth prayer. Not one of our daily devotions was performed faster, everybody seemed in a hurry to get it over. For those who did not wish to go out themselves (we and our mothers always required a special permission from our father or from his representative, which was rarely refused), or those who did not expect visitors, were sure to be invited by some one in the house, or received visits from brothers and sisters, stepmothers, stepchildren, or from other people. Coffee and lemonade, fruits and cakes were freely partaken of. There was a great deal of merry joking and laughing going on; some read aloud, others played at cards (never for money, however), or sang, or listened to negroes playing the sese, or sewed, embroidered, and made lace.

It is, therefore, quite a mistake to suppose that a great lady in the East does absolutely nothing. It is true she does not paint, nor play, nor dance (according to Western notions). But are there no other amusements to divert oneself with? People in our country are very temperate, and they are not given to a feverish pursuit of everchanging amusements and pleasures, though from the European point of view Oriental life may appear somewhat monotonous.

Our own personal attendants were, of course, all women; the menservants were dismissed every evening to their homes and families, and the eunuchs slept also outside the house.

Oil lamps are kept burning all night in the rooms and passages, but no candles are allowed after bedtime. Children above the age of two are no longer put to bed at a certain hour, they are left to themselves until they are tired. It frequently occurs that the children, overcome by fatigue, lie down anywhere and fall asleep, and then they are generally picked up carefully by some slaves and carried to their couches, sometimes a long way, without awaking to the fact.

Those people who have not gone out or received visitors generally retire about ten o'clock. On moonlight nights many take a walk on the flat housetops, which was a very delightful airing.

The fifth and last prayer ought to be said at 7:30 p.m., but as many are prevented at this time, it may be left unsaid until midnight or bedtime.

At bedtime all ladies of rank are waited upon by their female slaves, whose business it is to watch the falling asleep of their mistresses. One of them repeats the kneading process of the morning, while another fans gently, until they too may retire. I have mentioned already that all women go to bed fully dressed, and with all their jewels.

Chapter VII

OUR MEALS

We had two meals a day, as I have mentioned before. About nine a.m. we all met in the great saloon to kiss our father's hands. As a rule our brothers and nephews, even those who were married and who lived out of the house, shared our breakfast during the time our father lived in town with us. I do not remember, however, that he ever went out to take a meal with any of his sons or any one else.

The dishes were all arranged and placed by the eunuchs on the long sefra (dining-table). This sefra is made of wood, and looks somewhat like a billiard-table, only ours was twice as long, a little wider, and about three inches high, with a ledge of about a hand's breadth running round its sides. We do not have separate dining-rooms, and the sefra is carried into the gallery at mealtimes. Though we had some foreign furniture, such as couches, tables, and chairs, and sometimes wardrobes (my father's apartment contained a great deal of European furniture, which was more for show, however, than for actual use), we took our meals after the Eastern fashion, and sat down on the floor upon carpets and mats. Precedence was strictly observed at table. My father always took his place at the upper end of the sefra; next to

him, on his right and left, sat my elder brothers
and sisters, and the little ones (above seven years)
took the lower seats. The fashion of taking people
in to dinner is not practised.

There was always a great variety of viands,
often as many as fifteen dishes; rice dressed in
many ways. Of meat and poultry, mutton and
fowls were liked most. There was fish besides, and
Eastern bread, and all kinds of sweets and dainties. As all the dishes are placed on the table
beforehand, there is no attendance required; numerous eunuchs stand at some distance, drawn
up in line to carry out special orders. Their services were mostly required by my father, who
would send in portions to the smaller children
who were not yet admitted to table, or to sick
people. At Bet il Mtoni he used to make me sit in a
place where he could reach my plate. We had the
same food as the grown-up people, but it was
always a pleasure to us to have our dishes selected
by him, and he himself greatly enjoyed doing so.

On sitting down to table, every one said in an
undertone, but quite audibly: "In the name of the
merciful Lord," and on rising, "Thanked be the
Lord of the universe." My father always sat down
and rose first.

Clean plates were not handed to each person as
is the custom in Europe, but the various dishes
(with the exception of rice) were served up in
small plates, symmetrically arranged along the
sefra, and two people could always eat out of one
plate.

Drinks were not taken at meals, but after them
sherbet or sugared water was handed round.
There was no talking, unless some one was specially addressed by my father; the greatest silence

prevailed, which was very pleasant. Neither flowers nor fruit were placed on the sefra.

Shortly before and after each meal male and female slaves, smartly dressed, handed round basins to wash our hands. As a rule we used our fingers to eat with—knives and forks were deemed superfluous, and they were used only when European guests were entertained. Meats and fish were chopped up small beforehand, and we had spoons for all liquids. The upper classes perfume their hands after the washing, to remove any traces of the viands.

Fruit was never taken at meals, but either before or some time after. Each person had a certain quantity of the kinds in season sent to her rooms.

Half an hour after breakfast and dinner coffee was served by eunuchs in those well-known little Oriental cups in gold or silver casings. The coffee is very strong, boiled down to syrup, and filtered quite clear. It is taken without sugar and milk, and nothing is eaten with it, except, perhaps, a very finely chopped "areka" nut.

Coffee is always poured into the cup immediately before it is taken, and as the pouring out requires some skill, there are but few servants who can be selected for this office. The neat coffee-pot of tin, with brass clasps (china is never used), is carried in the left hand, and one of the little cups in its casing (called sarf) in the right one of the servant who pours out the beverage, an assistant following with a tray of empty cups and a large pot to fill up from. If he finds all the company still together, his work is quickly done, otherwise it is his duty to seek out each person.

It is well known that coffee is highly valued in the East, and great care is devoted to its preparation. The quantity required is roasted, ground, and boiled immediately before use, that it may be quite fresh. Neither the surplus of roasted beans nor the boiled coffee is ever kept; what remains is either thrown away or used by the lower servants if they like.

The second and last meal is taken every afternoon at four o'clock precisely, and nothing more is served after the same until breakfast next morning, except coffee and fruits.

Chapter VIII

BIRTH AND FIRST YEARS OF THE LIFE OF A PRINCE AND PRINCESS

Although the birth of a prince or a princess with us was not announced by the salute of guns, it was nevertheless always an event of importance, which caused much joy, but I regret to say much envy also. Our father and the respective mother were of course delighted at the birth of a child, and we little ones fully shared their joy. A new-born brother or sister had to go through all manners of ceremonies, and as such births occurred five or six times annually in our family, they were the welcome cause of as many family festivities to us.

No Mahometan will suffer the assistance of a medical man in such cases; midwives alone are allowed and admitted, and they are ignorance itself. The majority of them come from Hindustan, and are much preferred to native women; I do not know for what reason, for a midwife from Hindustan knows as little or less of her business than those from Arabia or from the Suahely country. In fact, mother as well as child may thank God alone, and their constitution, if they survive at all or keep well afterwards, for they owe no thanks to their stupid and foolish nurses.

After a warm water bath a kind of bandage is

wound round the child's body, its neck and armpits are powdered with some strongly perfumed vegetable powder, and it is dressed in a calico shirt of an ingrain dye, or in a muslin one. The little thing is then placed on its back, its hands and feet are straightened out to the utmost, and it is swathed in a swathing-band up to the shoulders, the tiny arms and legs being thus firmly confined. In this state the child remains for forty days, except while the band is removed twice a day to give it a bath. By this process the child's body, it is thought, will be made straight and faultless for life.

The mother always watches over the child herself, and never leaves it to the care of any of her servants. She rarely, however, nurses the child herself, except for a pastime, for each child has one or two wet nurses up to the age of two. Slaves are set incessantly to rock the cradle, which is of East Indian workmanship, and made of the finest wood beautifully carved.

If the child be a girl, she has holes pricked in her ears on the seventh day with a needle and thread of red silk, generally six in each ear, to which heavy gold rings are attached for ever when she is two months old. I say "for ever," because females who do not wear earrings either mourn a deceased relation or they have no holes pierced.

On the fortieth day a ceremony is performed to which European children could not be subjected: all the hair is shaved off the child's head. This may appear incredible, but many things in the South are different from what they are here. A bald-headed child would be considered as great a curiosity as a child born with a few tufts of hair is in this country. My Hamburg nurse was quite surprised when she saw for the first time my newborn daughter, whose black hair came down to her neck; nor was she satisfied until she had made my late husband bring home a small soft brush, with which she delighted in curling the baby locks two days old.

The shaving is done by the chief eunuch with certain ceremonies, in which fumigation with a species of a gum-arabic (somewhat similar to the incense used in Roman Catholic churches) plays an important part. The first hair is considered of much moment—it must not be burnt, nor carelessly thrown away, but buried in the ground, thrown into the sea, or hidden in some crevice of a wall. Twenty to thirty persons are always present during this ceremony, and the chief eunuch, who only on this occasion acts as barber, runs a great risk of crushing the soft and tender skull of the infant. He, as well as his numerous assistants, then receives a valuable present from my father.

The swathing band is removed on this day, rings are put on the arms and legs, and attached to the ears, and the child is dressed in a silk shirt and the kofije, a cap of gold stuff with ear-flaps. After this day everybody may go and look at it, for up to that time no one but the parents, the slaves on duty, and a few of the most intimate of the mother's friends were allowed to do so. This precaution is taken on account of the widespread belief in the evil eye and other dreaded species of witchcraft.

Little children of this age in the East look, beyond a doubt, much better than European ones, in whose dresses white predominates. My opinion remains unchanged on this point even after my long residence in Europe, and my own

children looked hideous to me in their baby
clothes when I compared them with my little
brothers and sisters in their pretty attire.

The smallest children are already strongly perfumed, and everything they use and wear—
dresses, sheets, bath-towels, and swathing
clothes—are covered all night with jessamine (different from that known here), fumigated with amber and musk, and sprinkled all over with attar of
roses before they are used. It must be remembered that windows and doors are open nearly all
day throughout the year, which mitigates to a
certain extent any bad effect arising from this
curious partiality for strong scents.

Several charms are also attached to the child's
body on the fortieth day to protect it against the
effects of the evil eye. They are called "Hamaye,"
or "Hafid," and consist of all sorts of things; the
lower class using an onion, or a bit of garlic, small
shells, or a piece of bone stitched up in leather
and worn on the upper part of the left arm. In the
upper classes these kinds of charms are replaced
by gold or silver plates, worn on a chain round
the neck, upon which sentences from the Kurān
are engraved. The boys wear them only up to a
certain age, the girls generally a longer period.
The favourite charm consists of a gold or silver
locket of pretty workmanship, likewise worn on a
chain, two inches long by one inch wide, enclosing
a miniature of the "hurs" (guardian). No person
wearing a charm like this, bearing the holy name
of the Lord, may enter an unclean place—a proof
surely of the great reverence of a true Mahometan
for his Lord and Creator!

From a very early age the child is fed (besides
mother's milk) from a long spouted cup several
times a day with milk soup, boiled with rice flour

and sugar; the sucking bottle was quite unknown in my time. It receives no other kind of food until it teethes; after that it may eat anything. It is not customary to carry the children about, they are put on the carpet and then left to their own devices.

Another festivity follows at the first attempt of the child to sit up by itself, for the exclusive benefit of its little brothers and sisters. To celebrate this festive event in befitting style, extra cakes and other good things are provided. The mother, the nurses, and the child are dressed in their best, and wear their finest jewels. The child is then put into a small square carriage on low wheels, stuffed with cushions. The little legs are steadied upon a board fixed perpendicularly to the poles, and the other children gather all round.

Grains of Indian corn, which have been roasted in a peculiar way, till they get as large as a thimble and soft as wadding, are then mixed with a quantity of small silver coin, and this compound is poured over the child's head; this done, the children rush upon their little brother or sister to obtain the coins, not seldom endangering the infant's life. The children of friends are sometimes invited on this occasion.

The child runs about barefooted until it is strong enough to wear sandals. Those worn by boys (watje) are much lighter than the kubkâb of the girls, and the latter are generally allowed to wear boys' sandals until they are able to put on the kubkâb. Stockings are not worn by either sex; ladies of rank use them at times upon riding excursions, as custom requires the ankles to be covered.

Besides the nurses, two or three slaves are ap-

pointed as personal attendants to each child when
it is three months old, after which they are its
property. The number of slaves is gradually increased as the child gets older, and in the case of
death of any of them the vacant place is filled up
by another, or a certain sum of money is paid
instead by my father. The little girls wear boys'
caps in the house up to a certain age.

Until their seventh year the princes live among
the women; they then solemnly embrace the
Mosaic faith, the ceremony being followed by
great festivities, in which the state dignitaries and
all high officials take part. This, if possible, is
enacted in the country and in the presence of our
father, and ends in public rejoicings of three days'
duration.

On this occasion the boy is presented with a
quiet mare, and with mounted attendants. The
boys are thus taught to ride from early youth, and
in time attain the dexterity of circus riders. It
requires, of course, a great deal more skill to gain
a firm seat on horseback without the good saddles
and stirrups used in this country. So great was the
importance my father attached to perfect horsemanship, that the slightest mishap while out riding would call forth a severe reprimand not only
on his sons, but on their incompetent riding masters.

Indeed not one of us was spoiled in the least.
My father's high sense of justice and unparalleled
generosity was combined with great and firm con-
sistency. We were expected strictly to obey our
tutors and teachers, be they Arabs, Abyssinians,
or Negroes. He was deaf to our entreaties or
complaints if ever we made any—a severity which
taught us to respect those in authority over us,

and to appreciate that authority when we had come to years of discretion.

The nurses, even those whose term of service had been but short, were highly esteemed and honoured as long as they lived. They are always slaves by birth, but as a rule they are freed as reward for their fidelity and devotion. The black nurses especially distinguish themselves by their great attachment to their charges; the most anxious mother may quietly leave her child with such a one who considers herself a second mother to the child and treats it accordingly. What a difference there is between this and the half-hearted interest shown by the nurses in this country! Many a time have I been unable to resist interceding in behalf of poor little nurslings when some flagrant carelessness forced itself upon my notice.

The contrast which exists between the wet nurses of these parts and our Arab nurses may possibly be explained by the fact that in most cases the former are compelled to forsake their own children in exchange for a perfect little stranger—a sacrifice for which, every mother will admit, no consideration of mere money will compensate.

The position of a black wet nurse with regard to the child entrusted to her by her mistress is quite a different one. She has been in the latter's service for years, may even have been born in her house: thus her own interests and those of her master's are closely knitted together. And further, there may be added a circumstance of much weight—a black nurse is not required to part with her child, but frequently, if not always, she retains it. The child of the nurse receives the same nourishment as its little foster brother or sister, shares its pap, its fowl, its bath, wears its old dresses, and by and by shares its toys. The child grows up into a slave, but always preferred to others except by very badly disposed people who can forget their foster relation.

This patriarchal state of things generates more faithful and devoted nurses than any European system could achieve. I have often reflected how very hard it must be for these poor women to part with their own children for the sake of lucre, though I have repeatedly been told that they are by no means so sensible of this as I supposed. This, however, I cannot understand. Could I ever entrust my poor helpless child to a perfect stranger, and with the greatest indifference too? Not for the world!

These black nurses, however, have *one* very bad habit: they are acquainted with all sorts of dreadful and absurd stories, which they tell the little children of three to five years to amuse and to keep them quiet. The lion (simba), the leopard (tshni), the elephant (tembo), and numberless witches (watchawi*) of course play a prominent part in these fairy tales, some of which are really blood-curdling. It is perfectly impossible to break them of this noxious habit.

Rearing children is unquestionably much easier in the South than in Northern countries: colds, coughs, and the other numerous assailants of European children are unknown there; yet although the climate is very hot, and indoor life is replete with enticing comforts, the children are not given to sluggishness and indolence; they are allowed to roam in full liberty, and from the mode of their garments their limbs are nowise fettered.

*A Swahili word, the singular of which is mtshawi.

Gymnastics are unknown, but boys from ten to twelve go in greatly for high jumping, some of their flying leaps taking them over two horses.

Swimming in the sea is practised as eagerly, and the boys teach themselves. At an early age they learn to shoot, and very passionately too, sham fights being very favourite pastimes. In spite of boys always going about armed to the teeth, provided with as much ammunition as grown-up men, one hardly ever hears of an accident arising from want of precaution.

I have already mentioned that the young princes live in their fathers' houses up to a certain age, after which a residence of their own is assigned to each, in which they generally keep house with their mother if she be living. They have a certain monthly allowance, fully sufficient to supply all their wants. In the event of marriage or an increase to the family, or even after a time of irreproachable conduct, an extra allowance may be looked for, but in no other case. However, on the arrival of our father's ships once a year with new goods, all our brothers and sisters living by themselves appeared with the whole of their family to claim their individual share, whether they required it or not. If any of them had the misfortune of exceeding their allowance they found it no easy matter to extricate themselves, as my father never countenanced the fact, and none would transgress more than once if he could help it.

In case of war, which was unfortunately rather frequent in Oman, all the princes, the half-grown included, were expected to join and take their part in the fight like the common soldier.

They were subjected to a very strict discipline, but this only caused the sons to look up to their father with greater respect and veneration. I often watched, as a child, how my elder brothers would hurry to the door, in advance of the slaves, to put the sandals my father had left there in readiness for him.

There is but little to say about the education of a princess: the first years of her life resemble that of her brothers, with the exception that the latter were allowed much more liberty out of the house after completing their seventh year. The only thing which deserves mention is, that at the birth of a princess—to suit the hairdress in our country—a broad comb, generally of silver, is placed under the back of the newborn child's head, to give it a flat shape. When a princess is married to one of her numerous cousins, either in Oman or in Zanzibar, she quits her paternal home, of course, in exchange for that of her husband. The former, however, remains open to her at all times, as the sole and real place of shelter against any vicissitudes of life, though she may go and live with a brother if she prefers it. Each sister has her favourite brother, and *vice versa;* they maintain a fast friendship in good and in bad times, and advise and help each other to their utmost. Though this might prove a source of deep joy in one way, it often gave rise to bitter jealousies which the stoutest heart had difficulty in overcoming—neither were the opportunities very rare in so large a family as ours.

It often happened, too, that a sister would intercede with our father in mitigation of some foolish deed of a favourite brother, and succeed entirely on the strength of his evident preference for his daughters, and his usual inability to refuse any of their requests. He was particularly kind and courteous to his elder daughters, walking towards them and seating them by his side on a sofa, while the elder sons and the little people stood by respectfully.

Chapter IX

SCHOOLING IN THE EAST

On the whole the school (madrse) is considered by
Eastern people, and likewise by us, as of little
moment and consequence. School in Europe is
the centre of life in Church and State, alike to
prince and to citizen; on its efficiency depends
essentially the cultivation of mind and knowledge
as well as most future prospects. In the East the
"madrse" is altogether a matter of secondary consideration, and for a good many people it does not
exist at all. Before discussing this point further I
wish to say something about what we called
"school" at our house.

Between the age of six or seven all children—
boys and girls—had to enter the mdarse; the
latter were only required to learn to read, the
former both to write and read. At Bet il Mtoni
and at Bet il Sahel there was only one lady
teacher, respectively, specially imported by our
father from Oman. I need not say that unforeseen
holidays, brought about by our teacher's occasional sickness, did not meet with proper regret
on our part.

We had no separate schoolroom; our lessons
were said in an open gallery, to which pigeons and
parrots, peacocks and ricebirds, found free in-
gress. We also had an uninterrupted view of the

courtyard and its busy life there. All the furniture
of the schoolroom consisted of a single large mat.
Our school property was equally simple—all we
required was a Kurān on a stand (marfā), a small
inkstand containing homemade ink and the well-
bleached shoulder-blade of a camel for a slate, on
which the writing with ink is easy, without the
irritating, jarring noise produced on the slate.
Slaves have to see to the cleaning of these blades.

The first thing we learned was the very complicated Arab A B C, after which, for want of any
other spelling-book, reading was taught from the
Kurān, and the boys copied from it. Those who
could read pretty fluently read in a chorus, and
rather loudly too. But this was the extent of our
schooling, for we never got any explanation of
what we were reading about. Hence the fact that
perhaps one only amongst a thousand really understands and is able to explain the sense and the
precepts of the Mahometan holy book, though
there may be eighty in every hundred who have
learned at least half of it by heart. To meditate or
to speculate upon its contents is considered irre-
ligious and condemnatory; people are simply to
believe what they are taught, and this maxim is
rigorously carried out.

After a repast of fruit we assembled at seven
o'clock in the morning on our mat, and there
awaited the arrival of our teacher, whiling away
the time with wrestling, boxing, jumping, and
with perilous attempts at climbing the railings,
&c. A watch was set at a corner of the gallery to
inform us, by a cough, of the teacher's approach,
upon which we would promptly seat ourselves,
looking extremely demure, only to rebound, like
so many indiarubber balls, respectfully to shake
hands with the dreaded one and to wish her good

morning. She always carried the much detested bamboo cane in one hand, and a large brass inkstand in the other. Until she had taken her seat we had to stand up before her in file, and were finally allowed to sit down ourselves cross-legged around her on the matting.

She now began to recite the first Sura of the Kurān, which may be called the Mahometan Lord's Prayer, echoed in chorus by us and concluded with Amīn (not Amen). Then we repeated what we had learned the day before, and took a new piece in reading and writing. Lessons lasted till nine o'clock precisely, and were resumed after breakfast up to second prayers at noon.

Each of us was allowed to bring some slaves to school to join in our lessons; they sat at some distance behind us, while we grouped ourselves as we pleased. There were neither fixed places nor a division into forms. Reports which are looked forward to with such feverish anxiety in European schools were unknown to us. Our respective mothers and our fathers received only a verbal report if any of us made very good progress, and in the reverse case, or if very good or bad conduct called for comment. Our teacher had received special orders to punish us severely whenever she deemed it necessary, and we gave her often enough occasion to make use of her cane.

Besides reading and writing, we were taught a little arithmetic, that is, ciphering in writing up to 100, and up to 1000 mentally; everything beyond that was thought of to be evil. No pains were taken with either grammar or orthography; the very complicated "Ilnahu" can only be acquired by much reading in after years. Of such sciences as history, geography, mathematics, physics, and others I never heard—I only was made acquainted with these branches of science when I came to Europe. I am not sure, however, that I am so much better off now for the smattering I have acquired of these things at great pains, than the people on the other side. This only I know, that my increased knowledge has not saved me from being repeatedly deceived and swindled. Oh, ye happy ones at home who are spared the inevitable sorrows which lie beneath the dazzling gauze of civilization!

The style of our tuition did not admit of home tasks of course, which take up so many hours in this country.

The teacher, feared as she may be, is treated with great respect by everybody, and by her pupils especially is treated with veneration in after life.

One thing, however, schoolchildren in the East and in Europe have in common—the natural instinct of gaining the teacher's favour by means of little bribes. When my children used to ask me for a few pence to buy a nosegay or a flower-pot for Miss So-and-so, I was always reminded of my own schooldays. This trait belongs, I believe, to every race and nation. Before we ever dreamt of the existence of foreign countries or of their schools and schoolchildren, my brothers and sisters and myself tried to ingratiate ourselves with our teacher by taking her all sorts of things, sweets in preference; every day she received a goodly portion of the French goodies our father gave us. I know not whether the other effect of this kind of present was a premeditated one, but certain it is that a repeated result was a violent toothache— and a holiday for us.

There was no fixed term for attending school. What was considered necessary to know had to be learned in any case; but it depended entirely upon the capacity of each individual if this knowledge was acquired in one year, in two, or more.

Fancy work was not taught at school, it was from our mothers that we acquired the art of sewing, embroidery, and lace-making, at which most of them were very proficient, though we were not expected to attain any particular standard. Some of my sisters, for instance, who had acquired great skill in such work, could easily have made a living by it, had they ever needed; others, again, never got beyond sewing on a button.

There exist some schools, but only for children of poor parents. Every one who is at all able to afford it, keeps a private tutor or a governess. Sometimes the secretary of the master of the house undertook to give lessons to the girls— however, only as long as they were quite young.

This brief mention is all I have to say of our schools. It is but natural that I should sometimes be tempted to draw comparisons between them and European ones, between the over-cultured here and the ignorance of the children there. I myself was born, bred, and educated there, and my judgment, which is based upon my experience both in Arabia and Europe, and which I feel to be quite free from any prejudice whatever, may perhaps be of interest.

In general I am of the opinion that Europeans exact just *that* too much from a school, as the Arabs demand too little. As yet no people has discovered the right middle course, nor will it ever be found; contrasts like these will exist as long as the world lasts.

There is hardly any science which the children are *not* taught here, and to such an extent that the childish understanding cannot possibly retain all.

With the beginning of school life parents see hardly anything of their children. The latter are so much overtasked, even after their regular school-hours, that home life and influence are almost at an end. There is a continued race and chase all day from task to task, and how much of these studies will be of lasting value to them? How much of it is crammed, only to be forgotten again as quickly! To my idea, a few extra hours spent in their home would leave a healthier impression on their minds and memories by and by.

For five or more hours daily the poor children are cooped up in a schoolroom which is insufferably hot and stifling. In one school, with more than two hundred children, I remarked that there were only four tumblers. Can any one be surprised under such circumstances if a child sickens? However much care and pains may be taken for its welfare at home, they are rendered quite useless by the effect of the foul school air. You need only look at some of these children to make your heart ache! Was not our large, lofty gallery a much fitter place? What is the use of all accomplishments if they are acquired by ruining health?

Of that feeling of respect which was inculcated into us in early youth for our parents, teachers, and tutors, and old age in general, there is not much to be perceived here. The lessons in religion also seem to me to miss their aim; the children are overburdened with learning numberless dates of ecclesiastical history, while their hearts remain a barren soil.

The word of God and His holy commandments should be taught more, and less time be bestowed on subtle inquiries into indifferent matter. It will surely always remain a vain longing of the short-sighted human mind to fathom the innermost secrets of nature and creation. I once read a beautiful and impressive simile. Man's short life was there compared with that of a moth, which first saw the light of day within the walls of a large cathedral; the moth's short span of life expired long long before it could realize one hundredth part of all the beauty and mystery surrounding it—such is the life of man amid the wonders of the universe. Let wise men continue their investigations and their broodings; but let them cease cramming children's minds with dry unprofitable stuff that the brain cannot digest and the soul sickens with and dies.

I was shocked, in looking over some statistics on lunacy, to find that the majority of these deplorable cases were returned from former students of high schools and universities. A good many of these surely were the victims of over-pressure. I could not help thinking of my native home, where lunatic asylums are not needed, where I never saw but two maniacs, and never heard of any others—and of these two, one was a negress, the other a native of Hindustan.

As I previously said, I have no desire to criticise European culture, nor am I able to do so; I only wished to speak of my own observations, which convinced me that there are many sad failures in the European educational system. But at all events, I shall be pardoned if I question the right which Europeans take upon themselves in deploring the fate of a people as yet "unenlightened," and their justification in forcibly imparting their civilization to the same. I am firmly convinced, Arab born and bred as I am, that all efforts on the part of Europeans to do away, at a sweep, with the incarnate ignorance of Mahometans, and to fly the flag of science and

learning, with even the smallest amount of pre-
cipitation, will meet with barren effect.

Other nations, like the Japanese for instance,
whose creed and precepts are less binding than
the Mahometan, probably offer a more grateful
soil—the more so as they are naturally more desirous of stepping into the footprints of Europeans.

People frequently deride the Turkish half-
culture, and yet the Turks have striven much
harder to become civilized than is at all good for
them. They have only weakened themselves without achieving the desired end, because foreign
culture is contrary and opposed to their funda-
mental views. Civilization cannot be obtruded by
force, and it will only be just to concede to every
nation the right of adhering without hindrance to
their views and institutions, which have in the
course of centuries been founded under the influence of ripened experience and practical worldly
wisdom. Above all, the pious Arab would be
deeply shocked if his civilization were to begin
with lessons on natural science, of which, according to the European code of education, people are
supposed to know something. What would be his
bewilderment if any one were to talk to him of the
laws of nature, who sees in all the universe, down
to its most infinitesimal details, but one source of
creation—the all-guiding and all-directing hand
of God!

Chapter X.

YEARLY OUTFIT. TOILET AND FASHION IN OUR HOUSEHOLD.

In Europe the father of a family generally makes his wife and his unmarried daughters a certain monthly or quarterly allowance for their dresses. This, however, is not the case with us. Zanzibar has no manufacture of any kind, therefore all the clothing and materials required for the entire population have to be imported from foreign lands.

My father carried on an extensive barter trade for the immense requirements of his various households. Several of his large sailing ships were annually despatched laden with produce (principally cloves) to England, Marseilles, Persia, to the East Indies and to China, and the net proceeds of these cargoes was reinvested by our agents in these countries in such goods as they had instructions to purchase. The master of each vessel took an endless list of the goods to be brought back, most of them being articles of dress and fashion.

The day for the yearly distribution of these goods depended, of course, upon the return of the ships. It is but natural that this event was impatiently looked forward to; it signified to us the beginning of a new season of fashion, and the style and quality of our finery for a whole year depended upon the contents of the ships lying in our ports.

To us children this time also had an especial charm: it brought all our beautiful toys from Europe. I remember my frantic joy on one of these occasions at being presented with a beautifully dressed doll—my first one—a doll that cried and had teeth!

Soon after the vessels had arrived in port, a day was fixed on which the distribution of the cargo was to take place to old and young, high and low, in the house. Our younger brothers generally tried to find out beforehand from the captains what toys they had brought back. There were always twenty to thirty cases, containing nothing but horses, carriages, dolls, whips, fishes and ducks, with magnets, musical boxes of all sizes, concertinas, flutes, trumpets, guns, and what not! Woe to the captain whose goods did not give satisfaction, for he was responsible for all he brought back, having full power and positive orders to buy only the best of everything, wherever he could get it, without regard to price.

The distribution took place at Bet il Mtoni and at Bet il Sahel, and it always took three to four days before each of the hundreds of recipients had received his share. The eunuchs had to do the unpacking, and my elder brothers and sisters were entrusted with the general apportioning. I regret to say, however, that this time never went by without a good deal of heart-burning and real or imaginary grievances.

The materials for clothing, costly and plain, were delivered to each member of the family, after which a lively exchange was carried on in the house for the next fortnight—resulting in a general satisfaction all round. There were musk, ambergris, numerous Oriental oils, attar of roses and rosewater, saffron (which, mixed with other ingredients, is used for dressing the hair), silks of all colours, gold and silver thread for fancy work, gilt and silver buttons—in short, every article an Arab lady could desire—besides which, to refund the outlay for various trifles, a certain sum of money (in Maria Theresia coins) was paid over to each, varying according to rank and age.

Sometimes it happened that an extravagantly fashionable lady spent more in the course of a year than she could well afford—in which case she would have to appeal to father or husband for help. Such requests were always kept very secret, for the lords of Arabian households are as averse to recklessness as their Northern brethren, and although the petitioner's request was generally granted, it was also accompanied with a wholesome reprimand.

Of course there were also people of economical propensities among the members of our household, and these were of the opinion that keeping slaves for mere show—a custom with people of rank and wealth—is a great piece of extravagance. They, therefore, had their young women-slaves instructed in different branches of trade, such as dressmaking, embroidering, and lace-making, while the boys were employed in saddlery, carpentering, and so on. The owners of such slaves managed thus to greatly reduce their expenditure, whilst those who were less provident gave their work out to be done, and paid heavily in proportion. The slaves who had been brought up to some kind of trade were more highly valued than those who had not had this advantage, and were better able to make a living when freed. In

Oman, where but few slaves are kept, it is a standing rule to have them taught a trade that will be of use to their masters as well as to themselves. For this reason, slaves are frequently sent from Zanzibar to Oman for a practical education. A negro or a negress of this class always obtained a higher price.

If any visitors happened to be staying with us at the time of distribution, they always received, by my father's orders, a share of the presents, and even of money—the residue of the cargoes being put aside in store for our numerous relatives that came to see us from Oman in the course of the year.

Our yearly outfit was of course adapted to, and very much simplified by, our close proximity to the equator, where we only know the four seasons by name. It would have been rather a difficult matter to provide garments for autumn, winter, and spring wear all at the same time. The only winter we have is the rainy season for some six or eight weeks, with a temperature as low as 70° F. During this more wet than cold season, velvets and stouter materials are worn.

All clothing was hand-made, as sewing-machines were unknown in my time. All dresses rejoice in a uniformly simple cut, alike for men and women, differing only in materials and trimmings. The abomination of tight-lacing, or lacing of any kind, has not yet found its way into the elegant world of the East—neither that fickle goddess, at whose shrine there is so much blind and reckless worship in these enlightened lands of Europe.

Of whatever rank or station an Arab woman may be, her dress consists only of a shirt reaching down to the ankles, trousers (*not* drawers), and a kerchief for the head. The material varies, of course. Rich people have gold brocades of many patterns, velvets and silks richly trimmed. During the hot season plain light calicoes or muslins are worn. Shirt and trousers are never of the same pattern. The shirt must not be too long, that it may not hide the rich embroidery of the trousers or the two anklets; a number of little golden bells are suspended from one of these, which make a pretty tinkling sound at every step. Two long tasselled ribbons hang loosely over the back or on both sides of the head, from the band that is worn round the forehead. The silk kerchief reaches down to the ankles.

In her walks an Arab lady puts on the "schele," which is shawl, waterproof, and cloak, all in one. The schele is a large shawl or mantilla of black silk, more or less richly trimmed with gold or silver borders, according to the wealth and taste of its owner. This is the only wrapper an Arab lady uses until it is completely worn out, its fashion never changing; even the greatest and richest ladies do not possess more than one schele at a time.

That an Oriental lady, in the idle indolence of her exotic home, and in the uncultured condition of her mind, should give her finery a good deal of thought, does not seem so very unpardonable. But what struck me, years ago, before I became accustomed to the fact, was that the ladies I came into contact with in my new European home, and who had, I knew, from their childhood up, received the most thorough and comprehensive mental training—that these ladies, I say, should never find any other topic of conversation but the all-important, all-engrossing one—dress.

During the rainy season the great Arab ladies

wear indoors the "djocha," a kind of cloak of cloth trimmed with gold and silver embroidery. It is worn open in front, only held together over the breast with gold lacing. The elder ladies prefer a Persian shawl to the djocha. This is the only covering to protect us against the comparative coolness of winter or rainy season.

I may mention that we had, in cases of emergency, a kind of heating apparatus. It consisted of a brass bowl, some 8 inches deep by 12 inches wide, on a three-legged stand, which was filled with burning charcoal, and placed in the centre of the room, the charcoal fire producing a very pleasant and mild heat. This "mankal" served at the same time to roast the green, freshly-gathered cobs of Indian corn. Doors and windows were, however, always left open, even when we had such a fire in the room.

Chapter XI

A PLANTATION

My father owned forty-five plantations, scattered all over the island. Fifty to sixty slaves were employed as labourers on most of these estates, and as many as five hundred on the larger ones, with an Arab overseer to each estate. Two only of the plantations had real palaces, six to eight had villas, and the remainder merely had houses for the officials, and farm-buildings. For a stay of any length we could only visit one of the first.

During my father's lifetime we could but seldom leave the town, and then for a short time only, as he was always too busily engaged, and preferred staying at home. But as we all very much enjoyed such visits to a plantation, we generally teased him till he granted us permission to go.

These excursions always required great preparations, since it was no easy matter to provide properly for so many people on a plantation some eight miles distant, to which all the provisions had to be conveyed upon the heads of negro slaves. Several hundred of these came some days prior to our departure to carry off all that was requisite. To the great annoyance of our cooks and chief eunuchs, into whose management it was given, so much was destroyed and lost on the road, that double the quantity actually required had to be

sent out. The overseers of the plantations we visited always came off very well on these occasions,
for they were allowed to keep for their own use
what we left behind.

The night before the start most of us were too
excited to retire to rest, so instead we went and
inspected our lovely white asses which were to
carry us, their tails having been dyed red with
henna.

But those who happened to have no ass of their
own had either to stay at home, or to borrow
one—my father having no time to trouble himself
with such matters.

Matters were, however, greatly simplified when
our destination was a plantation on the seashore,
for there were plenty of boats to convey us and
our provisions.

These excursions offered the welcome opportunity to all the ladies for showing off their finery.
How they vied to outdo each other in splendour!
Indeed, if one of the "belles" had set her heart
upon wearing a particular new garment, which
did not come home in time, she would bemoan her
disappointment by staying behind.

Our start was generally fixed for half-past five
in the morning, immediately after the first prayer.
For hours there has been noise and confusion in
the courtyard below—half-a-dozen voices calling
down the stairs, and as many shouting back;
slaves tumbling over each other, and vociferating
loudly—sometimes even cutting their arguments
short by kicks and cuffs. And mingled with all
these various sounds you heard the bray of the
asses, intended, no doubt, to remind you that
they have been saddled for the last hour.

Everything is ready at last, and the animals are
led into the road, and mounted. The slender and

weak eunuchs are likewise on horseback; the black slaves, however, are on foot. During the very pleasant ride which now begins, many harmless tricks are played and enjoyed to wile away the hour.

The whole cavalcade looks very picturesque: the white donkeys with their rich trappings of gold and silver plates, jingling at every step, their high saddles and splendid saddle-clothes, as well as our sturdy runners in their clean white robes and their glittering muskets. As the sun gets hotter, one of these slaves runs by the side of each lady's animal with a large parasol to protect the rider from the glare. Some of the slaves trot along with one of the smaller children, while the bigger ones, who cannot yet ride by themselves, are placed on the saddle with a eunuch.

We passed through the town at dawn, and kept close together as long as we were within the city walls; but as soon as we had emerged into the open country, all restraint was over, and we hurried along as best we could. However much the eunuchs might try to keep the procession together by calling out in their thin voices to the riders of very fiery animals, we generally arrived at the end of our journey in separate small detachments.

The first and oldest of our slaves and the family of the overseer, if he was married, were in attendance to receive us. But the overseer himself, conformably with Eastern etiquette, did not show himself during our whole stay.

Fruits of all kinds were handed round immediately after our arrival, and we sat down to breakfast at once in the same order of rank as at home. After breakfast we separated to amuse ourselves as we might, quite unrestrainedly, for here we could wander wherever we pleased, since no strangers were likely to surprise us in the grounds. Only at meals and at prayers the whole company met again.

Invitations from the adjoining estates soon followed, and the ladies from the neighbourhood sent word to announce their visits. Invitations and calls were always intended for all the family; while our guests were received and entertained only by our elder brothers and sisters, every member of the family was at liberty to accept an invitation.

As it was impossible to provide the necessary bedding for so many people, everybody lay down to sleep on horse and saddle-clothes, their arm for a pillow.

The quantities of eatables consumed on these excursions were really astounding. I have already said that these were conveyed by many hundred slaves for several days; besides all this, our kind neighbours insisted upon replenishing our store daily, in proof of their friendly feeling. I need not say that many cases of sickness occurred in consequence of this bountiful feasting.

Dear old Ledda, the head of the customs, had always shown, though a Banjan, rare loyalty and great personal attachment to our family, and nothing pleased the grey-haired star-worshipper more than to think of some new amusement for us children. He never forgot to send us pretty and curious presents, ordered from his Indian home, which invariably included, besides sweetmeats, several baskets of fireworks (fetâk). He always sent an extra relay of these latter when we made an excursion into the country, so that our evenings were made very pleasant, watching the effect of the beautiful Indian pyrotechnical constructions. But, failing those, we spent our evenings in the gardens, looking on at the games and dancing of the negroes. The negro dances are not nearly as ugly and uncouth as some African travellers describe them. When I first saw Europeans dance I did not admire the art either, for the continual turning round of the dancers made me feel giddy only to look. We generally took them with us to the plantations for our evening's entertainment. Their performances are very clever, and they are well paid for them. They may not receive the fabulous sums that are lavished on great dancers in Europe, still they are sufficiently well paid to enable them to return to their Indian homes in gladness, notwithstanding their extravagant habits. They are, however, held in little esteem in our country.

Such evenings in the East are truly romantic. Fancy a numerous company of all complexions, elgantly dressed—though somewhat fantastically and gaudily—standing, sitting, and squatting in all directions, laughing and making harmless fun with all the unconventional ease of Southerners—the whole framed in with the foliage of the most magnificent trees, and bathed in the silvery light of an intensive tropical moon! Description fails to do justice to a scene which, however, once beheld, can never be forgotten.

But the hour came at last, though not before the greater part of the night was spent, when we felt it was time to break the charm and retire to our rest.

On these excursions we often took a funny little French girl and her two wild brothers, fourteen and fifteen years old, the children of the French Consular doctor. They all three talked Suahely very well, and sang most amusing songs. The first time Claire came with us, she caused a general burst of laughter at bed-time, when she appeared in her white European nightgown. We had never heard of such a thing before, for everybody in the East lies down to sleep in the dress worn during the day—at least, in washing dresses, not in a costume made of velvet or gold brocade.

During a protracted stay, our father used to pay us flying visits of a few hours at a time, for he always returned to town in the evening. On such occasions mounted couriers kept up an uninterrupted communication between the town and our plantation.

We rarely undertook these excursions at harvest-time, so as not to interrupt the slaves in their labour. Cloves have a peculiarity of ripening quite suddenly, so that it requires the greatest exertions to gather in the crops at the right moment. Rice, too, makes a quick harvest, while more time can be taken over gathering in the sugar-cane, cocoanuts, sweet potatoes, and other produce. Cattle is never used for farming purposes, and scarcely any agricultural implements, not even the most simple plough, is known. All the work is performed by hand; the ground is dug with spades, and the rice cut in sheaves with a common little straight knife. The master or the mistress of the estate frequently joins in the work during the clove harvest, to stimulate their negro slaves, whose inborn idleness requires a great deal of shaking up; but since this cannot be done individually, they have a task set them, proportionate with their age and strength. Anything in excess of this task is rewarded, and the shortcomings are punished. The only really busy time of the year, then, is the harvest. The ground in that gracious clime almost takes care of itself. No manure is

ever used, except the straw that is sometimes
burnt.

The length of our stay was determinmed by my
father, and he fixed the day on which, between
half-past six and half-past seven o'clock, p.m., we
had to be back in town. The family of the overseer
received on our departure suitable gifts, which
my father himself selected, and we were always
accompanied some distance by our lady friends
from the neighbouring estates. An escort of about
one hundred and fifty soldiers was sent to meet
and conduct us into the city. In spite of their
heavy accoutrements (every man carried musket,
shield, lance, sword, and dagger) they always
managed to keep pace with our beasts.

We were not allowed to neglect our evening
prayers, even during the journey. The company
halted somewhere near the town, generally at
Ngambo, or at Muasimodja, and prayers were
said in the open air on mats which everybody
carried for the purpose. Supposing a mat was lost
or left behind, the worshipper would kneel on the
giant leaf of a moz tree (plantain), as none other
but a vegetable substance may be used.

When it was dark a number of very large lanterns were lighted; then we once more resumed
our saddles and entered through the gates like a
procession from fairyland.

Chapter XII

MY FATHER'S VOYAGE

I was about nine years old when my father determined to visit his old empire of Oman, on a tour of inspection, as was his wont in the course of every three to four years, my eldest brother, Tuēni (incorrectly called Suēni at times) acting as regent and head of the family at Mesket.

There was besides an urgent reason this time for my father's voyage. The Persians had made several incursions in the neighbourhood of Bender Abbas, which, though of little account in themselves, might easily have caused complications of a more serious nature. This small territory in Persia, rather important from the fact of its commanding the entrance to the Persian Gulf, had not only given infinite trouble, but proved a great expense to my father ever since his occupation of it. We were deprived of it again by the Persians at a later date, which was hardly a matter for regret; there was no peace for us till they had succeeded, neither could we blame their efforts.

We owned no steamers at the time I speak of, and the departure of our sailing-ships was retarded by the absence of fair wind. It took at least eight or ten weeks before all preparations were completed and all the provisions put on board;

the baking of the captain biscuits alone took up
much time, as about one thousand persons had to
be provided for ten weeks. Salt beef we did not
know, and preserves were of no use, as they were
"harām" (*i.e.*, unclean, according to our dietary
laws); it was therefore necessary to ship an immense quantity of live stock, and a dozen milk
cows; it is impossible to state what were the quantities of fruit supplied by our forty-five plantations for the voyage, but they amply account for
the many cases of dysentery which occurred.

All sons had permission to join in an expedition
of this kind; but only few of the daughters, on
account of the inconveniences caused by women
in travelling; and only a couple of the most
favoured Sarari.

Few of us cared much about going to Oman, as
the proud Oman ladies rather regarded Zanzibar
women as uncivilized creatures. Even our brothers and sisters there were not free from this con-
ceit, and all the members of our family born in
Oman thought themselves much better and of
higher rank than any of their African relations.
In their opinion we were somewhat like negroes,
as we had been brought up amongst these; and
our speaking any other language but Arabic was
the greatest proof of barbarity in their eyes.

A great number of my brothers and sisters and
countless relations lived in Oman, most of the
latter in reduced circumstances, and supported
by my father's bounty. All these expected presents
on his arrival, and, in consequence, his luggage
was somewhat formidable.

It was also a welcome opportunity for sending
messages to friends in distant Asia, with whom
none but the feeblest correspondence had been

kept up. The general ignorance in writing was a great hindrance to this, and it can hardly be conceived to what straits most people were put to meet this difficulty. They had to get their letters written by strangers, and strangers again were employed to read them. The services of my brothers and of all the male slaves conversant with the art were at such times in great demand; but if, from pressure of work or from unwillingness, not an unfrequent case, these services could not be secured, then the compositions were entrusted into the hands of utter strangers. Needless to say that such epistles must have greatly fallen short of what would be considered private and confidential in this country.

The following may, for instance, prove a case in point. A fine lady calls up her body-servant and says, "Feruz, go to such or such a Kadi, and ask him to write a beautiful letter to my friend in Oman for me; pay him whatever he asks for it." Then Feruz is told quite a number of things which the Kadi is to put into the letter. The Kadi, however, may be greatly pressed for time, as he has a dozen such letters or more on hand, therefore it can hardly be a matter of surprise that he jumbles up the different orders. And Feruz returns in triumph to his mistress: "Here are your letters, Bibi!" The lady, however, being of a cautious turn of mind, goes to some literate person, and desires to know what the letter contains. But picture to yourself her amazement and indignation when she hears that the letter, which was intended to convey her congratulations upon some joyful event, is couched in terms of the deepest condolence. Or in another instance the case may have been exactly reversed. Consequently nearly every letter has to

be written over several times and by different
people, until it contains at last something of the
desired meaning.

Everything was ready at last. The ship *Kitorie*,
i.e., Victoria (in honour of Her Majesty Queen
Victoria), was to convey my father and his family;
and two or three other vessels took on board his
retinue, the servants, and the luggage. This was
but a small fleet to carry such a crowd of pas-
sengers. However, Eastern travellers require very
little room and no cabin of their own; everybody
looks out for a place on deck at night where he
can lie down and go to sleep on his mat.

The retinue and the slaves embarked first; next
followed the women about five o'clock in the
morning; and, lastly, my father with his sons at
noon. My brothers Khalid and Madjid, with some
of the younger ones, accompanied the travellers
on board, and remained there until the ships
weighed anchor, the *Kitorie* firing a last parting
salute of twenty-one guns to the country and to
the family collected on the shore.

The house settled down now to great quiet,
though it was as crowded as before. Every one felt
the absence of the head of the family, and we led
henceforth a somewhat retired life. My brother
Khalid, as the eldest of the remaining sons, now
reigned in Zanzibar in my father's place; several
times a week he came to see us to assure himself of
our welfare, and he went as often to Bet il Mtoni
to look after its inmates there, but especially to
receive any orders our exalted step-mother might
wish to give.

As head of the family, Khalid was very strict,
and we often had reason to complain of his harsh
measures. It may suffice to mention two instances
here. A fire broke out at Bet il Sahel once, which

was fortunately soon extinguished. When it began we all rushed to the gates in our terror, but found them locked and guarded by soldiers, who had been ordered there by Khalid, to prevent our being recklessly exposed to public view in the broad daylight.

Another time he rudely turned a distant relation of ours, who possessed great influence in Zanzibar, out of the mosque because he had dared to propose for one of my sisters in that building, nor was the poor suitor permitted to show himself for months after, either in the daily assembly or in the mosque to which Khalid went to prayers. It however came to pass that the rejected suitor married another sister of ours some years later, after Khalid's and my father's decease.

The latter had appointed my sister Khole to act as lady superintendent during his absence both in Bet il Sahel and Bet il Mtoni, to the great annoyance of many. It may well be conceived that this "bright star" of our house felt anything but comfortable in her new position, reaping nothing but ingratitude and jealousy from her office, since, notwithstanding her sweetness of temper, she found it impossible to please everybody; few only were reasonable enough to consider that hers was but a limited power. It was no fault of hers that she was so much preferred by my father; unfortunately, however, envy was too strong—it positively blinded all reason in her opponents.

In the meantime our vessels had sailed several times between Oman and Zanzibar, and brought news and presents from our father, which always created much joy and pleasure in our midst.

Unfortunately, our brother Khalid was shortly after called away by our Lord. Madjid, the son next in age, now succeeded in the regency, and contrived to gain the goodwill of all by his kind and gentle manners.

A vessel arrived at last one day from Mesket with the joyful news that our father was about to leave Oman for Zanzibar. It soon spread all over the country, and caused great satisfaction everywhere, as he had now been absent three years, and had been missed very much. Those even who were not personally attached to him looked forward to his return with pleasure on account of the many presents he was expected to bring back with him from Oman for young and old, and preparations for his reception were made everywhere, just as if we were about to celebrate one of our great holy days.

However, the time which was generally allowed for the voyage from Oman to Zanzibar passed away, and no ships arrived, which caused great uneasiness to us and to the whole country. The Arabs are fond of consulting so-called seers in the future, and nowhere does this habit prevail so much as in Zanzibar. I verily believe no gypsies in Europe can in any way equal the craftiness and mendacity of their Swahilion brethren; but, then, where else would one find such unbounded and foolish credulity to encourage their wiles?

No means were left untried which possibly might help to throw a light on the whereabouts of the three overdue ships; some of the oracles then were fetched many miles off from the most remote nooks in the country, most of them belonging to the tribe of the Wachadimu—if old, they were brought in triumph riding on donkeys.

The most remarkable of all these diviners was supposed to be a woman, of whom the story went that she, or rather her unborn child, could look

into the future. Such a monster was quite beyond
anything that had ever been heard of before, and
had, therefore, to be procured at whatever cost it
might be. One afternoon (I have never forgotten
the scene) this prophetess, appalling and un-
wieldy in size, arrived. Her unborn child was said
to be omniscient—it could tell what things were
on the highest mountain tops as well as in the
nethermost depths of the sea. Now it was to tell us
how our father was, and why his return was so
much delayed. In quite an audible, squeaking
voice the monster reported its observations, while
the company stood around spellbound. It pretended to see several three-mast vessels far away
on the high seas steering for Zanzibar; then it
proposed getting on one of the mast-tops of my
father's ship to see what was going on on board.
After a while it reported with full details what
every one there was doing. Finally it ordered
sacrifices to be brought to the spirits of the sea to
secure their future favour with which to shield the
travellers from possible evil. As a matter of
course the commands of this mysterious voice
were obeyed to the letter, and the legion of profes-
sional beggars with which our beautiful island is
infested could for several days indulge to their
hearts' content in plenteousness of meat, fowls,
and rice, which were distributed amongst them,
together with clothing and money, as acts of pro-
pitiation.

I was not a little ashamed at a later time to
perceive that we had simply been duped by a
ventriloquist. At that time, however, we all firmly
believed in the wonderful child that could reveal
the invisible and read the secrets of the future as
from a book. Even now it is not quite clear to me
whether the woman was really a conscious im-

poster or a dupe herself. No one had ever heard of a ventriloquist in our country, so that, as no denunciation was forthcoming in the shape of a satisfactory explanation, we went on implicitly believing.

In our parts people are fond of everything supernatural; the more mysterious and incomprehensible it appears the more faith it receives. Everybody believes in spirits, good and evil. At the decease of any one the chamber of death is for days fumigated with incense, and as it is a general belief that the soul of the departed has a longing to return to and especially prefers to stay in its former abode, no person cares to enter the same in the daytime, and flies from it at night.

Superstition rules supreme. In cases of sickness, of betrothal, of pregnancy, on all possible occasions, the help of female prophets is called in—they are required to know and to tell if the disease can be cured, and how long it is to last, if the betrothal may be considered a happy one, whether the expected child will be a boy or a girl, and so on. If, as on frequent occasions, the very contrary happens, the prophetess screens herself behind numerous subterfuges and excuses. She declares herself to have been under the effects of an evil star that day, and trusts to be more successful next time; and this explanation is made to do—and does do. Certain it is they prosper and grow very rich.

Chapter XIII.

DEATH-NEWS.

Day after day and week after week passed away
without my father's return; the only pastime we
had was to listen to prophecies of the kind I have
just described, and which, if they did no other
good, at least shortened our suspense. One afternoon at last, while most of us were engaged at
prayers, the gladdening news spread that a fisherman had seen several ships bearing our flag on
the high sea, but that he had not dared to approach them on account of the stormy weather.
That could be no one but our father! All hurried
away to dress in their best, which had been kept
in readiness for weeks. We always expressed our
pleasure at the return of a dear relation from a
voyage or from a victorious campaign in this way,
while we showed our regret at parting by putting
on our plainest and most simple garments.

While the fisherman was still repeating over
and over again that he had reported the truth, a
mounted courier had been despatched to our high
step-mother at Bet il Mtoni to inform her of the
news. Cattle were slaughtered, the cooks had
plenty of work in the kitchen, and the rooms were
freshly perfumed. By the fisherman's report the
vessels might be expected to arrive within two to
three hours.

Madjid and his retinue hastened to join his father on board. They started in two cutters, battling against a heavy sea, which threatened to swamp them every moment. They hoped to be back again by seven o'clock in the evening with our father; but man proposes and God disposes.

Time went on. Seven o'clock had long since gone by and the vessels were not yet in sight. The whole town was in a fever of excitement—we in the house were of course the most restless of all. Many of us had forebodings of coming evil; still, we never dreamt of what we were to hear so soon. It was feared that Madjid and his companions had perished in the raging storm, and that my father's arrival had been retarded by witnessing this terrible accident. By degrees the belief gained ground that all the ships, both large and small ones had foundered in the hurricane. Conjectures upon conjectures were made, and nobody, not even the smallest children, cared to go to bed, until the absent ones had arrived safe.

News suddenly spread, which at first no one would credit. The whole palace was said to be surrounded, and to be strongly guarded, by several hundred soldiers. We rushed to the windows in hopes to get at the truth of this report. The night was pitch dark, and we could distinguish nothing but the gleaming matches of the soldiers, a sight which did not help to pacify us; moreover, it was said that the soldiers allowed no one to pass in or out of our doors.

What had occurred? why were we locked in? of course everybody wanted to know. Who, it was asked, had ordered such a measure? As far as we knew, Madjid had not returned; his house was likewise surrounded by the same gloomy, silent guard watching ours, and we could discern his people anxiously running about the house with lights.

We were the worse off, as all the eunuchs and male slaves slept out of the house, so there were but women and children left. A few of the stout-est–hearted gained the front hall of the ground floor, separated only by a door from the large guard-room on the other side of the portal, where they could easily speak to the soldiers through the hall windows. They, however, sternly refused all information, in obedience to their orders; and at last, when the slaves, one and all, lifted up their voices in wailing and lamentation, the soldiers threatened to fire on them.

The whole place was in a dreadful state of confusion; some women cried and abused the invisible evil power that kept us locked up, the most devout ones said their prayers, and the children shrieked and screamed on all sides and could not be pacified. Any one suddenly dropped in on this wild scene might easily have taken it for a lunatic asylum.

Morning dawned at last, and still we had not learned why we were kept prisoners and where Madjid could be. In spite, however, of the general excitement and anxiety, everybody grew orderly at the time fixed for morning prayer. But who can fancy our horror when, after prayers, we observed our fleet at anchor, and mourning flags flying in the breeze! How can I describe our grief when the gates were opened early in the morning and our brothers entered the house without our father!

Then only did we realize that the black flags were flying for him, and that we and the whole country had sustained an irreparable loss. Our dear father was no more! On the passage from

Oman to Zanzibar, surrounded only by a few of
his children and followers, he had been called
away by the Lord, whom he had faithfully and
humbly served all his life. The wound in his leg,
from which he had so long suffered, had put an
end to his existence.

He had not only been the most loving and devoted head of his own family, but also a most
conscientious king, and a true father to his people. The general mourning on his death proved
how sincerely he had been loved by all. Black
flags hung from every house, and even the smallest hut fastened up a piece of black stuff.

We soon learned from Bargash, who had been
on the same ship, and who had been present at
our father's death, all particulars of his illness
and of his end. To him we were indebted that the
dear remains had not been sunk into the sea, as is
ordained by the Mahometan law. It was at his
urgent request they were placed in a coffin and
brought on to Zanzibar. His great love and respect for our dear father had prompted him to
take this course, though he thereby seriously tres-
passed against our customs and our religion. Our
law does not permit the use of a coffin either to
prince or to beggar—the body is to be placed into
the earth, and so return to it once more.

We were also informed now of the reason why
we had been so strongly guarded the night before.
Madjid and his companions had suffered severely
from the storm, and had given themselves up as
lost. Their small boats were only built for coasting
service, so they stood in great peril of their lives
before they reached the ships they were in search
of. When they did at last board their father's
vessel they found Bargash gone. As eldest son he
had taken the command of the fleet, and when in

sight of the land had quietly gone on shore with the body, to have it interred secretly and unobserved in our burial-place.

There is an old tradition that, disputes on the succession to the throne must be settled in presence of the body of the deceased ruler, under the supposition that the veneration paid to the deceased will always assist the legitimate successor. Bargash wanted to be ruler, but knowing that his elder brother's claims were better supported, he resolved to act before he could be met with opposition. He relied upon carrying out his plan by the force of arms, and above all by the suddenness of his operations.

He had, therefore, on landing, ordered the troops to surround our house and Madjid's. But his plan miscarried, principally because he failed in taking Madjid prisoner. Bargash afterwards tried to plead in excuse of his conduct that he had been desirous to avoid a revolution.

Madjid, who had carried on the government of Zanzibar since Khālid's death, maintained it now, and proclaimed himself sovereign on the following morning. But doubts still prevailed whether he really were our legitimate chief, or whether our eldest brother, who always resided in Oman, would not endeavour forcibly to obtain the power to which he was entitled by birth.

Chapter XIV

OUR MOURNING

Many formalities had to be observed during our time of mourning. In the first place, old and young people had to put aside their costly garments, to replace them by coarse black cotton dresses, and plain black stuff instead of the richly-embroidered veils. Ointments and all kinds of perfumery were strictly avoided, and the woman who tried to remove the smell arising from the dye of her black dress by sprinkling over it some drops of rosewater or attar of roses was called heartless, or at least frivolous. During the first few days none of the grown-up people slept in their beds, in proof of their love for our departed father, whose body was lying wrapped in the cold ground.

For more than a fortnight our house resembled a large hotel. All persons, prince as well as beggar, were at liberty to enter and eat. It is an old custom to have the favourite dish of the deceased prepared on such occasions for distribution amongst the poor.

The wives of the departed, the legitimate and those purchased as slaves, submit to a special religious mourning for a period of four months. These unfortunate widows have to mourn their husband and master in a dark room all the time,

nor are they allowed to step out into the light of
day, much less into sunlight. A Terīke (widow),
who is compelled to leave her darkened apartment and to pass the gallery, throws a thick cloak
over her veil, and covers herself up in such a
manner that she can just see her way. In consequence the eyes get quite unused to the light,
and it requires always great caution to re-ac-
custom them gradually to daylight after the expiration of the term of mourning.

The widows are formally bound over to their
state of widowhood by the Kadi, before whom
they appear deeply veiled, and are released again
by the same person under like formalities after
the lapse of four months. On the day on which the
widows receive back their liberty they pass
through a great many ceremonies founded on
dark superstition. Firstly, they wash themselves
all at the same time from head to foot, while the
women slaves stand behind their mistresses beat-
ing together two sword blades over their heads
(poor people use nails as a rattle, for it must be an
iron substance). The number of my father's widows being too large to enable the performance of
this ceremony within the baths, it had to be done
on the beach, and a very curious spectacle it was.

The widow now puts on other clothing, and not
till then is she free to marry again. All the male
members of our family and our slaves had had
free access to the house up till then, but after the
lapse of these four months our mothers were only
visible to our brothers alone.

During the first year of our mourning some of
us regularly visited our father's tomb every
Thursday, on the eve of the Mahometan Sunday.
The tomb was a square building supported by a
cupola, in which several of our brothers and sis-

ters had been buried before. After saying the first Sura of the Kurān (the Mahometan Lord's Prayer) and other prayers, and after calling upon the Almighty to have mercy upon the departed, and to forgive their sins, attar of roses and other essences are sprinkled over the graves, which are also fumigated with amber and musk amidst loud lamentations.

The Mahometan has an implicit faith in immortality, and believes that the soul of the dead is allowed, unobserved of course, occasionally to revisit its former abode. For this reason people like to visit the graves of their dead, to keep up intercourse with their immortal souls by imparting to them all their own joys and griefs. Their memory is honoured in every way; and a Mohametan who swears by the head or by the name of his dead, would sooner perish than turn false to his oath.

During the mourning of our mothers, everything in our house remained unchanged, and no business was allowed to be transacted. Moreover, everything had first to be settled with our relations in Oman, to whom a vessel had been despatched with the news of our loss. Of course we discussed the question every day how Tuēni would act, who, as the eldest son, was the legitimate successor to the government: whether he would come to some amicable arrangement with Madjid, or involve us in a family feud.

Some months later our brother Mhammed arrived as the representative of all our brothers and sisters in Oman, to arrange about the division of the inheritance. He returned to Mesket immediately after having settled this matter. Mhammed was considered the most pious of our whole family, who from his early youth had never cared for worldly things. Averse to all show and splendour, and perfectly indifferent to worldly goods, he had never been happy in his station as prince. Disdainful of wealth, he had always dressed very plainly, and nothing vexed him more than the luxury and extravagance he met with at Zanzibar, to which he was quite unaccustomed in Omân; he never got over it all the time he was with us—indeed, his aversion to his surroundings made him hasten his departure to the utmost. In that primitive home of ours at Oman he could once more resume the life that was suited to his tastes and habits.

The question of the succession was still pending. Madjid, who had the power in his hands in Zanzibar, did not seem to trouble himself as to what Tuēni, who had succeeded in the government of Oman, might have to say about his usurped rights; but certainly Tuēni never acknowledged him as Sultan of Zanzibar. An agreement was afterwards entered into between them through the mediation of the English, in which the payment of an annual sum by Majdid to his elder brother was stipulated. The former, however, did not keep to the terms of the treaty, for he discontinued the payment, which he was afraid might be regarded as a tribute, and himself as a vassal of Oman. Tuēni had no means of defending his rights. He had more fighting than enough in the one territory of Oman, without engaging in a war with his wealthy brother, which must have resulted in the utter ruin of his country's resources. Thus, in the absence of a satisfactory compact between the two powers, Oman and Zanzibar have since remained two distinct and independent sovereignties.

No difficulty had arisen, on the other hand, in

the division of our late father's private property
between Mhammed and ourselves. Unlike European nations, we do not keep up a State with
public funds, or with an inland revenue. Neither
is there a public exchequer. All the proceeds arising from customs duties are paid into the sovereign's treasury, as also those accruing from his
plantations, he being the largest landowner in the
island. From this source alone all public expenses
are paid.

In my time there were no income or other taxes,
nor ground rents, of which there is such a plen-
tiful crop in Europe.

The whole of this private property was divided
between the brothers and sisters; even the men-
of-war were included and accounted for in Madjid's and Tuēni's shares, who took them over at a
certain valuation. The Mahometan law of inheritance favours sons much more than daughters,
for the reason that a man has to maintain a
family, which a woman has not. Each of the sisters
received in consequence only half of what fell to
the share of our brothers.

My brother Ralub, my old playmate at Bet il
Mtoni, and myself were declared of age at the
same time, though we were neither quite twelve
years old. This was rather early, even with our
customs, but the times were exceptional ones, and
many unlooked-for changes took place in our
family. Both of us received our share of the inheritance, and we had now to manage for ourselves,
young as we still were. Madjid acted as guardian
to our younger brothers and sisters, whose property he undertook to manage.

In his last will my father had directed that
those of his widows who had no children should
receive an annuity for life, while those who had

children were to have a capital paid down, which, however, was comparatively small. It was no doubt his intention that the children should make a home for their mothers, whose limited incomes made this dependence absolutely necessary. But our father had judged us correctly. I am happy to state, to the honour of all (there were thirty-six of us alive at the time of his death), that none failed in their trust. Our mothers were loved and honoured as before, and not one of us ever took undue advantage of the favoured position in which we found ourselves. Indeed, such an act would have justly deserved condemnation—for may she have been a born princess or a purchased slave, no one can replace our mother; she needs neither rank nor wealth with her child; with love and respect alone can we in a measure repay the sacred debt we owe her.

Shortly after the division of the inheritance our house, so crowded up to this time, became rather lonely and empty. A number of my brothers and sisters, with their mothers and their personal slaves, removed from Bet il Sahel to set up house for themselves. As my sisters Kole, Shewāne, and Asche were still staying on, I continued to live with my mother at Bet il Tani for some time more.

There were also many changes at Bet il Mtoni. Zemzem removed to her estate until she married, and Metle went to hers. It was indeed high time that those of us who were now independent left the large houses to make room for our younger brothers and sisters.

During our father's lifetime we had all, figuratively speaking, helped ourselves out of one dish, but things were now completely changed. Those who had received their share of the inheritance were supposed to manage for themselves henceforth; the old aspect remained the same only for the little ones, their mothers and slaves, and for the widows without children. It was Madjid's business to look after these now, for which purpose their allowances were given into his keeping.

Chapter XV

ABOUT SOME OF MY BROTHERS AND SISTERS

In the course of my narrative I have already spoken of several of my brothers and sisters. I do not know how many I had in all, as a great number died before my father, but I have reason to think that their total was about one hundred. Thirty-six of them were alive when my father died, eighteen sons and eighteen daughters. It would hardly be interesting to the reader to be told the history of each one. But I cannot refrain from describing some of them, feeling convinced that I shall thereby be able to invest the picture of my old home with some life and colouring.

1. Sharīfe.

My father, who was the head of and personally conducted all the affairs of government, found little leisure to occupy himself with his younger children, but to the grown-up ones he was all the more lovable. It made the little ones very jealous to have to remain standing before him like little waxworks while the elder sisters were allowed to sit on the sofa by his side. The object of my bitterest envy was my sister Scharīfe, and the thorn in my brother's side was Hilāl.

Sharīfe, the daughter of a Circassian, was of

dazzling beauty, with a complexion fair as a European's. She was very clever besides, and a much trusted adviser of my father's, who consulted her on every important matter, and, as I was told afterwards, he never once regretted having followed her advice. This surely proves that woman in the East is not quite a cipher.

For a short period only they had a slight disagreement. Following her own inclination, Sharīfe had married a cousin of ours who did not appear to my father to possess those qualities of character which he desired in the husband of his darling daughter. At first she kept aloof from her paternal home until my father's displeasure had subsided. She had, however, made a happy choice, and remained the only wife of her husband; her one child, Schaun, a very beautiful boy, whom she passionately loved, but brought up very strictly, was my playmate. Every Friday he came to us with his mother, always bringing me some trifling gift, in particular when the ships came from Mesket with the Monsoon (Arabic, Mossem). Sharīfe had many relations there, and was very fond of Mesket, where she died, having accompanied our father on his last trip to that place.

2. Khole.

When I went to Bet il Sahel first, Khole became my favourite in place of Scharīfe. She was also a special pet of my father's, whom she had won by her charming manners, her grace and bright spirits. I have never met with a more perfectly moulded figure. She dressed with great taste, and everything seemed to suit her. In plain cotton dresses she eclipsed all others wearing the most costly garments. Her opinion on all matters of fashion was considered as infallible as that of the Empress Eugénie in her time.

Her mother, who was from Mesopotamia, was so clever and circumspect, that my father appointed her superintendent of the household at Bet il Sahel. Khole had much to suffer from her sister Asche, who was considerably older, but she bore all with meek patience. She always turned a deaf ear on those people who wanted to slander Asche in her presence. It was only I who knew how deeply pained she was by her sister's conduct, for in spite of my youth she confided all her sorrows to me, and I knew all her secrets. She often said to me with tears: "O, Salme, what have I done, and how can I help it that my father is pleased to favour me? Do I not share with her all the presents he gives me? And am I to blame that he always requires my services?"

I am sorry to say there were many in the house who regarded her with the same envious feeling. Sweet words were not wanting to court her intercession with my father, but as soon as the desired end was attained her ungrateful suppliants again resumed their unloving attitude. She assisted her mother in superintending the household, and later on was herself called to fill this office, and, as it was impossible to please and satisfy everybody in such an overcrowded palace, there were opportunities enough for complaints. If among our huge supplies of provisions there should be found a flaw in either fish, flesh, fowl, or fruit, it was Khole's fault; if some of the purchases made for the house and distributed failed to give unequivocal satisfaction, the fault was laid at Khole's door; or even if the crop of roses in Turkey had failed, causing a short supply of rose-water and of

attar of roses, Khole was blamed and held responsible for it.

But the greatest soreness of all was caused by
my father taking her with him into the treasure-
chamber, or by sending her there by herself. So
spiteful were her enemies that I verily believe they
would have liked to have her searched on leaving
it, as they do the pearl fishers in the Persian Gulf.
Her numerous antagonists were very much star-
tled one day by the news that my father had made
her a present of a splendid and very precious
crown, which he had expressly ordered from Persia for her. This magnificent diadem was made of
golden palm leaves, richly set with diamonds,
decreasing in size from the large centre stone. It
was of a shape that could not be worn with our
head-dress, and it was intended more as a valuable investment in case of need. It may be conceived that the possession of so splendid an
ornament only increased the number of her adversaries. My father's marked preference was
greatly censured and resented; and yet not even
his great loving heart could have distributed such
love among all his children in equal shares.

All this bitter feeling it would seem only
brought out the goodness and sweetness of Khole's
disposition—the most cruel shafts she turned off
with a gentle, forgiving hand. As for revenge or
retaliation, they never entered her head. She
used merely to say: "Well, I shall be content if
only my father approves of my doings."

Khole took care of me faithfully, as long as I
was a child, and afterwards she was my dearest
friend. Our friendship became closer still when
she removed to Bet il Tani after my father's death.
We lived and dined together, talked till late at
night, and then retired to rest by each other's

side. It will be shown further on how great an
influence she had gained over me. After my reconciliation with Madjid our intimacy was troubled
for a short time only, but after that she loved me
all her life. After my husband's death in 1871, she
had a letter written to me (she could not write
herself), in which she asked me to send her one of
my children for adoption, to which I could not
accede, as the child would have had to become a
Mahometan.

Her liberality and kindness had grown quite
proverbial. She treated her servants very well,
pardoned all their faults, and always interceded
for other people's slaves. I had a Nubian slave
from Mesket, who was a splendid cook, and who
gave me great satisfaction in that respect; but I
soon found it impossible to keep her, as every
article she could lay hands upon vanished. No
admonitions or even convictions of her guilt could
alter her propensities, so that at last I decided to
sell the thief. No sooner had Zafrāne, as she was
called, heard this, than she escaped one night to
Khole's estate, to beg and pray her to intercede.
Indeed, she managed so well to touch my sister's
heart, that I had to keep the dangerous person
out of regard for Khole.

Khole, who had not inherited more than any of
us, bought with her share one of our finest plantations, which my father had been in the habit of
visiting most. There was a beautiful palace, splendidly furnished, on the estate, which, however,
was not a valuable property, though she had to
pay a high price for it. But in memory of the great
love our father had always shown to her she was
willing to make any sacrifice in order to possess
herself of his favourite resort. She went every
year to her plantation, called Sebe, for the clove

harvest. I look back with great delight on those days, when we used to walk about the fragrant gardens hand in hand, talking to the numerous children of the slaves, or looking out from the windows to watch the people at work.

My father's richly-furnished room was never occupied, and was only opened and shown to distinguished visitors at their special request.

Khole was very hospitable to the many people who were attracted by the beautiful situation of Sebe. She had some of the rarest exotic plants in her gardens, which were kept by her faithful overseer in the same state as in my father's time.

A very pretty stone building had been put up just outside the high garden-wall, overshadowed by a magnificent tree, higher than the tallest oak-trees in Europe. This building contained one saloon only, paved with marble, mirrors covering the walls up to the ceiling; and it was furnished with bamboo chairs and numerous coloured lamps. When at Sebe, my father used to receive his visitors and take coffee in this place. We could now quietly visit this beautiful shady spot, enjoy ourselves like children, and talk of our dear departed parent.

My dearly beloved Khole, she, the object of such great love and such bitter hate, is of this world no more; I lost her in the year 1875. It is said that she fell a victim to a dastardly act of poisoning, but that belief is too much shrouded in mystery to give it foundation. She will always be with me in spirit.

3. Ashe.

It rarely happens that two real sisters are more whimsically endowed by nature, than were Khole and Ashe. The latter was small and dark, Khole tall and fair; Ashe was pockmarked, while her sister possessed a countenance of perfect Oriental beauty. Ashe was reserved and even cold in manner, Khole a radiant sunbeam, though perhaps she was not so clever as her sister. A greater contrast could not well be conceived, and it was difficult sometimes to convince our Asiatic relations that they were really sisters.

Poor Ashe was very well aware of her plainness, and the marred expression of her features; and for this reason she never appeared unveiled, even to her relations and servants. For the same reason she did not pay much attention to her outward appearance, and, for her station, she dressed very plainly and even meanly. One Abyssinian female slave, very clever as a hairdresser, attended her in this capacity, also as milliner and lady's-maid all in one.

She was, however, reputed far and wide as a person of refined culinary taste, and she kept, indeed, the best table for miles round. Young people were frequently sent to learn the secrets of cookery from her cooks, and my brother Madjid partly boarded with her, getting five or six dishes daily from her place, for which he paid a fixed sum monthly.

On account of her good common-sense she was often chosen to settle disputes, and very clear her judgment was, too. She was a capital manager, and kept her financial affairs in exemplary order, for which few of us deserved praise. Her exchequer was never at an ebb, not even before harvest-time, which we always looked forward to as the tide in our purses. It is true that persons of extravagant habits put a very uncharitable construction on her possessions: they said she was miserly and selfish.

Poor Hilāl was her favourite brother. She was devotedly attached to him and took a motherly care of his eldest son, Sūd, after his death.

4. Khadudj.

Khadudj, Madjid's sister, is already known to the reader. She was much better liked than Ashe, but she did not often come to see us, as she lived with her brother, whom she very fondly loved.

In later years she took the mother's place with our youngest brother Nasor. With him she went to Mecca, weary of life, after Madjid's death, as the last refuge of the Mahometan, and both died there within a short time after their arrival.

5. Shewāne.

When I went to Bet il Sahel, Shewāne, though older than myself, became my playmate. She was very sensible, and possessed a power of expression in her eyes that might have subdued a lion; these qualities combined made her play an important part in our house. She installed me at once as her errand-boy, thrashed me every day, and under fortunate circumstances requited my services with the doubtful compliment: "You white ape!" For she was the daughter of an Abyssinian, a race well known with us for rudeness and violence as well as for cunning. I had a "white" mother, and this fact exposed me to a good many attacks from my dark-complexioned relations. My brother Djemschid had still more to suffer from them, for he had not only his mother's fair hair, but also her blue eyes.

In early youth she had lost her only brother Ali, who was much more good-natured and more generally liked in consequence; her father and mother died within a short time of each other; and thus, still quite young, she found herself alone in a world totally different from what she wished it to be. Madjid was the only one of her numerous brothers whom she cared for a little out of regard for Ali, who had been his intimate friend.

Her majestic figure and the almost classic beauty of her features made her a very dignified and even imposing personage. She possessed a strong spirit of self-reliance, and would never take advice from any one, or betray by word or look what she intended to do. Thus she fell into the hands of a crafty negro slave, who took advantage of her inability to write, and robbed her right and left. With all her rough manners, however, she was very charitable, and a severe but just mistress to her servants.

She always tried to pick out and to own the handsomest slaves, whom she loaded with the most costly weapons and jewels. Everything about her showed a fairy-like display of riches and splendour.

I was the only one of all her sisters who managed to get on with her, notwithstanding the bad treatment I had suffered at her hands in early years. Once when I seized a favourable moment to represent to her how much she was blamed for her extravagant habits, and especially for keeping such a great number of slaves, she quietly replied, that she was sure she would not live long, and that she intended partly to spend her money on the poor, partly on herself, as fast as she could, so as to leave us nothing. She was very rich, having inherited a considerable fortune from Ali, besides her own share, but she always continued to live in our paternal home, regardless of the general feeling of dislike entertained for her.

The opinion of her fellow-creatures troubled her very little. Though residing under the same roof with several hundred people, she took no notice whatever of any of them, and only lived for and among her slaves. Thus it came to pass that we were informed too late of her severe illness. Exasperated at what she considered want of sympathy on Khole's part and on mine, she refused to receive our visits, and much as we were grieved we could not force ourselves upon her and violate that firm will of hers. When she felt she was dying from rapid consumption, she made all her servants swear solemnly that no one should see her in death, except the woman who would perform the last offices. Her commands were carried out to the letter, for the moment she expired her rooms were locked. We were only admitted after the body had been laid out, covered with camphor and wrapped in a sevenfold winding-sheet, the face included, as prescribed by our religious rites. Overwhelmed with grief, I knelt down by the body and embraced it, unmindful of the scared bystanders, who wanted to drag me away, and who warned me of the danger of infection.

In spite of the difference of our characters, I really had liked Shewāne; I always took her part, for she deserved to be loved by all who could overlook her rough manner and her eccentricities. Pride and ambition were her besetting sins—no wonder she made many enemies, especially among her elders.

Before her death she made ample provision for her town slaves and for the upper slaves on her estates. She not only set them free, but be-

queathed all their costly arms and jewels to them,
besides one whole estate for their maintenance.
She did not wish that those who had worked for
her so long should have to begin life again among
strangers.

6. Metle.

Like Shewāne, Metle was the daughter of an
Abyssinian; but she had so fair a complexion that
nobody could have guessed her descent. She and
her brother Ralub were my playmates during my
stay at Bet il Mtoni. Her mother was totally para-
lyzed, and could not devote herself much to the
rearing of her children; nevertheless, they turned
out excellent and worthy persons.

The poor sufferer was obliged to live on the
ground–floor, which was intended only for store-
rooms, and naturally very damp and unsuitable
for an invalid like her.

A sheltered place had been erected in front of
her room, close to the banks of the Mtoni, about a
yard in height, to which the sick one was carried
in the day, and where she was attended on by her
children and her slaves. Her step-children and
their mothers frequently came to keep her company; and my mother in particular used to read
to her from the Kurān and other holy books, for,
like most of the other women who became members of our family after they were grown up, she
could not read herself.

Metle and Ralub were a dear little couple; they
loved their mother fondly, and only thought of
pleasing her. Metle especially, my senior by some
years, was very sweet, and a most unselfish playmate.

After my father's death she was my nearest

neighbour on her estate, and during our stay in the country we met daily. Ralub delighted to break in upon us unawares with his friends, and so cause a great deal of confusion, as we were not allowed to show ourselves to strangers; and I am bound to say he always succeeded!

After her mother's death, Metle used to spend the rest of the year at Bet il Mtoni, until she married a distant cousin in the town. She was very happy with her two charming boys, whom she always carried about or had on her knees when I came to see her.

She was the most unassuming and contented person in the whole house, the very opposite to Shewāne. But even this did not please everybody—her tastes, they said, were far too simple for a princess; to which she replied that nothing would change her, nor did she consider it at all derogative to her dignity or to her station, to treat prince and beggar with the same kindness. "What matters it," she said, "if I do not choose to be always dressed in silks and velvets—am I worth less on that account than my brothers or sisters? Do I not remain my father's daughter at all times?" I must own to my shame that I had not sufficient good sense then to understand this kind of philosophy, which I only learned to appreciate properly afterwards.

7. Zeyāne.

Zejāna and Zemzem are sisters by an Abyssinian mother. I have already mentioned, that during our stay at Bet il Mtoni an intimate friendship existed between my mother and Zejāne, who had a great weakness for me, and spoiled me more than my mother approved of. Our apartments were far apart, and as it took me a long time to get to their rooms, I often stayed there all day, to my mother's annoyance, who vainly sent messenger after messenger to bring me back, until she came herself, and in her turn stayed all the evening with my sisters.

Zeyāne was the first to teach me pillow-lace making, at which she was very clever. Alone, or with my mother, she invented the prettiest designs, which no one was permitted to see until they had been successfully completed. She made many friends by her kindness, and was never tired of nursing the sick and helpless.

The days that my father did not spend at Bet il Mtoni, the women had permission to go out; and on these occasions Zeyāne could always be seen in company with some slaves, loaded with many presents, which she distributed amongst the families of officials.

It was a very sad parting when we removed from Bet il Mtoni, for both Zeyāne and my mother knew well that they would now see but little of each other, for Zeyāne rarely went into the town, which she disliked. Before we left, I was much with her, and she gave me many keepsakes, at the same time exhorting me to be always good to my mother.

I was the more strongly impressed with our sad leave-taking, as we had to go immediately afterwards to our overbearing stepmother, Azze bint Sef, to bid her a cool good-bye.

8. Zemzem.

Much prettier than Zeyāne, Zemzem possessed all the good and noble qualities of her sister, who was taken away from us much too soon. I only knew her more intimately at a later date, when we had become neighbours on our estates. She was very practical, not given to extravagance, and fond of simplicity and solidity—and things prospered more under her management than in any other Arab household. I may say that, taken on the whole, she came nearest to the ideal of a good European housewife.

She was very motherly to me, as I had been her dear sister's favourite. When I did wrong, she looked at me with her large, expressive eyes, and said: "What a pity that your mother had to leave you behind so young in this wretched world! Zejāne would have been a second mother to you, if she were alive, and you would have remained a child much longer. For after all you are a child yet, with very little common sense." And to appease me, she added: "Don't be angry with me for speaking to you thus, if I do it is only for love of Zeyāne, to whom you were so dear. Others, you see, commit the same follies, but I never take the trouble to reprove them!"

She was of great assistance to me in my farming—she rode with me over the plantations for hours, and pointed out any improvements she considered necessary. Once she turned to my "Nakora,"* or overseer, and said: "Your mistress is a mere child still (in Swahili, *mtoto)* and does not understand these matters; you must therefore look after her interests, and my Nakora will always be ready to advise you." This was not very flattering to my self-esteem, but as she meant well I could not be angry with her.

Zemzem married rather late in life our distant cousin Humud. (It is the custom with us to marry as much as possible in the family, so as not to be linked with people of lower rank.) Humud was the

*Nahoda (Swahili) meaning overseer or ship's captain

same who had once dared to ask Khālid in the mosque for another sister of ours, and had been so harshly repulsed on that occasion. After Khalid's death he made personal advances to the lady, but with no better success—and when he had recovered from his great disappointment, he proposed to Zemzem and was accepted. They were married immediately after, but very quietly, for Humud was exceedingly stingy, and not even hospitable, as all Arabs traditionally are, though he was one of the richest men in Zanzibar. He was fanatically orthodox, and made a great display of rigorous devoutness; but this mantle of hypocrisy was seen through by most people, since he did not hesitate to commit the greatest cruelties on the slightest provocation. For this reason he was almost universally despised—and yet no one ventured to show open hostility to so rich and influential a person.

After her marriage I saw but little of Zemzem. She seemed to live happily with her unpopular husband—in her practical way I suppose she managed to get on even with him.

9. Nunu.

I will say a few words about a sister, treated badly by nature, who deserved to be greatly pitied. Nunu was the daughter of a Circassian, who received the name of Tadj (crown) on account of her marvellous beauty. She had been greatly distinguished by our father, and became the object of much envy and jealousy. When her child, as beautiful as herself, was born blind, many looked upon it as a punishment to the mother, who had been guilty of being my father's favourite. This misfortune bitterly distressed her, and only the firm belief that God had so willed it made her bear it. Nor was she spared long to her blind child, for soon after she died of a kind of dropsy.

Poor blind Nunu was now quite alone. But in her case also the old saying proved true, "that God's help is nighest in our extremity." A trustworthy Abyssinian slave had solemnly vowed to the dying Tadj to look after Nunu and never to desert her as long as she lived. She kept her promise in an exemplary manner, and shielded her little mistress from all mischances of life, though she had often more than just cause to complain of her. She took orders from no one but my father, who in his love for the poor blind child took more care of her than he had been able to do of his other children, and this again gave rise to much envious talk.

Nunu was the wildest and most unruly child I have ever seen, and the terror of all mothers with little children. From the age of six until she was ten years old, she waylaid all her younger brothers and sisters, on purpose—incredible as it may appear—to scratch out their eyes! When told of the birth of one, her first question was whether it could see and had sound eyes. After a time it was deemed advisable not to tell her the truth, and it then pleased her much to know that there were others also who would never be able to see the sun or the moon. Her little soul was filled with the most bitter envy. A very pretty little brother of ours was greatly admired for his beautiful long eyelashes. His mother having gone to dinner one day, and the nurse having turned her back for a moment, the child was heard to scream fearfully; and upon their rushing back, they found that Nunu had cut off the eyebrows and eyelashes of the child with a pair of scissors!

No child in the house was from that time left unguarded for a single moment. Nunu possessed knowledge of locality hardly credible in a blind person, and she moved about with the greatest ease and quickness. She was to be found everywhere, and as busy as a wicked little fairy. Her greatest pleasure was to smash whatever she could lay hold of, china, glassware, and particularly our pretty Asiatic watercoolers.

One of her peculiarities was that she insisted on being treated as though she could see. When the guns announced sunset, she ordered her room to be lighted up. She insisted upon selecting her wardrobe herself, and when she was being dressed by her servants she always stood before a looking-glass. When she heard that any one had fine hair, or beautiful eyes and brows, she subjected those parts to a critical examination, only to observe that she was either disappointed or pleased.

To the great satisfaction of all, Nunu bcame more reasonable and sedate as she grew up, and in consequence she was no longer regarded with such horror; indeed, she gained on everyone's affection as her good qualities began to shine more prominently The poor unfortunate girl lost her faithful nurse soon after her parents, and as she could not live by herself without some help and supervision, our sister Asche took charge of her and kept house together with her.

10. Shembūa and Farshu.

I must not omit to mention in this place two nieces of mine, Shembūa and Farshu, who were at school with me and who afterwards had the same party views as myself. They lived opposite our place, and as the streets in Zanzibar are very

narrow, we could easily talk together from our
windows without deaf and dumb language—dis-
cuss fashions, household matters, and politics. In
the last case we observed the precaution of sta-
tioning such servants at the corner as would not
be likely to attract attention, who would warn us
of the approach of an enemy by dropping a stick,
by coughing, or by a low whistle. About these
times I shall have to say more further on.

Shembūa and Farshu were my brother
Khālid's only children, and from their earliest
youth they had been so fond of each other that
they were almost inseparable. This brought them
frequently into conflict with their mothers, who
were exceedingly jealous of each other. Schembūa, some years older than her sister, was gentle
and modest, just the reverse of Farschu, and so
sensible that she took almost a mother's care of
her.

They were both very rich, having inherited the
whole of their father's large fortune. In their love
for each other they resolved not to divide their
property, but to live together and share their
possessions. But this arrangement greatly displeased Farshu's mother, an Abyssinian, who
wanted her daughter to shake herself free.
Farschu, who was very determined, refused to
accede to this demand, and declared she was
firmly resolved not to divide the fortune as long as
she and her sister remained unmarried. Her
mother, deeply hurt by this refusal, and finding
that things in other respects, too, were getting
unbearable, left her home and her child secretly
one day, taking with her only a small parcel and a
very small sum of money. At first no one knew
where she had gone, and it was generally believed
she would return to her daughter after a while.

But it was soon discovered that she neither intended returning to her child nor living by her bounty—and would, therefore, gain her living by her own work. I have previously alluded to the circumstance that at the death of her husband the widow is made almost entirely dependent on her children, and that in some cases, as for instance in this, the law proves a disaster instead of a protection.

The place of the unhappy mother's concealment remained perfectly unknown as long as her scanty means lasted; and she only came to Bet il Mtoni, after having spent her last "Pesa," to see my elder sister Zuēnē, who had formerly been on very friendly terms with Khalid. With her she continued to live on condition that Zuēnē would never attempt to bring her and her daughter together, unless the latter came of her own accord to acknowledge her wrong. Farschu, however, remained perfectly indifferent to this state of affairs, nor did she take any steps to be reconciled when her mother began to sicken. Neither entreaties nor even the severest censure took the least effect on her. Repeatedly but in vain, I tried to remind her of a child's duty—she remained obdurate. It was almost impossible to believe in so much unrelenting hardness in so small and pretty a being; but from the flash of her dark eyes one might have guessed how inflexible was her resolution. Soon after my departure from Zanzibar, Farschu died of consumption, and I have never been able to learn whether she was ever reconciled to her mother before her death.

The finest estate that belonged to my nieces was the grand and superb plantation "Marseilles;" Khalid predilection for France and for everything French had made him select this name. The walls of all the rooms, except those set apart for prayers, were covered with large mirrors, which had a wonderful effect when lighted up. The floors were inlaid with black and white marble slabs, producing a pleasant freshness much appreciated in a southern clime. A large collection—such as a clock of ingenious construction, from which dancing and playing figures stepped out at the striking hours; glass globes reflecting the most grotesque distortions; large round quicksilver balls like those put up sometimes in gardens, and a variety of other works of art— gave the palace quite the look of a museum, especially to all simple and uncivilized persons and to our relations from Oman. Frequently I heard expressions of wonder and surprise, such as "Truly, the Christians are real devils!" At "Marseilles," perhaps the best insight into the real ways of Eastern life was to be gained.

I have spent many a happy day on this estate. The house was always full of guests, and as my nieces were rather emancipated and very tolerant in religious matters there was no constraint put upon intercourse. The cries of the runners and outriders: "Sumila! sumila!" (make room), and the announcing of visitors by slaves never ceased. All people here were gay and merry, and seemed to know of no care. The amiable hostesses often induced ladies to stay for more than a fortnight who had only come for three days, much to the displeasure of their respective fathers and husbands.

Everybody could spend the day as he or she pleased best, without being considered impolite, for it is only true hospitality that grants full liberty to guests. In the evening about sunset the whole company met to stay till one or two o'clock in the splendidly lighted saloons, or, on moonlight nights, in the park. When there was no moon, piled up stacks of wood saturated with palm oil were kept burning in various spots all the time.

Unfortunately, this splendid and pleasant place was soon after destroyed. My brothers Bargash and Abd il Azia fortified themselves in the castle during our rebellion against Madjid, and the closing and decisive battle was fought here. The estate was totally ruined in consequence, and my nieces were great losers thereby. But their great wealth made them soon get over this loss, nor did they like to have it much talked about, "as it was not worth while losing a word about the matter!"

11. Hilāl.

I will speak of two of my brothers only in this place, of Hilāl and of Tuēni, both of them unhappy men; the one by his own faults, the other a victim to his own son.

It is well that the Mahometan religion forbids the use of all spirituous liquors, and our sect, which does not even sanction smoking, is in this respect much more rigorous than the Turks or Persians. By degrees a sad report began to gain credence that our brother Hilāl (Newmoon), seduced by Christians and in particular by the then French consul, had taken to drinking. He then had frequent attacks of giddiness, the smell of wine was noticeable about him, and the unfortunate man had not the strength of mind to conquer the evil spirit that possessed him. Hilāl was the favourite son of our father, to whom this caused a bitter anguish. He tried to reform the seduced son by having him at first confined to the house, but soon found himself compelled to banish him altogether from our family circle.

Our sister Khadudj suffered most of all, as she was very fond of Hilāl. He still visited her at our paternal home after his banishment, but could only gain admittance under the greatest difficulties and dangers, and when he stayed overnight with her and some others, who had remained faithful to him, the room was kept dark so that his lights might not betray him. No one ever found the heart to apprise our father of these visits. He kept him very short to prevent him from indulging his vice, but Khadudj assisted him largely, though greatly to his own ruin.

Hilāl sank deeper and deeper under his evil passion, until he was scarcely ever sober, and he was soon released from this misery by death. In spite of all that had occurred, our father's grief for his favourite son was unspeakable. He often locked himself up in his chamber, and the traces of tears could be seen afterwards in the place where he had knelt down to pray. Something which had never happened before: he gave vent to his grief even in words like these: "How great is my despair and my grief for thee, oh, Hilāl!"

Hilāl left three sons, Sūd, Fesal, and Mhammed. The last and youngest was adopted by my stepmother Azze bint Sēf, who was childless. The boy completely won her over, an attempt in which none of us had ever succeeded. She had always been reported to be mean and ungenerous, and nobody could believe their eyes when Mhammed commenced living very extravagantly, with her money of course. No one had ever before dreamt of keeping dogs—he ordered a whole pack of hounds from Europe, amongst them such splendid beasts as had never been seen in our country. His whole time was taken up with these dogs and some really beautiful horses. He would not allow

his favourites to be fed on garbage, but had a
separate kitchen put up for them, where a variety
of food was prepared. The fattest fowls, the best
joints of meat, and the largest fish, were picked
out for them. Report even had it, that his dogs
and horses got no water to drink, but only cham-
pagne. I cannot say whether this was true; at all
events people said a great many bad things of
Mhammed, that were probably not entirely without foundation, for his was the refinement of extravagance.

Sūd had a great weakness for European habits
and style of life; in his manners he resembled his
father most.

The third of Hilāl's sons was very different
from his brothers. Gentle Fesal, who had not the
luxurious habits of Mhammed and Sūd, was always so modestly dressed that he might sooner
have been taken for a plain citizen than for a
prince. He was of a philosophical turn of mind,
very averse to all material pleasures, and always
remained a puzzle to his brothers. In after years
he bought a small estate near my own and often
came to see me. He went hardly ever to the town
without bringing me back some small present, if it
was only a bundle of fireworks, which I liked very
much.

Misunderstood by his brothers, the poor fellow
was very unhappy; he had a gentle and noble
disposition, which is thought much too lightly of
in this world. But by his gentle and amiable manners he won the friendship of all who saw more of
him. He had lost his mother when very young and
had hardly ever known true love. "It pains me the
more," he used to say to me, who, though I was
his aunt, was much his junior, "that my brothers
look on me as quite superfluous, and care not one

jot for me. I care not whether I live or die, for no
one will ever miss me." My heart ached when I
heard him talk so, for he really deserved to be
loved. How truly happy a monastic life would
have made this man, who felt a stranger in his
own land and an alien in the world!

No one regretted more than poor Fesal, when I
yielded to my brother Madjid's request to return
to the town. In the course of time he had become
quite accustomed to telling me of all his thoughts
and sorrows, as if I had really been a sensible
aunt, and not what I was, a wild and inexperienced girl.

12. Tuēni.

Our eldest brother Tuēni was born at Mesket,
and spent all his life in Oman. He never came to
Zanzibar, and could not be shaken in his prejudice against that birthplace of most of his brothers and sisters. Since a Mahometan is not allowed
to have his portrait painted, a commandment
which is strengthened, if possible, by superstition, and as photographs were not yet known with
us at that time, Tuēni always remained a perfect
stranger to those of us who had not been to Mesket. We had only heard a good deal of his gentle
manners, of his courage, and his bravery in war.
His soldiers idolized him, and his presence alone
inspired them with confidence. Like our father, he
was very fond of warfare, and a more accom-
plished soldier than any of my brothers. He had
spent the best part of his life in the camp, to the
great sorrow of his legitimate wife Ralie, our
cousin, by whom he had several children. During
my father's residence in Zanzibar, Tuēni acted as
his representative in Oman, but having enough to

do to look after the defence of the frontiers of the empire, he left the real government in the hands of our pious second brother Mhammed, who was possessed of the same prejudice against Zanzibar. Tuēni would either fight about Bender Abbas with the Persians, or resist the invasions of the wandering tribes of central Arabia. These numerous tribes are very poor, and most of them live only by pillage. An Arab of the desert seldom possesses more than a camel, some indispensable arms (such as musket, sword, dagger, lance, and shield), one or two iron cooking pots, a bag of dates, and at best a milk-goat. The men, young and old, carry their arms into battle, followed at some distance by their wives and daughters on foot, and met after the fight with cool water, milk, and viands. Oman was invaded every year by larger or smaller hordes, and the country was kept in a continual state of activity by them. None but the most resolute and energetic ruler could hold his own against their incursions.

Such was the state of affairs at the time my father died on his return to Zanzibar. Had his death taken place at Mesket, Tuēni might have been in a position to possess himself of the government of Zanzibar, instead of Madjid, our fourth brother, who, taking advantage of favourable circumstances, caused himself to be proclaimed Sultan of Zanzibar. I have already stated that Madjid agreed to pay an annual sum to Tuēni, but that he soon afterwards withdrew from this engagement. His conduct was universally condemned, the more so as Tuēni's position became daily more difficult. The continued campaigns were a heavy drain on the country's resources, and just at the worst time the supplies from Zanzibar began to fail. Money at last became so scarce that he saw

himself compelled to levy duties on various articles of merchandise. Luckily for Oman, public
loans, which have been the ruin of more than one
Eastern State, were then unthought–of. But even
these light taxes raised a spirit of discontent, and
the malcontents unfortunately succeeded in gaining great influence over Tuēni's eldest son, Sālum,
who at last became guilty of the heaviest crime
man can commit.

One day when Tuēni, after having been to an
assembly, had thrown himself, greatly fatigued,
upon a couch, to take a little rest, his son stepped
up, and peremptorily demanded the suspension
of all taxes and duties, for which unjustifable
proceedings he was naturally called to order.
Whereupon this unnatural, cowardly son drew a
revolver, which he had kept hidden until then,
and shot down his father where he lay!

But the misguided youth did not long enjoy the
fruits of his evil deed—a speedy retribution was
in store for him. He had hardly installed himself
as ruler of Oman, when his brother-in-law Azzan
determined to depose him. He surprised Mesket
one night, and put the capital to massacre and
pillage. His action was much facilitated by the
great exasperation of the people against Sālum, as
no righteous man would take up arms on behalf of
a parricide. The wild invaders met with little
resistance—they carried off all they could, and
destroyed the rest. Sālum's palace in particular
was sadly wrecked, and he succeeded under great
peril in escaping on board one of his men-of-war,
saving nothing but bare life.

His unfortunate mother and her other children
just managed to save themselves on board a ship,
and she, too, lost her all. A young Indian merchant, called Abd il Rab (servant of the Lord),

had the good fortune to buy the greater part of her precious jewels for a mere trifle from a Bedouin (it was said for about three hundred dollars), and the honest fellow restored the lost property to the unfortunate princess as a gift!

Azzan, the invader, was himself soon after turned out by my third brother Turki, and he again suffered the same fate at the hands of my younger brother, Abd il Aziz (also, servant of the Lord). The latter, Khole's ward, was much distinguished by intelligence, courage, and energy. At the age of twelve he had already taken our side in the conspiracy and conflict with Madjid, and he lived afterwards for a time in Beloochistan*, whence most of our soldiers used to be drafted. He succeeded in the end in restoring peace in Oman for a short period, but was not able to maintain himself in power for long. Turki returned, and possessed himself anew of the government, whereupon Abd il Aziz sought a refuge again in Beloochistan, where he still lives.

Surely a sad page, these family feuds! They can only be understood by those who are personally acquainted with the ambition of Eastern princes and with the passionate dealings of Eastern people in general. I, myself, was not to remain a stranger to these; indeed among the first I was to be a sufferer from them!

*Baluchistan—between Persia and India, but now part of Pakistan.

Chapter XVI

WOMAN'S POSITION IN THE EAST

Before proceeding with the account of my personal adventures, I desire in this place to include some chapters describing various phases of Eastern life. I do not intend to enumerate all our customs and habits, as I am not writing strictly for instruction; I only wish to enable the European reader to form a more correct idea of the prominent features on the general aspect of Eastern life. I hope I may not be led away to speak of matters wholly uninteresting—though I would like to come as near as possible to completing a picture that will impress itself on the mind.

I will turn at once to the most momentous of all these questions, to the description of woman's position in the East. I find it rather difficult to speak of this matter. I am convinced that, as a woman born in the East, people will be apt to think me partial, and I fear I shall not succeed in eradicating altogether the false and preposterous views existing in Europe, and especially in Germany, on the position of the Arab wife in relation to her husband. In spite of the easier ways of communication in these days, the East is still too much considered the land of fairy-tales, about which all sorts of stories may be told with impunity. A traveller making a few weeks' tour to

Constantinople, to Syria, Egypt, Tunis, or Morocco, sets about at once to write a big book on the life and the customs of the East. He has been able to judge only quite superficially of these, and has seen absolutely nothing of domestic life. He contents himself with setting down the distorted stories and second-hand accounts of the French or German waiters at his hotel, or of sailors and donkey boys, and considers these sources of information perfectly reliable and trustworthy. But even from these there is not much to learn, and accordingly he throws the reins over the neck of his imagination, and gallops away into fable-land. The only necessary merits of his book are he thinks, amusement and entertainment, which are the sugar-plums between the pages, and lure the reader on, and his production is pronounced "such a success!"

My own experience, I admit, was somewhat similar—for I myself judged things in Europe at first by their outward appearance only. When I first met in European society faces beaming all over with smiles, I was, of course, led to believe that the condition of husband and wife must be much better regulated, and that connubial happiness was a thing much more frequently met here than in the Mahometan East. When, however, my children had outgrown the age when a mother's continual presence is more desirable than her absence, and I was able to go more into society, I soon perceived that I had completely misjudged men as well as the general state of affairs. I have watched many cases of what is called "wedded life," in which the parties seemed to be chained together expressly to make each other suffer excruciating torments. I have seen too many of such unhappy cases to make me believe that Christian wedlock stands on a higher level or renders people much happier than the Mahometan. To my mind married life, in the first instance, cannot be made more or less happy by any particular religion, or by existing views or habits alone; matrimonial happiness can depend alone upon real congeniality and harmony between husband and wife. Where these exist, happiness and peace will always predominate, and from them will spring in time that harmonious sympathy which wedlock truly ought, and is intended, to be.

Taught by this experience I will try not so much to give my own opinion, but simply to define the position of women—and of married women in particular—in the East. I admit that I know intimately only the state of affairs in Zanzibar, and tolerably well that existing in Oman. But it is just in Arabia, and with the Arab people, that the true Mahometan spirit, upon which the views of other Eastern nations are founded, has maintained itself most pure, and for this reason my description may claim to be applicable to the entire Mahometan East, with the exception, of course, of such cases of degeneracy which have arisen from, and grown out of, a closer connection with the Christian occident.

In the first instance, it is quite a fallacy to think that woman in the East is placed socially on a lower level than man. The legitimate wife—the purchased Sarari are of course to be excepted—stands in all respects on a par with her husband, and she always retains her rank, and all rights and titles emanating from it, to their full extent.

The mere circumstance of her retired way of life makes the Arab woman appear more helpless and possessed of fewer rights. But this is a custom existing with all Mahometan (and also with many non-Mahometan) nations in the East, and the higher the rank the more rigorously it is observed. Only her father, her sons, brothers, uncles and nephews, and her slaves are allowed to see her. When she appears before a stranger, or has to speak to him, the law requires her to be shrouded and veiled; part of the face, the neck and chin, and, above all, the ankles, must be completely covered. As long as she keeps to this rule she may move about freely, and walk abroad in open day. Poor people, who have but few or no slaves at all, are obliged, on this account alone, to go abroad more in the daylight, and consequently enjoy more liberty. Ask a woman of this class whether she does not mind exposing herself so freely, and she will reply: "Such laws are only made for the rich, and not for poor women!" I must say that ladies of higher rank often envy their poorer sisters on account of their advantages, of which especially the women in Oman avail themselves, who, owing to the poverty of their country, are prevented from keeping many slaves.

I have already stated that the lady of rank too may walk abroad in the daytime. For instance, if one of her near relations falls sick she may visit the invalid veiled; in the same way she may appear before a judge to plead her cause in person, for luckily we know nothing of lawyers. But custom requires that this right be only put into force in most urgent cases, and vanity has a good share in upholding it, as the veil disfigures women to a degree, and makes them look like walking mummies.

I fully admit now that this swaddling in the East is carried too far, though I cannot say that I find the European customs any better. In my opinion

the *want* of dress in the ball costume of a fashionable lady is carried much further still.

It is true that a single woman is an object
deserving pity. Shut out completely by precept
and custom from any intercourse with men, and
without any protection, her position frequently
becomes a painful one. As she is not allowed to see
or speak to her own officials and managers, if
these be Arabs, she is often robbed by them; and
I am myself acquainted with several ladies who
only married to save themselves from being at the
mercy of these frauds and impostors. This proves
that the seclusion of women has its unmistakable
drawbacks, and that this also is carried too far.
There is, on the other hand, a great deal of senti-
mental pity wasted on the Eastern woman. She is
perfectly unaware that any constraint is put upon
her, and habit makes the greatest inconveniences
bearable after a time.

Pity is also lavished upon her because she had
to share her husband's love with one or many
others. By law the Muslim is permitted to have
four legitimate wives at one time, and to marry a
fifth if one of the former dies or gets divorced
from him. Sarari, or concubines, he may buy as
many as he pleases, and can pay for. But I have
never met with any man who really had four wives
at once. Of course a poor man can only afford to
have one; the rich man restricts himself to two at
most, who live apart and keep house separately.

In the East there are, of course, women too who
know how to take care of themselves; who first
take the precaution to inquire whether the suitor
to their hand has a wife already, and who stipu-
late the clause of a formal promise in the mar-
riage-contract that he will wed no other wife or
purchase a Surīe.

Practically, and in most cases, monogamy predominates. Whenever a man avails himself of the
full liberty granted to him by law, the relations
between the different wives become rather uncomfortable. Ruffled tempers and envy soon turn
into raging jealousy with the hot-tempered southern women. Apathy and indifference do not
create jealousy; this comes only when we have
reason to doubt our power over the object we love
and want to keep to ourselves alone. Do not these
frequent outbursts of passion sufficiently prove
the fact that woman in the East can love more
deeply than her cooler northern sister?

By jealousy polygamy is turned into a source of
great vexation and torment—and that is well.
Many a man of sufficient wealth to facilitate this
has a horror of daily scenes, and therefore he
prefers monogamy, which acts as a further check
to this bad custom. No sensible man, and surely
no woman, can excuse or defend polygamy. But
now comes another question. How is it with
Christians? how about wedded life in civilized
Europe? I will say nothing of the fact that in a
Christian state the Mormons, a sect who call
themselves Christians, are publicly and openly
avowed polygamists. Is wedlock always considered
a sacred institution in moral Europe? Is it not
bitter irony and delusion to talk of only "one"
wife? The Christian may, of course, marry one
woman only, and that is the great superiority of
Christianity; the Christian law requires the just
and the good, the Mahometan allows the evil; but
custom and practice mitigate to a great extent in
the East the evil consequences of the law, while
sin is rampant here in spite of it. I should say the
only difference in the position of a married

woman in the East and in Europe to be, that the former knows the number as well as the characters of her rivals, while the latter is kept in a state of considerate ignorance about them.

Of course only a wealthy man can purchase Sarari. Slaves by birth, they become free as soon as they have children. It happens very rarely, and then only in the case of very hard-hearted men, that the Surīe is resold by her master after the death of her child, from necessity or because he is weary of her. In case of the husband's death, his Sarari are absolutely free and have no other master. And if they are married again to a brother or to any relation of the deceased, they become, as free women, the legitimate wives of such.

It is an absolute myth that the Arab husband treats his wife with less regard than is the case here. This is already provided for by religion, which, though neglecting the wife in some points, recommends her, like a helpless child, to the protection of the husband. The believing and pious Mahometan has as much humane feeling as any highly-civilized and moral European; he is perhaps even more strict and rigorous to himself, believing in the ubiquity of the Lord, who made the laws, and carrying the firm conviction to the grave that his good acts and his bad will by and by meet with just retribution.

Certainly there exists in Zanzibar as well as in this country the uncomfortable character known as the domestic tyrant. But I may state upon my conscience that I have heard here a good deal more of loving husbands who sometimes think fit to establish their argument by physical manipulation. Any decent Arab would feel ashamed and dishonoured by such an action. It is different

with negroes, for I have frequently had to separate couples fighting on my plantations and make
peace between them.

Neither is the wife obliged to submit uncondi-
tionally and for ever to all the whims and
humours of her husband; in such cases she always
finds shelter with her relations, or, if she stands
alone, she has the right to make a complaint to
the Kadi in person. Frequently, too, she has re-
course to the law.

A lady, with whom I was very intimate, married
at the age of sixteen a cousin of hers, who was
many years her senior, but by no means worthy of
her. Continuing to lead his former gay life, he
thought he could treat her as he pleased; but he
was not a little surprised when he found one
evening on his return home a very strongly-
termed letter instead of his wife. I had always
been accustomed to go to my friend's estate without being first announced, as I knew that her
amiable husband was never at home, and preferred the pleasures of the town to his wife's company. After the above-mentioned occurrence,
however, my friend called upon me one day to tell
me that I could no longer visit her without being
announced, as her husband was again living with
her on the estate. Remorseful and repenting, he
had followed and implored her pardon; and having once learned what a determined little wife he
possessed, he took good care to mend his ways. I
could speak of many instances of this kind.

When married people meet they kiss each
other's hands, and they take their meals in company with their children. The wife performs all
kinds of friendly services for her husband. She
fastens on his weapons when he goes out, and
takes them off again on his return; she refreshes

him with cool drinks; in fact, shows him all those trifling acts of attention which make life more pleasant and affectionate. But all these services are voluntary, and by no means the duties of bondage.

The household stands entirely under the control of the wife, and there she is absolute mistress. She does not receive a certain sum for housekeeping, as is customary in Europe—she has full liberty to dispose of her husband's funds. When the latter has two wives living apart, his income is equally divided between them.

Of course much depends upon the individual disposition of husband and wife, how far the latter may venture in using her authority. I had once invited a large party to one of my plantations, but the invitations had been issued too late to allow all the ladies to order their riding donkeys in time, and I was afraid, therefore, many of them would have to decline. In this plight a young married lady, a friend of mine, at once placed a large number of fine donkeys, fully harnessed, at my disposal. Before accepting her generous offer I wanted her to ask her husband's permission first—upon which she very quietly replied that she was not accustomed to let her husband interfere in such trifles as these.

Another lady of my acquaintance in Zanzibar had still greater control over the household and all the property. She managed quite by herself all her husband's large estates and his town-houses. The latter was not even aware of the extent of his income, nor did he consider it derogatory to his dignity to ask her for money whenever he wanted any; he knew well enough that he could not do better than leave the entire management of his affairs to his prudent and sensible wife.

The education of the children is left entirely to the mother, whether she be legitimate wife or purchased slave, and it constitutes her chief happiness. Some fashionable mothers in Europe shift this duty on to the nurse, and by and by on the governess, and are quite satisfied with looking up their children, or receiving their visits, once a day, In France the child is sent to be nursed in the country, and left to the care of strangers. An Arab mother, on the other hand, looks continually after her children. She watches and nurses them with the greatest affection, and never leaves them as long as they may stand in need of her motherly care; for which she is rewarded by the fondest filial love. Her children repay her in a great measure for all the disadvantages of polygamy, and their affection renders her life more happy and contented.

If foreigners had more frequent opportunities to observe the cheerfulness, the exuberance of spirits, even, of Eastern women, they would soon and more easily be convinced of the untruth of all those stories afloat about the degraded, oppressed, and listless state of their life. It is impossible to gain a true insight into the actual domesticity in a few moments' visit. And the conversation carried on on those formal occasions hardly deserves that name; there is barely more than the exchange of a few commonplace remarks—and it is questionable if even these have been correctly interpreted.

Notwithstanding his innate hospitality, the Arab has the greatest possible objection to having his home pried into by those of another land and creed. Whenever, therefore, a European lady called upon us, the enormous circumference of her hoops (which were the fashion then, and took

up the entire width of the stairs) was the first
thing to strike us dumb with wonder; after which
the very meagre conversation generally confined
itself on both sides to the mysteries of the different costumes; and the lady retired as wise as
she was when she came, after having been sprinkled over by the Eunuchs with attar of roses, and
being the richer for some parting presents. It is
true, she had been to and entered a Harem, she
had seen the much-pitied oriental ladies (though
only through their veils), she had with her own
eyes seen our dresses, our jewellery, the nim-
bleness with which we sat down on the floor—and
that was all. She could not boast of having seen
more than any other foreign lady who had called
before her. She is conducted upstairs and downstairs again by the Eunuchs, and is watched all
the time. Rarely does she see more than the reception room, and more rarely still can she guess or
find out who the veiled lady is with whom she
conversed. In short, she has had no opportunity
whatsoever of learning anything of domestic life
or the position of Eastern women.

It is essential to know another fact in order to
understand oriental wedded life properly. The
marriage of a girl neither changes her name nor
the rank she has held previously. The wife of a
prince, descended from the family of a simple
citizen, will never think of demanding equality of
rank with her husband—she remains always the
daughter (bint) of N. or M. On the other hand, an
Arab prince or chief often allows his daughter or
sister to marry one of his slaves. He reasons thus:
"My servant will remain her servant, and she will
always be his mistress." Only he ceases to be a
slave after marriage, but he, of course, addresses
his wife as "Highness" or "mistress."

If a man has occasion to mention his wife in the course of conversation, which he avoids doing if he can, he never calls her, "my wife," but always "the daughter of N. N." At best he uses the expression, "Um Ijali" *i.e.*, "mother of my family," whether she has children or none.

It stands to reason that people who marry, being previously unacquainted with each other, do not always agree; or there may arise difficult and painful circumstances from other causes, such as I mentioned in the cases of my father and Shesade and of Madjid and Ashe. In cases like these the Mahometan law has the great advantage of facilitating a divorce. It is decidedly preferable that two people completely at variance in their views and disposition should be able to separate in peace, to being compelled to remain chained together—often a cause for crime. In such a case the wife has her whole dowry returned, the disposal of which also rests with her during her wedded state. If the divorce has been initiated by the husband, she also retains the marriage settlement made by him, which, however, she cancels on suing herself for the divorce.

I trust the above will suffice to demonstrate that woman in the East is not at all the degraded or oppressed and outlawed being she is generally believed; she is by no means a cypher. What power and how great an influence some women may gain I have already pointed out in speaking of my stepmother, Azze bint Sēf. She ruled our father completely, and court and public affairs depended in most cases on her verdict. All attempts on the part of her step-children to weaken her influence completely failed, although their efforts were, if at no other time, perfectly united in this aim. Any request of ours, made to our father in person, was invariably referred to her final decision, even in matters that might be thought to have been beneath her consideration. While my father lived she ruled with a rod of iron.

Here is a case in point: The daughter of the commanding officer of one of our fortresses in Oman came over to Zanzibar with her husband. They were pretty well off, and had no children— "fortunately," as the lady told me herself. She was very clever and witty (wit is nowhere more valued than with us) but frightfully ugly. Her husband, nevertheless, adored her, and bore all her whims and humours with an angelic patience. When she walked out he had to accompany her, whether he liked it or not. He could never dispose of his time himself, and in the morning after prayers he had to wait for orders from mistress Ashe, to know if she deigned to remain at home with him or intended to go out for the day. He was altogether her slave.

I will only speak of one more member of our family, whose history contradicts better than anything else all the fabrications about the inferiority of Eastern women. My great-aunt, my grandfather's sister, is to this day held up as the model of a clever, courageous, and energetic woman. The history of her life and of her deeds is told over and over again to old and young, and listened to with awe.

My grandfather, the Sultan Imām, of Mesket, in Oman, left at his death three children: my father Saīd, my uncle Slum, and my aunt Ashe. My father was only nine years old at the time, and a regency had to be established. Contrary to all custom, my great-aunt at once declared in the most decided manner that she would carry on the government herself until her nephew was of age, and she suffered no opposition. The ministers, who had never anticipated such a thing, and who had already in secret congratulated themselves on the prospect of ruling the country for some years, could do nothing but submit. They had to make their reports to her, and to receive her instructions and commands every day. She closely watched and knew everything, and nothing could remain concealed from her, to the great vexation and annoyance of all the disloyal and idle officials.

Personally, she put aside all rules of etiquette; regardless of what people might say, she merely wore her schele in the presence of the ministers, and went her own way with energy and firmness.

Her courage was soon put to a very severe test. Not long after she had taken up the reins of government a very serious war broke out—unfortunately, a frequent occurrence in Oman. Some of our next of kin had thought it an easy affair to overthrow the government of a woman, to extinguish our house, and possess themselves of power. Their hordes ravaged the country with fire and sword, and advanced close to the gates of Mesket. Thousands of country people from the sacked provinces had already fled for shelter and protection into the city, leaving all their goods and chattels behind. Mesket is strongly fortified, and well able to stand a siege, but of what use are the strongest walls when provisions and ammunition are exhausted?

But in this terrible distress my great-aunt proved herself equal to the occasion, and she even gained the admiration of the enemy. Dressed in men's clothes, she inspected the outposts herself at night, she watched and encouraged the soldiers

in all exposed places, and was saved several times
in unforeseen attacks only by the speed of her
horse. One night she rode out, oppressed with
care, having just received information that the
enemy was about to attempt an entrance into the
city that night by means of bribery, and with
intent to massacre all, and now she went to convince herself of the loyalty of her troops. Very
cautiously she rode up to a guard, requesting to
speak to the "Akīd" (the officer in charge), and
did all in her power to seduce him from his duty
by great offers of reward on the part of the be-
siegers. The indignation of the brave man, completely allayed her fears as to the fidelity of the
troops, but the experiment nearly cost her her
own life. The soldiers were about to massacre the
supposed spy on the spot, and it required all her
presence of mind to make good her escape.

The situation grew, however, to be very critical
at Mesket. Famine at last broke out, and the
people were well-nigh distracted, as no assistance
or relief could be expected from without. It was,
therefore, decided to attempt a last sortie in order
at least to die with glory. There was just sufficient
powder left for one more attack, but there was no
more lead for either guns or muskets. In this
emergency the regent ordered iron nails and peb-
bles to be used in place of balls, the guns were
loaded with all the old iron and brass that could
be collected, and she opened her treasury to have
bullets made out of her own silver dollars. Every
nerve was strained, and the sally succeeded beyond all hope. The enemy was completely taken
by surprise, and fled in all directions, leaving
more than half their men dead and wounded on
the field. Mesket was saved, and, delivered out of
her deep distress, the brave woman knelt down on

the battle field and thanked God in fervent prayer.

From that time her government was a peaceful one, and she ruled so wisely that she was able to transfer to her nephew, my father, an empire so unimpaired as to place him in a position to extend the empire by the conquest of Zanzibar. It is to my great-aunt, therefore, that we owe, and not to an inconsiderable degree, the acquisition of this second empire.

She, *too*, was an Eastern woman!

Chapter XVII

ARAB MATCHMAKING

In Arabia matches are generally arranged by the
father, or by the head of the family. There is
nothing peculiar in this, as the same is done even
in Europe, where man and woman are allowed to
meet freely. Does it not often happen here that a
reckless father who has run deeply into debt sees
no way out of his difficulties but by the sacrifice of
his pretty daughter to some creditor; or that a
fashionable, pleasure-loving mother hurries her
child into marriage for the sole purpose of obtaining an undisputed sway?

Amongst the Arabs there are just as many despotic parents, who care as little for the happiness
of their children, or listen to the voice of conscience. But it is not abuse of power alone which
makes parents in those parts choose for their
children; they are compelled to do so by the retired life of the women; though even by this seclusion a meeting with men cannot always be
prevented. But it is a general rule that a girl must
not see (except perhaps from the window) nor
talk to her future husband before the evening of
her wedding. Yet he has not been quite a stranger
to her—his mother, his sisters and aunts have had
frequent opportunities of describing him, and

telling her everything about him that may be of interest.

Sometimes the young couple have been acquainted in early youth, as girls are permitted, up to their ninth year, to associate freely with boys of the same age. In such a case the young man goes to the father of his old playmate to ask for her hand, after having secured her own consent through the mediation of his mother or sister.

In all such cases the cautious father asks: "But where have you been able to see my daughter?" To which the reply is made: "As yet I have never had the good fortune to see your honoured *makshume* daughter—but I have heard a great deal about her charms and virtues from my own people."

If the candidate does not suit, he is straightway refused by the father, though, as a rule, the latter asks for some little time to take the matter into consideration. He does not mention a word at home about what has occurred—but secretly and rigorously he watches the conversation between his wife and daughter. Occasionally, and in quite an indifferent manner, he will speak of his intention to give a small gentlemen's party in a few days, mentioning the names of his friends with as little concern as possible if the women require to be told them. If they appear to be pleased at hearing the suitor's name mentioned, he knows that some understanding exists already between the two families. Then only he informs his daughter that N. N. has asked for her hand, and asks her opinion. Her yes or no are almost always decisive—only a despotic father takes the decision upon himself without waiting for his daughter's acceptance or refusal.

Our father, too, showed in such questions his sense of justice, and left his children to decide

their own lot. A distant cousin of ours, Sūd,
proposed for my elder sister Zeyāne when she was
barely twelve years old. My father disapproved of
his proposal on account of her youth, but did not
like to decline it altogether without having first
consulted his daughter. Zeyāne had lost her
mother, and having no one to advise her, she was
so pleased with the idea of being a married
woman soon, that she insisted upon accepting
him, and my father gave his consent.

There are cases, it is true, in which children
are affianced and married in very early youth.
Two brothers had agreed upon the intermarriage
of their children, and, as it happened, they had
only one child each, the one a son, the other a
daughter. The marriage was already talked of
when the boy was seventeen, and the girl seven.
The boy's mother, who lived on an estate not far
from my own, a very prudent and sensible
woman, often complained to me of her husband
and her brother-in-law, who insisted upon her
accepting a little child as daughter-in-law, whom
she would have to nurse and educate first, while
on the other hand the girl's mother was inconsolable at having so soon to part with her daughter.
But they both only so far succeeded as to have the
wedding postponed for two years. I do not know
how the matter was finally settled, as I left
Zanzibar soon after.

All friends and acquaintances are formally informed of the engagement by handsomely-dressed
female slaves, who, sometimes to the number of
twenty, go from house to house with the an-
nouncement and the invitation to the wedding, for
which message they are richly rewarded at each
house.

The paternal home of the bride is now the scene

Princess Salme

Sultan Saīd bin Sultan of Oman and
Zanzibar, father of Salme

Sultan Bargash bin Saīd, brother of Salme

Sultan Madshid bin Saīd, brother of Salme

Zanzibar town, circa 1880

Slave market in Zanzibar, circa 1870

House of Wonders, Palace of the Sultan

House of Wonders, Interior

House of Wonders, Seaview

The Palace of Syed Saīd at Mtony

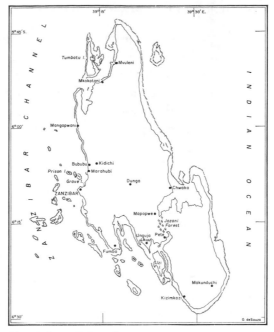

Zanzibar Island

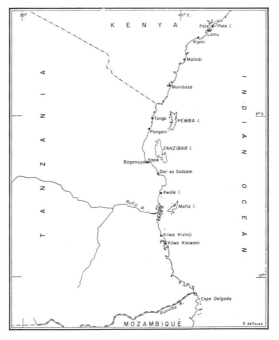

Part of the East African coast, showing the islands of Zanzibar and Pemba

of much life and bustle, for the wedding generally takes place within four weeks. Under any circumstances the betrothal never lasts long, as but few arrangements are necessary in our blessed South. There we know nothing of the hundred and one things considered indispensable to Northern people on such occasions, and an Eastern bride would become speechless with surprise at the sight of a European trousseau. Why are people in these parts so very fond of loading their new bark with such a quantity of unnecessary ballast?

The dowry of an Arab bride is comparatively a small one; according to her rank and wealth it consists of rich dresses, jewellery, male and female slaves, of houses, plantations, and ready money. She gets presents from her parents, from those of her affianced husband, and from the latter himself. All this remains her personal and private property, and the cost of her dowry is never deducted from her share of the patrimony.

The making of the bride's dresses takes some time, for a lady of rank has to change her toilet twice or thrice a day during the first week after her marriage. A bridal dress, like the white robe and veil here, is not worn in the East, but the bride must put on perfectly new garments from head to foot—the colour of the dress is left to her taste. Some appear in all the colours of the rainbow, yet their costume is neither ugly nor without taste.

Special perfumes are prepared, which play an important part at the wedding feast—the Rhia, a costly mixture of powdered sandal-wood, musk, saffron, and plenty of attar of roses, is used as an ointment for the hair, and a pleasant incense, made of the wood of the "ud" (a species of the aloe), of the finest amber, and of a great deal of musk. An Eastern lady never can get too many perfumes.

Then come the baking, the preparing of sweet-meats, and the slaughtering of cattle, which occupy all hands fully.

The bride herself has yet to go through several unpleasant and tiresome ceremonies. During the last eight days she has to stay in a dark room, nor must she put on any of her finery, so that she may appear all the more resplendent on her wedding-day. All this time she is a much-to-be-pitied creature—visit follows upon visit, all the old women whom she knows, and her nurses foremost of all, whom perhaps she had not seen for years, come to her with hands open ready to receive. The chief of the eunuchs, who has shaved off her first hair, and who is very proud of this service of honour rendered to her once, gets to offer his congratulations, and returns his way with a souvenir—either a costly shawl, a ring for the little finger of the left hand, a watch, or some guineas.

The bridegroom is spared this imprisonment in a dark room, but otherwise he has to undergo quite as many trials. All those who have ever been in his service or in that of his bride come to him before calling upon her, and in this way they obtain double presents.

The bridegroom stays at home during the last three days, and only his most intimate friends visit him. But there is a lively intercourse between the two families—for there is no end to the interchange of compliments and of presents between bridegroom and bride.

The great day appears at last. Generally the nuptial ceremony is performed in the evening at the bride's house, and not in the mosque. The act is performed by a Kadi, or, if no such is to be had, by a reputedly devout man. It may appear strange to a European, that the principal person, the bride, is not present herself during the solemn act; she is represented by her father, her brother, or some other near male relation.

She only appears before the Kadi in person if she has no male relations at all, to be united to her bridegroom with the customary ceremonies. In this case, she enters the empty room first, completely muffled, after which the Kadi, the bridegroom, and the witnesses are admitted. After the conclusion of the ceremony, in which the voice of the bride is barely audible, the gentlemen leave first to let the newly-married wife retire to her apartments.

All the gentlemen, the bridegroom included, partake of a sumptuous feast. Whilst this lasts, the room in which it takes place is richly perfumed with incense of ud and of attar of roses.

The surrender of the bride to the bridegroom does not always follow upon the ceremony, but in most cases three days later. Numerous persons are now engaged in dressing her in her finest garments, and at about nine or ten in the evening of the third day she is conducted by her female relations to her new abode, where the bridegroom receives her in company with his male relations. Before the entrance to the private rooms, leave is taken with many congratulations and blessings, and the company then retire to the reception-rooms on the ground floor, to celebrate the marriage by merrily feasting for several days.

Some rules of etiquette are always to be observed when the bridegroom has entered the bride's apartment. If her rank is higher than his, she remains quietly seated, nor deigns to speak to him until he has first addressed her, and meanwhile still retains her costly mask, which covers her features. Then, to prove his affection, and as a bribe for the removal of the mask, the young husband places at her feet such presents as his means can afford. A few pence will suffice with poor people—but by rich ones large sums are spent on these offerings.

On the same evening, a general entertainment commences in the house of the young husband, which lasts three, seven, and even fourteen days. Friends, acquaintances, strangers—all are welcome, and may eat and drink as long as they will. There is, of course, neither wine nor beer, and even smoking is not allowed with the sect of the "Abadites," to which we belong—but that does not prevent people from being very merry and jolly. There are plenty of good things to eat, and almond milk, lemonade, &c.; songs are sung, warlike dances are performed, and stories are listened to. Eunuchs perfume the rooms with ud and sprinkle rose-water over the guests, out of silver dishes.

The ladies always remain together till midnight, but the gentlemen stop all night till they are called away to prayers in the morning.

Wedding tours are not known in the East. The young couple spend their honeymoon quietly at home the first week or fortnight, invisible to the outer world. After this time, the young wife receives visitors, and in the evenings her apartments are filled with her female friends, who have come to offer their congratulations.

Chapter XVIII

AN ARAB LADY'S CALL

I have repeatedly mentioned that we made many visits to, and received as many from, our friends and acquaintances. It may be interesting to the reader to learn a little more of such calls, and also about the etiquette observed and the conversation on such occasions.

If we wished to call upon any one, we had ourselves announced on the same day by well-dressed female slaves; we rarely ventured to go without having done so. In town our visits were made on foot, in the country we rode. The finest dresses are, of course, worn on such occasions, not only in honour of the friend to be visited, but also to exhibit our costumes and jewellery—just as is done here!

An Arab lady is not permitted to show her face; at home it is generally, and walking abroad it is always, covered by a mask, which is not like those worn by Egyptian women, which are ugly, and render respiration difficult. Our masks are nicely made of black satin, trimmed with splendid lace of coloured silk, and of gold and silver thread. They are in two parts, the upper portion covering

*The views expressed by Salme, in this chapter and throughout the memoirs, about Asians reflect the prejudices of her time, class, and cultural milieu.

the forehead, the lower hiding the nose and part
of the cheeks. The eyes, the tip of the nose,
mouth, neck, and half of the cheeks remain free.
The mask is fastened with long chains, twisted
several times round the head, serving at the same
time to keep the head-dress in its place.

Generally, Mahometan ladies do not walk
abroad into the public streets during the day—
they mostly do so early in the morning or in the
evening, after sunset. The streets in Zanzibar
were not lit up in my time; we took lights with us
to walk through the narrow, uneven, and dirty
streets. There was a great deal of luxurious display in the carrying of these lanterns, of which
the larger ones sometimes were more than two
yards in circumference. The prettiest were sometimes small facsimilies of a Russian church, a big
cupola in the centre and four smaller ones at the
corners. The light in each of these towers was
reflected through glass windows, white, red,
green, yellow, or blue. A lady of rank always had
two or three such lanterns carried before her, and
it required very strong slaves for that. Common
citizens use one lantern only.

Rainy days, though they occur rarely, hang
heavily, as they admit of no sociability out of the
house, and prevent all intercourse with the outer
world. Umbrellas, these indispensable companions in the North, are not owned by every one in
the East, nor is it easy to get one borrowed for a
walk. The middle classes, and sometimes the
negroes, carry immense umbrellas of Indian
make, covered with yellow, green, or black oil-
skin.

Ladies of rank are accompanied by a large
troop of armed slaves, who look more martial
however than they really are. These attendants

are very expensive, as their weapons, with the
exception of musket and revolver, are always very
costly and richly inlaid with gold and silver. But
that did not prevent the rogues from selling their
arms for a mere trifle, or pawning them at some
usurer's (these nice fellows are generally Hindoos
or Banyans) for the mere sake of quenching their
thirst for once in "Pombe" (palm wine). In such
cases the mistress can do nothing but redeem the
weapons at a tenfold rate, or equip the rascal
anew, and let a well-deserved, severe chastisement
be administered to him at the same time. Nothing,
however, could break them of their equanimity in
disposing of their masters' property, which was
always a heavier item than the buying of the
slaves.

The vanguard was led by ten to twenty of these
armed fellows, two or three in a line carrying
lanterns; the mistress, with an Arab companion,
followed; and a number of well-dressed female
slaves closed the procession.

The slaves turned all people, high or low, passing in the street at the same time, out of the way;
and to let the procession pass, they were obliged
to take refuge in a by-street or in some open
doorway. This measure, however, could only be
carried out by members of the reigning family—
other great ladies were not so easily obeyed, and
the lower classes rarely disposed themselves with
alacrity to clear the way.

It was a very pretty spectacle to see such a long
procession move on with lanterns; and although
Southern custom prescribes that perfect decorum
be observed in the public streets, it would be
almost too much to expect that such a merry
party could proceed many yards in total silence—
and there is a general rush to doors and windows

to see it pass. If a sister or lady friend was met in the street, the processions joined and formed into a large one.

Having arrived at the place of destination, we were at once announced; after which, we followed the servants into the reception rooms, or, on moonlight nights, up to the clean paved roof.

The hostess is seated on her "Medde," a seat some six inches high above the ground, which is covered with rich cloth of gold, reclining against a "Tekye," a cushion put against the wall. It is not customary for her to rise and meet her visitors as courtesy requires in this country; she only rises to express her pleasure, or in honour of the rank and station of the calling lady.

Arab women are very reserved with strangers, whether of high or low station; but whenever they meet you as friends the difference in birth and rank disappears at once. It is true that Southern women are more easily inclined to be jealous, but they also love more intensely than the children of the cold North; there the heart is allowed to speak for itself, while here the cool, calculating mind alone rules—which no doubt is as well, considering the different mode of life.

The visitors kiss the hands of the hostess, her head, and the hem of her shawl (persons of equal rank only shake hands), and they then seat themselves. Only a lady of the same rank can sit down on the Medde—those of an inferior station in life have to sit at some distance.

The mask is retained; with the exception of the shoes no part of the dress is removed, not even the Schele. In walking, the wooden sandals are replaced by the richly-embroidered "Kosch," a kind of leather slipper with broad heel. The shoes are slipped off before entering the room, and this custom is followed from the sovereign down to the slave. It is the business of the attending slaves to place these shoes, which are all much alike, in such a way that the owner on leaving can at once step into them. Even in this there is a strict rule of etiquette maintained: the slippers of the lady highest in rank are placed in the centre, and all the others round in a circle.

Coffee is then handed round in little cups, and this is repeated whenever a new visitor appears; fruits and sweetmeats are served besides.

The hostess is not required to keep up the conversation, and certainly not such a formal one as in these parts, from mere politeness. People are perfectly natural, and talk about everything they can think of. There are no theatres or concerts, balls or circuses, that can be talked about; nor are there any bright remarks made on the state of the weather. The conversation turns mostly on personal affairs and on agricultural pursuits, for which every lady of rank has a taste. There is nothing to check or restrain good spirits, and jests are exchanged without anxious regard to dignity. It is one of the greatest blessings Southern people enjoy, that they are nearly always bright and merry. Why should they not be so, when their serene and bright sky at all times sets them so good an example? And how should they have fits of the blues when Nature grants them so bountifully all they need and can wish for?

During visiting hours the master of the house does not come into the room of his wife, daughter, or mother. The sovereign only, and his nearest male relations, are dispensed from this rule; but whenever a lady cousin of equal rank from Oman was present, even our brothers and nephews were not allowed to enter without being announced.

The husband of a married sister, upon whom I call, remains in his reception room until I have departed. If the master of the house is compelled to talk about some matter of moment to one of his female relations, he has her called into another room. The same is done by ladies who wish to speak to their male relations, when these are engaged with their friends. This custom is rigorously observed even if a lady stays with her friend all day, say from half-past five a.m. to seven o'clock p.m.; and the gentlemen are frequently put to a great deal of inconvenience to avoid coming across strange ladies.

Still the Oriental bears the inevitable with incredible patience; for he has been reared in these views, and has lived no other life. The force of habit and its influence remain alike everywhere. I do not at all deny that many things in the East are exaggerated, and may appear superfluous. But are people in Europe quite free from such conventional tyranny and foolish customs? In one country the strictest reserve is observed in the intercourse between men and women; the most licentious liberty prevails in the other. There, a state of muffling up and wearing of masks in spite of the heat; here, in the cold North, the fashion of low dresses, and so on. All these are extremes; both things are overdone, and the happy medium has not, as yet, been put into practice anywhere.

Amidst very lively conversation these calls generally last from three to four hours. At last the time has come to part. The slaves must be roused to get into order for the procession; the lanterns are always kept lighted during the visit—a perfectly useless extravagance—but it is "swell" to do so.

Before separating, the hostess presents each

visitor with a parting gift, however trifling, and the same compliments are exchanged as at the arrival. It always takes some time before the different processions form into proper order to return home; but home must be reached by midnight, this being the hour for night prayers.

The Arab ladies possess another great advantage over their European sisters: they are never required to thank their hostess at parting for their entertainment, and make pretty, hypocritical speeches. It is bad enough to be compelled to go to a tiresome party; it is worse still to have to express thanks for it afterwards. I have often heard ladies in this part of the world highly complimenting their hostess on the great success of her delightful party, and immediately afterwards picking them both to pieces. What degrading hypocrisy! Would it not bring us nearer to our Creator if everybody endeavoured to meet his neighbour in a kindly, yet a straightforward, spirit? Why carry on such an eternal masquerade?

Chapter XIX

THE AUDIENCE. VISITS BETWEEN GENTLEMEN

Twice a day, by an old-established custom, all the
male relations, the ministers and officials—in
fact, all those who wish to see or speak to him—
are allowed free access to the sovereign in the
morning after breakfast and later in the day, after
fourth prayer. The audience chamber *(barze)* was
on the ground–floor, in a wing of the palace, built
close to the seashore, and at high tide the water
came right up to its walls; there was a magnificent
view far out into the sea from its windows. It was
a very large chamber, and yet not sufficiently so
to contain, at times, all persons who appeared.
The furniture was in the same plain style as in all
Arab rooms, consisting only of some carpets, of
tall looking-glasses, some clocks, and a number of
chairs ranged along the walls.

As no Arab of rank goes out by himself, there
was always a crowd of some hundreds of followers
outside the doors waiting for the return of their
masters and friends. As many of them as could
find a place sat down on the stone seats provided,
the remainder stood about in the open court of
the palace. To us this was always a very interesting spectacle—for the gentlemen appeared at the
audiences in their state-dresses, that is to say,

with turbans, and in the long overcoat *(djocha)* reaching down to the ankles, with their scarves girt round.

At home the Arab covers his shaven head with a white skull-cap, which is sometimes very handsomely embroidered, but whenever he walks abroad he puts on his turban *(amame)*. It requires a great deal of skill to twist it up, and takes some people more than half an hour to arrange it properly. It must be taken off very carefully, so that it may not collapse; but, as a rule, it is built up afresh every time it is worn. The cloth used for it is not expensive, and only costs some five to eight dollars; much more costly, however, is the material for the scarves *(mahsem)*, their price varying from twenty to two hundred dollars each; it is of silk richly interwoven with gold and silver thread. A man of rank possesses a great many scarves, and changes them as frequently as people in this country change ties; old and devout men, who no longer care for fashion, wear only mah–sems of plain white or black silk. The Arab's full dress is not complete without his weapons, as I already mentioned before. They are generally handed to him by his wife or daughter, or by his son, when he is about to leave the house.

Before entering the audience-chamber, the gentlemen slip off their shoes, and by the manner in which this is done the different ranks can be easily distinguished. The common people, for instance, take off their *watyes* some distance from the door; those of rank and station just in front of it. This is not ordered by some "despotic" law, it is an established and voluntary action. The Arab is accustomed of old to pay respect to every station, and his sentiments to his sovereign and to his house are instinctively loyal.

As soon as the audience-chamber is full, the sultan opens the proceedings. During my father's life, the procession was formed in the following manner: A detachment of negro guards came first; then a number of young eunuchs headed by the chief eunuchs; behind these my father, followed by his sons, the youngest closing up the column. In front of the entrance to the barze the guards and eunuchs formed into double line, through which my father, with his sons, passed into the chamber. All rose to salute him, and the same order of procession was repeated when he retired from the assembly. If a man of rank wished to leave the room before the audience was over, my father used to walk with him a few steps, and the whole company rose. To Europeans this may appear peculiar, and the liberty allowed to every one to come in and go without being dismissed by the monarch, or until the latter had left himself, is to a certain extent quite in opposition to the usual ceremonious bearing of the Arab.

At the morning audiences coffee was rarely served, but this was always done at those of the evening, after which business began. Everybody had a right to come forward and prefer a request, or to bring in a complaint, and to ask for a decision in his case. Nearly all the proceedings were verbal ones—either to settle affairs or give judgments in writing is much disliked. Petty business was mostly referred to the ministers or to the *kadis* (judges), and even to the chief eunuchs. The audience continued for two to three hours; people who had not got their business settled within this time, or who had come in too late, were ordered by the chief eunuchs to let the arbitration stand over till next day.

From the age of fourteen to sixteen the princes

are permitted to assist at the assembly; afterwards they are even obliged to. In the same way
every notable is obliged to put in an appearance,
to show his·loyalty and respect to his sovereign,
unless he be prevented by some urgent reason. If
any such notable absent himself for several days
running, the reason for his absence is at once
inquired into at his house, and in case of sickness
he may count upon a speedy visit from his master;
not even the most contagious diseases, such as
cholera or smallpox, will prove a hindrance—
indeed, this will prevent no one from going near
him, for all things are predestined and ordered by
God. The nurses of the sick man, his wife,
mother, or other females, of course leave the sickroom while other men are present.

Every Arab of standing has such a barze on the
ground floor of his house, quite apart from the
ladies' rooms, and there he generally lives and
receives his friends. In most cases, the floor is
paved with black and white slabs of French marble, and to keep the chamber cool there are neither carpets nor mats in it.

The gentlemen have the same visiting hours as
the ladies, after seven o'clock in the evening. The
Arab never goes out without a certain aim or
object; he never dreams of taking the so-called
constitutional walk, and if he sees a European
pacing up and down on the roof of his house in
the evening, he thinks he is saying his prayers in a
fashion peculiar to Christians.

I need not add anything about the ceremonials
or the conversation carried on at these gentlemen's calls; they are much the same as with the
ladies, only there are more topics to be talked
about, such as the affairs of town and country,
the features of the last audience, the petitions and

various lawsuits either pending or settled. To all these parties, and to the audiences especially, Europeans are freely admitted, and thus the patriarchal way of living with us, its advantages and disadvantages, are much better known in the North than anything connected with an Eastern woman's secluded life.

Chapter XX

THE LONG FAST

Most people may have heard that the Mahometans have to fast some time every day for a whole month, until the sun has sunk below the horizon, but the Mahometan fasting is not like that of the Roman Catholics, which is very easy in comparison. Every Muslim fasts himself and makes his children do so after their twelfth year. My mother being very devout, I had to keep the month of the Rumdān (thus pronounced by us, and not as it is here generally, Ramadān) from the time when I was nine years old.

It is indeed no easy matter for a child of that age to eat and drink nothing whatever for fourteen hours and a half every day. Thirst being much more trying in the tropics than hunger, and having very little conception of religious duties at that age, I admit I more than once quenched my thirst secretly with water. When questioned by my mother, I ruefully confessed my sin, and was only forgiven after promising not to trespass again. The rules are so strict, that it is even considered wrong to swallow the saliva, and for the first few days I was in such a drooping state, that I was sent away to sleep, to pass the time.

The beginning of the fast is signalled at four o'clock in the morning by firing from the ship;

from that very moment you cease eating, you put down the cup untouched that you were about to raise to your lips. After these shots no grown-up person in sound health touches either meat or drink; people sleep, however, a good deal during the day, to enable them to enjoy the pleasures of the table at night.

The sun sets at six o'clock; at half-past six, after prayers, the fast is broken. Beautiful fruit and cool water are taken as first refreshment, and then the whole family meets, and with every conceivable variety of delicacies makes up for lost time.

During the month of Rumdān, the Arab completely puts aside his ordinary simple habits, and devotes himself completely to sumptuous feasting.

On the whole, it is a very social time—hymns are sung throughout the evenings and nights, stories are told, while eating and drinking go on uninterruptedly. At midnight a gun gives the signal for those who have gone to sleep, to get up for the night meal (Suhur), which is taken between three and four in the morning, and even the little children who have been put to bed at ten o'clock, are roused to take part in it. The Suhur is generally served to all persons separately in their own rooms.

In this manner the whole month is passed. Fainting fits occur frequently at its commencement, and people grow visibly thin and slender— but gradually they get more accustomed to this mode of life, and they sleep less in the daytime than they did at first.

The fast is kept very strictly, and the head of the house keeps his slaves to it, especially those engaged in the household and the personal attendants. An exception is only made with slaves working on the plantations, who, having for the most part no religion at all, are at liberty to fast or not.

Children and all invalids are dispensed, of course, but the latter have to make up, after recovery, for the days missed, by an equal number of unbroken fastings in the course of the year. The same rule is valid for people travelling at this time.

The fasting season is not meant to be a mere probation to the outer man—it is intended to be a time of serious reflection to the devout Mahometan. He endeavours to discover his own deficiencies, and prays for forgiveness of his sins, in the same way as a good Christian spends Lent and the Holy Week. Even dangerous beasts are spared during this holy time, and every one endeavours to do as much good as he can. Thus the Rumdān is intended to be, as far as possible, a time of "Peace on earth, and goodwill towards men." Those who may at all other times lead a heedless life, are in this month's rigid service of their Lord brought nearer and raised to Him.

The traditional hospitality of the Arab never shows itself more than in this period, when it is considered a religious duty. All those who have a family or a household of their own, entertain as many strangers as they can find, often without inquiring their names. They request the warden of the mosque they habitually attend to send them a certain number of poor to their evening meals. The persons invited are not necessarily poor people, they are often rich men of high rank, who, being strangers in the place, have no home of their own during this holy season, and the true and hospitable Arab is only too happy to supply this want. No one considers it derogatory to be

entertained by a man poorer than himself, nor
would he in that case think of offering to pay for
the hospitality received. Selfishness cannot become a national sin where such principles prevail.
Happy those nations where charity is practised as
a sacred duty.

The Rumdān is in some respects like Christ-
mastime. A great many presents are distributed
on the first day of the following month, Shewāl,
which is one of the great feast days of the Mahometans. These presents consist but rarely of
ladies' fancy work; in general they are articles
purchased ready made. The best business is done
by goldsmiths and jewellers—nearly all of these
are Hindoos and Banyans, and they are without
exception the most mendacious crew. They are,
however, very clever workmen, and have succeeded in driving all the Arab goldsmiths out of
the field. They have plenty to do before the feast;
they get more orders than they can execute, but
undertake them nevertheless. To insure our orders being executed in time, we had to send a
couple of armed slaves to the workshop to watch
our work being done, and to prevent other orders
being finished first. These may seem rather strong
measures, but we had no choice else. One of my
sisters first suggested this expedient.

The presents most preferred consisted of arms.
To European ladies it may sound odd that a
woman makes a present of weapons to her husband, her brother, her son, or her bridegroom.
But it must be remembered that these are not
ordinary arms, but perfect gems of workmanship,
and Arabs do not mind paying fabulous sums for
them—when they are intended as presents.

Many other things are bestowed besides jewels
and arms, such as beautiful horses, white riding

donkeys, and—it will shock the civilized European to hear it—even slaves!

The last week of the Rumdān is spent with great preparations in every household for this feast, and as the first day of Shewāl draws nearer, there is much bustling in getting the presents and everything else ready in time. The night of the twenty-seventh day is considered the most holy one, it being the "night of value," in which Mhammed received the Kurān from heaven. The prayers on this particular night are uttered with the full conviction of their being granted.

On the last day of the month, the twenty-ninth or thirtieth (our months have only twenty-nine or thirty days, and our year three hundred and fifty-five days), all try to be the first to discover the new moon. In our country only scholars are initiated into the use of the almanacs—but on this occasion its prognostications alone would not avail, as the new moon must be clearly seen before the fast can be said to be at an end—a discovery which is rarely retarded by clouds in our deep blue southern vault.

Opera and field-glasses are passed from hand to hand—friends and acquaintances from a long distance send to get the loan of one for a short time. Keen-eyed men are sent up to the roof of the fort (a remnant of the Portuguese dominion) and to the mastheads of our ships to signal the first approach of the silvery crook.

The greatest excitement always prevailed in our palace. Forgetting that a shot fired off on board the ships right in front of us could hardly have passed unnoticed some one cries out every now and then, "There's the signal," "Hark!" all of which of course are false alarms, till at last a crash shakes our building from roof to basement, and immediately on that follow cries of joy from every soul in the town, with the words, "Id mbarak" (a happy feast to you). People on distant plantations despatch mounted messengers into the town to learn and bring back the longed-for news, or they send slaves up into high trees to watch the horizon; but should any false alarm cause the fast to be broken before its lawful termination, then the shortcoming must be made up, which is a harder trial while it lasts than the whole month put together.

Chapter XXI

THE LITTLE FESTIVAL

As I have already said, the preparations for the celebration of this feast begin a week beforehand. A large supply of bullocks, sheep, goats, gazelles, fowls, and ducks, has been provided (veal is not used, and pork forbidden to Mahometans), and the stalls are barely large enough to hold all the beasts. The eunuchs of rich people are very busy changing gold pieces and guineas for silver dollars, to be distributed during the festival among the poor, especially among the numerous poor from Oman.

Immediately after the signal, announcing that the celebration of the so-called "little festival" is to take place on the morrow, a very picturesque and lively spectacle is enacted in every Arab house. People, whose usual demeanour is staid and dignified, rush about hurriedly to offer congratulations to all their dear ones, and in this high-water-mark state of general brotherhood inveterate enemies are frequently seen to shake hands. There is such hurrying and scurrying, such talking in various languages, and such quarrelling among the slaves, who have yet to get through some work, all through the night, that it is impossible to get any rest whatever.

The butchers (slaves) rush upon their bellowing

and squeaking victims, and despatch them with the words, "In the name of the Lord, the merciful"; the throats of the animals are cut in a strictly ritual manner, the heads quickly severed from the body, and after being skinned the animals are sent into the kitchens at once to be prepared for the festive meal of the morrow. On such an evening our slaughtering yard was changed into a lake of blood; for this reason all the Banyans at Zanzibar, who are vegetarians, looked upon our feasts with much horror, and took care not to come near any such places at this time. I have already spoken of these Banyans as the principal traders and money-lenders in the town, and in the last capacity they are, beyond a doubt, the greatest cut-throats imaginable; they are bitterly hated on this account, and on occasions like these there is a splendid opportunity for their victims to take revenge upon them. Among the lower-class people it is a standing joke to entice the Banyans, who never allow any chance of business to slip out of their grasp, under pretence of some important order, into these blood-streaming yards, which is the greatest insult that can be offered to the star-worshippers, of whom it can be said, however, in spite of their low moral standing, that they adhere religiously to their code in being strict vegetarians.

In some of the ladies' chambers the burning question of dress is still being gone into or revived before the morning. Every fair one desires to surpass the other. Three complete costumes are required for the three feast days, every item of which must be brand new. Incredible quantities of fresh roses, jessamine, orange-blossom, musk, amber, and all kinds of the finest Oriental perfumes and essences are used during this time.

Many an Arab lady spends more than five hundred dollars on perfumery alone, and no nerves could stand these conglomerate strong scents if the doors and windows were not always kept open.

The henna is an important article of an Eastern lady's toilet, particularly on festive occasions; it is prepared from the leaves of a medium-sized tree, and serves to dye the feet of the women and children red. This henna, so indispensable to Eastern ladies, is used for two purposes—as a remedy for boils, prickly heat, itching, and the like, and as an ointment for the hands and feet. The leaves, resembling those of the myrtle, are not efficacious if used alone; they are dried, pulverized, and mixed with some lemon-juice and water. A stiff paste is made of this, which must be exposed to the sun for several hours; when used it is again softened with lemon juice.

The lady who is about to undergo the dying process is stretched out full length on her back, and is not allowed to stir. The paste is put on the sole of the feet, the toes included, about an inch thick—the upper part of the feet is never dyed; soft leaves are then applied as a covering, and the whole is tightly wrapped in linen. The same process is gone through with the palm of the hand and the fingers. To keep the application in its place, she must remain all night perfectly still without moving; for no other parts but those named must have the dye, and a smudge on the back of the hand or on the finger-joints is considered a great disfigurement.

All this time she is dreadfully teased by the swarms of mosquitoes and flies, but she dare not move to drive them away. In the upper classes women slaves have to watch all night by their mistress, to keep these plagues off with fans until the paste can be removed in the morning. The same process must be gone through three nights running, to obtain the desired dark red tint; then it sticks for about four weeks, and resists all washing.

I remember reading once about a fashion that prevailed in France at one time, of employing only one particular hairdresser who was very clever, and that this man, in order to satisfy on festive occasions his numerous customers, had to begin his work on the previous day, and that the ladies were compelled to pass all night seated in their high-backed chairs without stirring, so as not to disarrange their fashionable head-dress. This story reminded me very much of my youth in the East, though the sufferings we had to undergo for vanity's sake were even worse.

Middle-aged ladies and little children are not subjected to this tormenting process; they only employ the henna as a cooling ointment, and wash their hands with a liquid solution thereof.

The festive day has at last arrived; as early as four o'clock all are in full dress. More time is spent over prayers, and more fervently this morning than usual. At half-past five some ladies may be met already hurrying along the gallery in all their magnificent finery, showing their new dresses and jewels to particular friends. It would not do to postpone this to a later hour, for the general splendour by and by would preclude any close and individual inspection, and swallow up the due share of admiration. The scene is something like that in a European ball-room, with the difference that quieter colours or white dresses prevail there. I wonder what a European belle would think of an Arab lady's "full dress," and

whether she would care to exchange her gauzy
and delicately tinted ball costume for the following combination: a loose red silk dress, richly
embroidered with gold thread in different patterns, elaborately trimmed with gold or silver
lace, and satin trousers of bright green. It sounds
odd, I own, but habit soon does away with a great
many of our scruples. I was struck with something of the same feeling, but from a perfectly
opposite cause when for the first time I saw people
in Europe dressed in sober grey and black. I was
far from overjoyed at having to adopt these dark
shades myself, and being told that they were con-
formable to good taste and breeding.

The first gun is fired at six o'clock, to be followed by the firing of a succession of shots in
honour of the Feast of the Faithful; if there are
any foreign men-of-war in port, they also fire a
salute of twenty-one guns. Every Arab shows his
joy on such a day by letting off as many fireworks
as he can—a stranger might almost fancy himself
in a bombarded city. Every ship in port runs up
whatever flags she has, as do our own men-of-war.

An hour later all the mosques are crowded to
excess—no Arab stays at home on this day—and
those who cannot find a place within say their
prayers in the open street. Mahometan worship is
attended with a great deal of bodily exertion; it
prescribes bowing down very low, and touching
the ground with the forehead repeatedly. To have
to do this in a dirty ill-paved street is decidedly
unpleasant. The faithful must not let their
prayers be interrupted by rain or thunderstorm,
and on festive occasions, it is specially ordained
to say them either inside or close to a mosque.
Our father always went to the nearest mosque on
such days shortly before the hour for prayers,

followed by his numerous sons, and by a very
large retinue.

Meanwhile, there is a great deal of bustle in our
house to get everything ready for the entertainment of the numerous people, who come to offer
their congratulations on the return of the gentlemen from the mosque. As soon as the conclusion
of the worship is made known by the guns, everybody is free to enjoy the good cheer offered, for
the fast only closes when the prayers in the
mosque are over.

We waited for our father's return in his apartments, from where we could see the crowds of
visitors arrive. On his entering the room, we all
rose to congratulate him, and to kiss his hands.
This kissing of hands continues all day, only, however, between people of high rank; the middle
class kiss the head, or rather the cloth on the
head of those superior in station, and common
people kiss the feet.

The moment for the distribution of the presents
had now arrived. Accompanied by my sister
Khole and by Djohar, the chief of the upper eunuchs, both of whom were not a little envied for
this proof of confidence, my father went into his
treasury, which contained a great variety of precious objects, such as costly arms inlaid with
precious stones, all kinds of women's trinkets,
from the plainest to the most expensive, rare
materials for dresses, ordered expressly from
Persia, Turkey, or from China, attar of roses and
other varieties of fine essences in large jars, from
which smaller bottles were filled, and any amount
of glittering gold pieces.

It was impossible to expect that our father
should know how much and what kinds of jewellery each of his wives or daughters possessed, or

what they desired to have; he generally inquired a few days beforehand to learn the wishes of each, but Khole would again refresh his memory when he selected the gifts.

The sorting was done by the eunuchs in our father's presence, the name of the recipient was attached to each article, and handed over by the eunuchs. The presents were of course inspected at once, and it occurred frequently that they were returned to our father with the request to change them for something else, which was granted in most cases, as he was extremely good-natured. He was always very liberal, but never received anything in return. It is a beautiful custom in Europe for children to offer presents to their parents on their birthdays or at Christmas—the head of an Eastern family does not fare so well. Arab children never give a present to their father.

Hitherto, I have only spoken of the presents made by my father to his family; his obligations did not, however, end there. On this day everybody expected something; he had to remember all high African or Asiatic chiefs who happened to be in Zanzibar at the time, his officials, the soldiers and their officers, the captains of his ships and the crews, the managers of his forty-five estates, and last, but not least, all his slaves, exceeding 8,000 in number. The various gifts were, of course, suited to the rank of the receiver; the slaves, for instance, merely received materials for dresses. To all these many hundreds of poor may be added, who sometimes came a fortnight afterwards to claim a present; on the whole, it was not a bad time for the poor, who received rich donations from all the wealthy people.

A similar and quite as comprehensive a distribution of presents took place at Bet il Mtoni. I

often wondered at the inexhaustible produc-
tiveness of the treasure chamber to withstand
such a drain, particularly on ready money, as was
made upon it during these three days, which
proves, I think, that our father was an excellent
manager, and a clever business man.

Chapter XXII

THE GREAT FESTIVAL

The Mahometan celebrates only two great festivals in the course of the year, and to a Roman Catholic with his numerous saints' days this may seem very strange. Two months intervene between the little feast and the great feast—called Id il hadj, and generally known in Turkey and in Europe by the name of the great Beiram feast.

It is a repetition of the one I have just described, with the difference only that it is celebrated in a still more beautiful and grander style, and is altogether of a more solemn order. It is the time of the great pilgrimage to Mekke,* which is the dearest wish of every one of the Faithful to undertake at least once during life. The devout Muslim cannot be deterred by the danger of cholera and other epidemics, which carry off many thousands of the pilgrims at times; countless crowds join every year to seek forgiveness of their sins in the holy city of the Prophet. These poor people have to travel on foot over long distances; and the manner in which they are conveyed in overcrowded ships is really dreadful. Still they go, putting their trust in the Lord, in whose hands their life is. Truly, such faith, which knows not

*The word is pronounced as written above, and not Mecca.

fear, and shuns no hardship to carry out this religious duty, may well hope for mercy.

This, the greatest feast of the Mahometans, falls on the tenth day of the twelfth month of the year, and lasts from three to seven days. Many hallow the same by a nine days' fast, beginning on the first day of the month, in the same way as is done by the devout pilgrims to Mekke.

Whoever can possibly afford it, procures a sheep, which is killed on the first holiday, and distributed among the poor. The law prescribes, that the sheep, intended for this purpose, be of the very best quality, and perfectly sound; it must not have lost even a single tooth. It is, of course, next to impossible to procure so faultless a sheep, and we used to send slaves all over the island a fortnight and more before to obtain what we required, but if none were to be had near home, the slaves crossed over to the African continent, where there is a greater abundance. The owners knew that Arabs of high rank were ready to pay any price for really fine sheep, and made their charges according; so that, added to the other expenses incurred in the purchase, each specimen represented a somewhat disproportionate value.

No part, however, of the immolated animal may be consumed by any of the family nor by the slaves—every particle must be given away to the poor.

To them, the great feast is the most important event of the whole year, as on this occasion one of the most commendable of all Mahometan customs is made manifest, viz., the self-taxation in favour of the poor.

With the exception of such half-cultured States as Turkey, Egypt, and Tunis, public funds and shares are things quite unknown in the true East;

nobody understands the meaning of the word investment. All the property consists in plantations,
houses, slaves, jewels, and ready money. Religious
law exhorts every Mahometan to give to the poor
a tithe of the yearly profit on his crops, the rental
of his houses, or any other source of income. At
the same time he must get all his property, consisting of precious stones and gold and silver,
valued by experts, and relinquish the tenth part
for the same purpose.

All this is done without any authorized civic
supervision or control. Alone the voice of conscience prompts to the performance of this duty.
This law of the Prophet is kept particularly sacred, and none but people of really bad character
ever try to elude it. Moreover, this act of charity is
never talked about or inquired into, but is carried out on the precept that the left hand shall not
know what the right hand doeth.

This may account for the fact that such a great
number of beggars, if I may say so, are quite an
indispensable institution in every Mahometan
state, and also for the reason of this self-taxation.
But these poor people must not be compared with
the poor in these parts, who have far better
claims on our charity. For one-half of the Oriental
beggars possess more perhaps than they want.
Begging is their trade—it has become their second
nature, and they would never be fit for anything
else. Their craft is more often than not a heritage,
and you may happen to be accosted thus: "Why,
don't you know me? I am the daughter (or the
son, the sister-in-law, &c.,) of So-and-so, to
whom you always used to give so much, when they
were alive. Now I have taken their place, and if
you have any alms to give, please be good enough
to send them to such or such a place."

Hundreds of such poor used to assemble for their share of the alms we distributed in fulfillment of certain vows we made during the year. They gather also under the windows of sick people, and alms given in such cases are called "Satka." No Mahometan will refuse the poor on such occasions, even if he has to part with all he has. Whatever his motive may be—real charity or the hope of being acceptable in the eyes of God, I think it a beautiful custom.

Many of these beggars are covered with wounds and sores—some go about minus some feature, and otherwise horribly maimed and disfigured. They are the victims of a very bad disease called Belas,* which attacks hands and feet first, and leaves these snow-white ever after. Everybody flies from them, as the taint is thought to be contagious. I cannot say whether this is leprosy or not, but these unfortunates always receive rich alms.

The giving away of presents does not, however, stop with the feast itself. For those who may have been ill or absent at the time do not forego their right to their share of the alms. Weeks and months may have passed away—the new feast may already be close at hand—still they come and claim their overdue present.

There is no other religious holiday for the next nine or ten months—nothing to interrupt the even and regular course of life, unless it be by some such festivities already described or about to be described in the next chapter. Birthdays are not celebrated in our country.

*leprosy

Chapter XXIII

AN OFFERING AT THE SPRING TSHEMSHEM

When I was about fifteen years old, I wore one
day for the first time a red dress of silk brocade;
and on the very next day some kind of inflamma-
tion spread over my whole body. Old and experienced people declared at once that I was
bewitched, or that some jealous being had cast an
evil eye on the pretty dress. I had, however, always been a great sceptic in this respect, and
declined to part with my new dress, which, in
spite of all warnings, I put on again. Perhaps the
dye really contained some poisonous substance—
or from some other unexplained reason—I was
taken ill again, and had to stay in bed. The matter was now perfectly clear—I was not allowed to
wear the dress any more; therefore, to settle the
point, I gave it to a courageous citizen's wife, who
believed no more in witchcraft than I did. Had I
acted strictly in accordance with the prescribed
precaution in such cases, I should have ordered a
"spell" to be said over it, or had it burnt so as to
completely destroy its evil effect.

The above may serve as a little sample of the
kind of superstition that prevails in the East. I
have spoken on this subject before, and some
more details may follow now, connected with the

rites of a certain oblation, also originating in superstition.

Some springs are believed to possess special miraculous powers—not their waters, but their presiding spirits. Such a spirit will do all it can for those who implicitly believe in and do honour to its power; it can cure the sick, restore lost people to their homes, arrange a good match for those who wish to marry, give childless parents their desire; it can soften angry parents, reconcile husband and wife and friends, restore lost property (such as gold, slaves, cattle, and so forth) to its owners, make poor people as rich as Crœsus; indeed there is no feat with which such a spirit is not credited.

The favorite spring in the island of Zanzibar is called Tshemshem; it is situated some miles out of the town. A visitor to this miraculous spot would gain the impression that its spirit must be easily contented, to judge from the poor quality of the gifts presented. Poor people spend only a small bit of cloth, two inches wide, left dangling about in the wind, or an eggshell. The spirit is also rather partial to all kinds of sweets (Halwe),* to perfumes, and incense; but to make quite sure of success, the tribute must be paid in blood.

Tschemschem is visited by many afflicted people, who have vowed to bring some such offering. There is, however, always a cautious proviso attached to these vows—the wish must be granted within a certain stipulated time, otherwise the spirit goes without his offering. If the spirit is not punctual to time, the promise is cancelled, and there is an end of it. In the reverse case the promise is faithfully kept, often by the relations

*Halva

of those who have died before their vow was fulfilled.

When quite a child, I was frequently taken to one of these sacred springs, and we always had a very pleasant time there. But after I ceased to be called "Kibibi," or little mistress, and had become "Bibi," or a real mistress, and when I was old enough to observe and to think for myself, I only assisted at one more oblation, which was, however, very grand.

My sister Khadudj, now dead, had been seriously ill for a long time, and her anxious attendants made the vow that she should go to Tschemschem herself to present an offering if she recovered life and health; and when this came about she went to carry out the promise made on her behalf.

Four weeks before the day appointed invitations were issued to several of her favourite sisters, and preparations on a large scale commenced at the same time. Ten invitations to balls in Europe, all received at once, would not cause such anxiety and expense as this single one to our impending pilgrimage. It was not a case of simply providing dresses for one's self or daughters, but a whole regiment of slaves of both sexes had to be equipped with dresses and jewellery suitable to the wealth of their mistress, not to speak of a great number of donkeys that the occasion would require. Artists and workmen were over head and ears in work; the jewellers, who never keep any stock, but make everything to order, had consequently most to do, besides superintending the polishing up of the gold and silver ornamented harnesses and the weapons of the slaves. A pilgrimage of this sort is always something of a pageantry—all the riding gear must look beautifully new and resplendent; no expense is spared, and many an article of jewellery is paid tenfold its value on account of the great demand.

As early as half-past five on the appointed day, I rode to my sister's house to join her there; the crowd was so great that I despaired ever getting there at all. At last the signal was given to start, and we had a long and brisk ride in the pleasant morning breeze to the spring.

The spot, at other times so lonely and deserted, had been changed for this day into the most wonderful fairy palace. For days the grand preparations had been going on. The long grass was cut, carpets spread under the big trees, mirrors nailed to their trunks, and every possible comfort provided; a sumptuous meal had been prepared the day before.

Breakfast was taken soon after our arrival in the shade of the magnificent trees. The picture of this scene deeply impressed itself upon my memory; the gorgeously-attired people, with their costly jewels, gracefully reclining in front of the merrily bubbling spring, and surrounded by the romantic rich vegetation of a tropical wood; truly it was a picture that no painter's fancy even could devise—indeed, like the enthralling descriptions of "The Arabian Nights."

Two hours later we prepared to make the offering, the object of our excursion. The spirit of the spring was to rejoice this day in the blood of a beautiful, choice bull, and in smaller tributes, such as sweetmeats and immense numbers of fresh eggs, dashed to pieces on the water's edge. Two flags were likewise dedicated—a red one, our insignia, and a white one—as a peace-offering.

Our camping place was only a short distance

from the spring, and the whole company rose to assist at the ceremony. One of my sister's chamber-women advanced close to the water's edge to make a little speech. She spoke of the severe illness of her mistress, and how the vow had been made in the last extremity. She thanked the kind spirit for its assistance in restoring her mistress to health, who had now come in person to present the promised thank-offering.

The bull was brought forward and killed; the blood was carefully collected and sprinkled over the spring from all sides. Musk and ambergris were thrown upon burning charcoal in silver incense pans. The ceremony concluded with some prayers, which were said standing.

Besides the blood of the immolated animal the invisible spirit received the heart, liver, and a few other parts, which were strewed all round, cut up in small pieces. The remainder ought to have been distributed amongst the poor, for neither the person making the offering, nor any of her relations, are by custom allowed to partake of it. As the spring Tshemshem is, however, too far removed from town, and as there were no poor people to be found in its immediate neighborhood, an understanding with the spirit had been come to when the vow was made, that, to overcome this difficulty, the immolated beast was to be eaten on the spot, and thus it formed part of our afternoon's repast.

When the company all sat round again to rest, one or the other of our party might be seen to disappear quietly for a while, but no notice was taken thereof, for we knew that the secret visit had been paid to the miraculous spring, and to the discreet and powerful spirit were confided many griefs and afflictions, physical and mental

troubles, or, may be, the burden of an unrequited
love; but for all of them its intercession was
craved.

The hours up to four o'clock passed away in
feasting, walking about, playing, resting, and
praying. The horses and donkeys were then
brought back to be saddled. It generally took
above an hour before we were quite ready to
start, as one of the bad habits of negroes consists
in forgetting the most necessary things at the last
moment.

On our return we stayed at Mnasimodja, or at
Ngambo, for prayers, and after dusk we all re-
entered the town to accompany my sister home.
The magnificence and splendour of this feast
formed the main topic of our conversation for
many weeks after.

Chapter XXIV

DISEASES AND MEDICAL TREATMENT—POSSESSED PEOPLE

People in the East grow up without paying any particular attention to their body or their health; rarely, and then only in cases of severe sickness, nature is aided a little, but the remedies used for this purpose are, as a rule, more than useless.

The detestable practice of cupping plays a great part, and only the very smallest children are spared this torment. Letting blood is considered the universal remedy for all kinds of ailings—it is made use of alike in attacks of cholera and small-pox, or in any other case of suffering. It is also employed as a preventative remedy, for people in perfectly good health have themselves cupped once a year at least, as was the custom in Europe formerly.

In the upper ranks bleeding takes the place of cupping, but no particular precaution is ever observed in this practice. I once had a great fright in one of the dark passages at Bet il Mtoni, seeing one of my sisters being carried past quite motionless, and looking as if she were dead. My screams alarmed the whole house, and I would not be calm till they told me that she was not dead, as I had feared, but that she had only fainted after having been bled too profusely. She recovered very slowly from the critical state into which the careless treatment had thrown her.

I am not competent to judge whether such profuse issues are, from time to time, beneficial to the health in a hot climate; I fancy, however, that the manner in which they are practised must be extremely dangerous.

The kneading of limbs and joints produces a very pleasant effect. I have spoken of this as being done regularly every morning and evening, and of the great proficiency our slaves had acquired in it. In cases of ordinary indisposition, especially indigestion, it is much practised.

Emetics, prepared of the most nauseous herbs, are frequently taken. It is sometimes next to impossible to swallow these concoctions, the mere smell of which is sufficient to produce the desired effect.

In cases of severe illness the aid of God is alone invoked, and to this end sentences from the Kurān are considered the best cure. These passages are written by a person, generally admitted as devout, on a white plate, with a solution of saffron. This writing is dissolved with water (generally with rosewater), and the whole mixture must be swallowed by the invalid, like a dose of medicine, thrice a day, morning, noon, and night; but to do any good, not the smallest particle of this sacred liquid must be spilt. I myself had to take this remedy once for some time during a violent attack of fever.

In exceptional cases, and if the sick person was a special favourite of our father, a real medical man, or a sorcerer, was admitted to the bedside. My sister Khole once suffered severely from pains in the ear, which would not get better, in spite of all the quackeries employed. At last it was

thought advisable to call in a Persian doctor
(*hakim*), very famous at the time. I was quite a
child then, and was permitted to stay in the room
while he was consulted. Khole was wrapped up so
completely in a schele that nothing of her whole
body was visible but the ear. My father stood on
the right, and my brother Khalid on the left of the
couch on which she was seated, and my other
brothers formed a circle round her, all of them
fully armed. The doctor was conducted into the
sick room by a number of eunuchs, while others
were placed as guards at different parts of the
house, to give the female residents the signal to
retire on the approach of the Persian. The hakim,
of course, was not allowed to speak to the sick,
but his inquiries had to be addressed to my father
or to my brothers, who also replied.

When I was down with typhoid fever, at a later
period, and had been raving for some days, my
aunt Asche, my father's sister, resolved at last to
call in a European doctor, as none of our Arab or
Swahili remedies would answer. My father's death
having made me personally independent, the cer-
emonial just described was no longer needed. The
doctor, who was well acquainted with Arab
customs, insisted upon being allowed to feel my
pulse, which demand was granted by my aunt
after long consideration. A number of eunuchs
had, however, been put in requisition, and I was
completely covered by my schele, although quite
unconscious of what was going on around me, and
was only told afterwards by my aunt. But when
the doctor required to see my tongue, Djohar, the
chief of the eunuchs, aghast with horror, flatly
refused this unheard-of demand, so that the doctor withdrew quite furious, without having prescribed anything.

Such panacea are, of course, only made use of
in countries where the deepest ignorance prevails
of the human frame, as well as of its functions,
and the ailments to which it is subjected. The
Arab is perfectly ignorant of all these, and quite
unable to distinguish one case of sickness from
another. He divides all inner complaints into two
classes—pains in the stomach and pains in the
head. No matter which be the internal organs
affected, the disease goes always by the same
name; and every complaint that affects the head,
up to softening of the brain and sunstroke, is
called headache. But as to the origin of all these,
the Arab remains in utter darkness, and when all
the home cures have been tried and have failed, a
eunuch is perhaps sent to one of the consular
doctors to ask for some medicament. A medical
man who can, however, not see the sick person,
and who obtains only the vaguest information
about the disease itself, labours rather under a
disadvantage. Consequently, the sufferer often
gets a wrong medicine, or an innocuous one at the
best.

No one knows what is meant by observing a
certain diet. A person attacked with cholera, ty-
phus, or small-pox is allowed to eat whatever he
chooses, or what he can get. Nature is supposed to
be proof against anything, and with the belief in
predestination, the Muslim does not even guard
against the danger of contagion; people taken
with small-pox, for instance, are never isolated.
Needless to say, that with such rampant ignorance
precautionary measures can never be effected,
and that all attempts to confine cholera epidemics, or to set a strict watch over the great
caravans of pilgrims, have so far failed.

I wish to say a few words more about some
kinds of diseases. Small-pox, unfortunately, rules
permanently in Zanzibar, and kills off many
thousands. The person attacked is rubbed all
over with an ointment of Djiso *(curcumac)*, and
placed in the sun; in some cases the skin is saturated with cocoanut-milk, which is preferable to
Djiso. The only other means to ease the invalid
consists in removing him from his bed to a soft
mat, or by placing him upon a large plantain leaf.
Internal remedies are not given, and, above all,
care is taken that no water comes near him.

Cases of consumption, especially of a rapid
nature, are frequent, but they are taken no notice
of, nor is any treatment of the disease known. Yet,
of all, it is the most feared; it is thought to be
contagious, and not unjustly so, as many European physicians assert. Any one suffering from
consumption is almost an outcast; nobody likes to
occupy the seat just left by such an one, or touch
his hand, much less drink out of the same cup
with a consumptive person. One of my stepmothers, a young and very beautiful woman, was
very ill with consumption, but to the last she was
able to leave her bed and visit her friends.
Though still quite a child, I could plainly perceive
how unwelcome she was to all. I felt very sorry for
her, and used secretly to go and be of some use to
her when she could leave her couch no more: she
had only one little boy, and no daughter to tend
her.

Many of my dear relations have succumbed to
this malignant disease, and the majority of them
at an early age. The property left by consumptive
people is treated with the greatest precaution;
their dresses and bedding are carefully washed in

the sea, gold and silver objects even are put
through a process of firing to guard against contagion.

Whooping cough is as frequent with us as it is
in this country. The children are given large
quantities of "dew-water" to drink, which is collected in the morning from the giant leaves of the
plantain. A remedy, founded on superstitious belief, is likewise used. A number of round pieces,
of the size of a shilling, are cut from the dried
skin of a kind of pumpkin, called hawashi, and
these pieces are suspended round the child's
neck.

Sores and boils are very common and very
painful. They are covered up with the skin of
onion and with dough.

The simple home remedies are all tried in
turns, but medical aid and treatment—never, in
the absence of which it can hardly be a matter of
surprise that people trust in the miraculous instead, and address themselves for help to fortune-
tellers. These Basarīn, as they are called, are
consequently in great request, and do a thriving
business. We generally consulted, in cases of sickness, an old, one-eyed woman from Hadramaut,
who was a "Shihrie." Her magic implements consisted in a dirty bag, containing a variety of
things, such as small shells, sea-pebbles, bleached
bones, quantities of broken bits of glass and
china, rusty old nails, bent copper and silver
coins, and so forth. When she was wanted to
answer a question, she prayed first for aid from
above for a revelation of the truth, after which,
she opened her bag, mixed its contents well, and
then emptied them out. Her answer was always
regulated by the position of the articles she had
thrown out of her bag, and then she stated

whether the sick person would get better or not, &c. Chance appeared to favour this Basara a great deal more than any of the other fortune-tellers; frequently her predictions proved true, and she made a good thing out of it, for in these cases she was rewarded by large presents, quite out of proportion with the small preliminary fee.

External hurts are of course cured more easily than inner diseases. To stop bleeding tinder is generally used; though broken bones are cases of a more dangerous nature. I broke a forearm once, falling downstairs; my aunt and my brother Bargasch at once bandaged the broken limb, but unfortunately they did not understand how to set the bone properly, so I have a somewhat crooked arm in consequence to this day.

I have not yet touched upon a very important subject—the devil! It is well known that in the East nearly everybody believes in the devil, and that he prefers taking up his residence with human beings. I do not remember a single child with us, that had not been possessed of the devil once, at least. A new-born child, that is more restless and more inclined to cry than is usual, must surely be possessed, and the exorcising of the evil spirit is at once set on foot. Little onions and bits of garlic are strung like pearls and sus-pended from arms and neck. The remedy is a very simple one, and not quite so foolish as it looks, for if the poor devil has any olfactory nerves, he could hardly withstand such an attack upon them.

Grown-up people are also frequently possessed— men but rarely, but many women, and of the Abyssinian women, nearly one-half. Convulsive attacks, want of appetite, and general apathy, the desire to remain shut up in dark rooms, and such propensities, are taken as sure signs. A person, thought to be possessed, is treated with a tremendous amount of respect, or rather—fear!

A special examination takes place to find out whether a person be really possessed. For this ceremony a party is invited, of which all the guests must be acknowledged habitations of the evil one. These pitiable victims form a kind of secret society, in which they keep their movements quite dark.

The newly attacked woman sits down in a dark room, wrapped so completely in her schele, that she cannot be touched by the slightest ray of light. She is then, in the true sense of the word, smoked out, a vase containing strong incense being held close to her nostrils. The company round her begin to sing a strange song, wagging their heads all the time to and fro. Some Abyssinian concoction, composed of corn and dates, which tastes rather pleasant, is a beverage necessary for the occasion. I have been told that all these combined influences put the victim into a state of second sight; she first talks incoherently, until at last she raves with foam at the mouth. Then is the time that the spirit has taken possession of her. The company present enter into conversation with this spirit, and request to be informed what it wants; for it must be understood that the sick are not plagued by evil spirits alone—there are also good spirits, that may have taken a special fancy to a person, wishing to protect her in life. Sometimes it occurs that two spirits, a good and a bad one, contest for the same person, and during this exorcism they are sure to manifest themselves. It is said that frightful scenes sometimes ensue on such occasions, which none but the very bravest can face out.

Frequently an expert woman will drive out an evil spirit; with a good one a kind of agreement is made, allowing it to pay visits to its victim at times, when it would be well received, on condition that it predicts what may befall the possessed one, as well as her relations.

Possessed people are in the habit of drinking the blood of immolated animals, such as fowls and goats; they devour eggs and meat raw. Of course the poor people who have undergone such an examination suffer from its effects for many a day afterwards.

In these cases I was also able to observe how fast a bad example is followed by others. In spite of the superstitious views of all Mahometans, the Oman people are far from believing in all the nonsense I have just described. When they come to Africa, they look upon everything at first as only fit for negroes, and would wish to return home at once. After a short stay, however, they are more susceptible and credulous than all the rest put together.

But enough of this melancholy subject!

In conclusion, I should like to ask if it would not be more humane to import female physicians into Zanzibar instead of those horribly demoralizing spirituous liquors? Must corruption always precede civilization? There is a great opening here for Christian charity, that would bear fruit hundredfold, without any great obstacles in the way. For my part I am perfectly willing, in case a society undertake to send out a qualified person, to instruct the same in Arabic and Swahili; this is the least service I can do my dear native home. But it must be a female physician; she will be able to do more good in the East then ten medical men combined. A kind woman with pleasing manners would be received with open arms by all Eastern ladies. She would not only find herself well rewarded, but soon acknowledge herself that she is doing a good and charitable deed.

Chapter XXV

SLAVERY*

This chapter treats of one of the most controversial subjects of the day. I am perfectly aware that I shall not make any friends by the opinions I hold, but nevertheless consider it my duty to state them frankly. I have met everywhere with a great deal of ignorance in regard to this question, and even these people who are more intimately acquainted with it frequently overlook the fact that it is not called into existence solely and purely by humane efforts on the part of Europeans, but that political interests are often a secret incentive.

I was still a child at the expiration of the term after which, as convened between my father and Great Britain, the slaves of all British subjects in Zanzibar, the Hindoos and Banyans, were to be set free. These were hard times for the owners, who complained bitterly; many of the upper classes sent their wives and daughters to entreat our intercession, which, of course, was utterly outside our power. Some of them had a hundred or more slaves on their estates; all these received their liberty on one day, which caused the ruin of

*The views expressed by Salme, in this chapter and throughout the memoirs about black Africans and about slavery reflect the prejudices of her time, class, and cultural milieu.

their owners. The latter could procure no men to
work their plantations, and consequently they
could get no revenues from them; besides which,
our beautiful island had the questionable good
fortune of suddenly finding itself saddled with a
few thousand idlers, vagabonds, and thieves.
These great children thus set free enjoyed their
liberty as a release from their bondage, and its
inflicted duties, but what was their physical condition in life on waking from their short dream of
happiness? They found themselves for the first
time in their lives thrown upon their own resources, homeless, and utterly without means of
maintenance. The apostles of the anti-slavery
unions, after fighting hysterically for the liberty
and rights of citizenship for the slave classes,
disappeared on having gained their point, making
no more provision for their *protegés* than if they
had been lilies of the field, except in so far—and
probably to complete the grim farce—that their
ladies at home sent woollen socks for the lilies on
the burning soil of Africa. Everybody who has
lived in the United States, Brazil, or any country
where there are negroes, will corroborate the fact
that, apart from many good qualities, the black
race cannot be induced to work, but only forced.

As I said, only British subjects were henceforth
forbidden to keep slaves. The English could not
interfere with the laws and customs of our country, and slavery exists to this day in Zanzibar as
well as in all Mahometan States of the East. One
must, however, be careful not to judge slavery in
the East by the same standard that is applied to
slavery in the United States or in the Brazils. The
slave of a Muslim is in quite a different and far
superior position.

The worst features of this institution are the

slave trade and the transport of these poor people
from the interior of the continent to the coast.
Great numbers perish of fatigue and of hunger
and thirst, but all this is shared also by their
leader. It is absurd to suppose that the slave
traders cause these great hardships and priva-
tions on purpose; their own advantage requires to
bring out the people in the best possible condition, as they have often invested their whole
fortune in such an enterprise.

Once arrived, the slaves are for the most part
well cared for. They have of course to work for
their masters without wages, but they have no
care themselves, and their welfare is always stu-
diously looked after. Is every non-Christian of
necessity a creature without a heart?

The negro, above all, is fond of his ease—works
only when he is compelled to, and then requires
the strictest control even for the little work he is
required to do in our parts. Neither are they an
easy family to rear and keep, for there are a great
many thieves, drunkards, deserters, and incendi-
aries among them. What is to be done with these?
To overlook their sins would be to encourage them
in their practice. Imprisonment they would not
resent, but on the contrary, court it, and revel in
their cool retreat, eating, drinking, and dreaming
their time away.

Under these circumstances there is only one
expedient—corporal punishment. A great outcry
is raised about this in Europe, especially by those
who are more richly possessed of fine-sounding
theories than of practical knowledge and insight.

Cruelty and depotism is justly condemned
everywhere, may its victim be a poor negro or a
civilized person languishing in a Siberian mine.
But all things must be fairly considered, nor is

every institution alike justifiable or applicable.
With Eastern nations slavery is a very ancient
institution. I doubt if it could ever be completely
abolished, and in any case it is folly to attempt
sweeping away old customs in a bluster of enthusiasm. Every good thing must take its time, and be
confronted with good examples. There are a good
many Europeans in the East who keep slaves
themselves, and who buy them if they find it in
their interest to do so. Such things are, of course,
not reported home, or they are excused on the
plea that they have been done "in the interests of
science." Science must serve as a pretext for
many an evil. The morality, however, remains the
same, whether the Arab puts his slaves to field or
domestic work, or whether they be employed as
carriers and porters by Europeans, the latter
being much harder and more trying work. Nor
are these European slave-keepers always humane
enough to set the slaves they have bought free
when they require them no longer, as the Arabs
often do; they simply resell them. The Mahometan population of Zanzibar were greatly in-
censed on one occasion against an Englishman
who, before returning to Europe, secretly sold his
woman-slave to an Arab official.

With one or two more such cases of inconsistency on the part of Europeans that I could quote
it is not surprising if Arabs look on their civilized
visitors with an eye of suspicion, and wish back
those happy times when they had nothing to fear
from their subverting ideas. They have taken it
into their heads that the object of suppressing
slavery was solely to work the slow ruin of their
nation, and ultimately of their God.

If people really think that slavery can be abolished by degrees, and that other important

changes can be effected beyond that, then the
greatest caution will be necessary, and slow advancement step by step. The negroes must first be
trained to think and to work, and their masters
must be taught in an intuitive manner, and in a
form admitting of no doubt as to its disinterested
motives, that by employing good agricultural implements and machinery they could easily do
without those hundreds of slaves which are now
required to cultivate their lands. The Arab must
be brought to understand that there is no intention to ruin him, and that he is to be treated and
weighed in the same balance as the negro.

In my opinion it would have been more judi-
cious to adopt the slow and sure course, than
ostentatiously to build a church on the slave market, for which there was no need, as two existed
already, one Catholic and the other Protestant,
and both with very meagre congregations. That
this must have been offensive to Eastern people
will easily be understood by those who know a
little about things there. The Arab, like all Eastern races, is conservative by nature, and adheres
with great tenacity to his traditions. He must not
be hurried into innovations which appear to him
impossible and incomprehensible. His objections
are peremptorily put down to Mahometan fanati-
cism and religious intolerance. But the following
may show that this intolerance is by no means so
great as it is described. When I revisited Zanzibar
after a nineteen years' absence all came to meet
me with the greatest friendliness—the people even
left the mosques to welcome me and to wish me all
blessings; and if my countrymen had really been
the religious fanatics they are reported to be, I, as
a renegade, would have deserved and roused their
indignation much more than a born Christian. It

is therefore not intolerance which governs them, but a sense of self-preservation, increased and intensified by the fact that their most vital interests and rights are encroached upon by reckless, high-handed innovators, and often by utterly worthless, inefficient representatives of civilization and Christianity.

The negro, however, is at present still very indifferent to religious matters, and certainly such is the case in Zanzibar with the greater part of the black race. Many become Christians merely from selfish motives. An English missionary who has worked for many years at Membase (Mombasa, a little island to the north of Zanzibar) complained to me once that the number of his converts had always risen and fallen with the duration of the supplies he received from England. Hence I regret that, before familiarizing the negro with higher doctrines, his religious sense must first be awakened and nursed with an untiring care! For this reason many of those brave men may have failed after risking their strength, their health, and their lives even in the attempt to deepen the shallow level of the negro soul, and then to lift his race into culture and Christianity.

The objection might be raised against me that I am not a fair judge on the slave question; that, having grown up with Eastern views, I am unable now to release myself from them or weigh the matter calmly. In vindication of which I here produce as momentous evidence the views of some ultra-Europeans on this subject.

The African traveller, *P. Reichard*, wrote in 1881 from Gonda:

"In the night of the 12th of October, I was aroused by the shrieks of a woman who asked for admittance. I sent Askart to discover the reason of this noise, and was told she wanted to get into my place, having quarrelled with her husband, and smashed some object of value, that she might, by the custom of the country, become our slave. Three similar cases happened to a native Arab within a short time, who, however, obtained compensation, and it is by no means an uncommon occurrence for a free man, dissatisfied with his position, again to become a slave in this way. This is a clear and distinct proof of the exaggeration and one-sidedness of many of the reports on slavery, which depict their condition in dark, and I might say, non-existing, colours. . . .

"The position of a slave once settled down, is by no means worse, at least as good, and frequently much better, than in his own country. The tribes south of the Tanganika, for instance, are governed by very cruel sultans, and slaves coming from that place to this would on no account go back again.

"The slave of the Arab is not at all overburdened with work, and criminals alone are condemned to corporal punishment; greater severity than that which exists would necessitate many more overseers, and an enormous additional expense. Moreover, the slaves of Arabs are generally set free after having served faithfully ten to fifteen years.

"Slaves owned by natives are considered as members of the family, and enjoy their own free will. They are not punished even when they show their masters open defiance—as, for instance, going down to the sea-shore and hiring themselves out as pagasi (porters)."

An Englishman, Mr. Joseph Thompson, says in his book, "Expedition to the Lakes of Central Africa":

"All classes of society show a cheerfulness and happiness, which would appear uncommon everywhere, but this is an ideal land, where four shillings and sixpence suffice all day to live in plenty. Half-starved or ill-treated slaves are nowhere to be seen; for as soon as any cases of barbarous treatment come to the knowledge of the sultan (of Zanzibar) the sufferers are at once set free, and protected against the cruelty of their masters. It would seem, indeed, as if this class here is in a particularly comfortable position, and enjoys ten times more liberty than thousands of our clerks and shop girls."

Another Englishman, who had lived long in the East, and who knew the state of things there well, once expressed himself to me in a shorter and more drastic term; he simply called the anti-slavery movement, with its countless meetings, "bosh."

In conclusion, I should like to call attention to one more fact. Gordon, who at one time was one of the greatest adversaries of slavery and the slave trade, began his second short government of the Soudan by abolishing his former laws. He may not have been convinced of the necessity of slavery in Africa, but he may have been sensible of the necessity not to suppress at one stroke an institution so deeply rooted, but to gradually mitigate its effects before abolishing it completely.

Chapter XXVI

MY MOTHER'S DEATH—A PALACE REVOLUTION

Since my father's death I had lived with my mother and Khole at Bet il Tani, happy in their friendship and love, for about three years, when suddenly a fearful cholera epidemic spread over the town and the whole island, and snatched away many people in our house. It was during the hottest season, and finding it impossible to get any rest in bed, I had one night got a soft mat spread out on the floor to lie down upon, but was not a little shocked, upon waking in the morning, to find my dearly beloved mother writhing with pain at my feet. To my anxious questions she replied that she had been there half the night already, and that feeling herself attacked by cholera, she wished to die near me at least, if it was so decreed. I was well-nigh distracted at seeing my dear mother suffer with the malignant disease without being able to help her. For two days longer she withstood its attacks, then she was taken from me for ever.

My grief was boundless, and without heeding the warnings of my friends, who were afraid I might catch the disease, I clung frantically to the dear body. My only desire was to leave this world together with my mother, but God willed that I should be spared, and to His will I at last found strength to resign myself.

I was now barely fifteen years old, an orphan, a ship without a rudder tossing in the sea. My mother's prudence and good sense had always guided me, and now I was all of a sudden to take upon myself the duties of a grown-up person, and the responsibilities, not only for myself, but also for the welfare of my servants. When I came to a clear understanding of my position, God helped me to do my duty and to manage my affairs without the assistance of others. Nevertheless, trials did come, and I succumbed to them, for, without knowing myself how it had been brought about, I found myself drawn suddenly into a conspiracy against my noble brother Madjid!

It was just as if my father's death had been the signal for general discord amongst us, instead of uniting us more, as it ought to have done. It certainly may be difficult to maintain perfect concord and unanimity amongst thirty-six brothers and sisters, and thus we divided into groups of threes and fours, according as affection drew us together. Our position was quite incomprehensible to strangers, and even our friends became, quite against their wills, involved in our feuds. A loyal friend of my brother's, or a true friend of my sister's, must needs become my most bitter enemy—unless these belonged to my special circle—whatever their personal feelings toward myself might be. Such utter disunion could of course only end in disaster. Still, with hot passion we pursued each other blindly, and hated without a cause.

We soon ceased to have any personal intercourse with our belongings, but instead kept numerous spies, who took care to widen the gulf by informing us secretly of every word said, and every project made by our adversaries. These worthy persons always made their appearance at night to receive their reward, which varied according to the gravity of the news they had to report. Gold coins had never slipped so fast through our fingers before; frequently we did not even count them, but took a handful of gold from our *kis* (pocket) in acknowledgement of some daring and successful deed. Sometimes we were roused at night by a muffled person demanding to be admitted by the gate-keeper—and such nightly visits not only lightened our purses considerably, but often kept us from going to sleep again if the messenger had communicated some particularly perturbing news. Indeed, we seemed to be, one and all of us, labouring under some sudden attack of madness, and no pains were spared when we could annoy or thwart an antagonist. If one seemed inclined to buy a fine horse, a house, or an estate, his opponents promptly out-bid him four and six times beyond the value, to the great satisfaction of the owners. If one sister appeared with a new article of jewellery, the jeweller was sure to receive orders from all sides for one just like it, or a still more beautiful one. The people soon found this out, and merchants and workmen rapidly learnt how to turn our discord to their advantage.

Madjid and Khole had been on very good terms up to this time, at which I was delighted, for I was very fond of both; after my mother's death they had treated me like a child of their own. But the good relations between them began gradually to get cooler on account of my brother Bargash, and this ended finally in a complete rupture. I was always strongly attached to Khole, but in truth I

am bound to state that the fault was hers and not
Madjid's. I cannot here give an account of all the
circumstances which preceded this rupture, only
that we were all, as it were, completely blinded
and maddened.

It was a period of great conflict for me. I lived
in one house with Khole; we took our meals together and were hardly apart all day. Without any
reason, she commenced to avoid Madjid, and
ended by wishing him every possible evil. At first,
I hoped to be able to remain neutral, and I even
ventured to take my brother's part, whose only
guilt was his being sultan instead of Bargasch.
But passion knows no justice, and Khole continued to nurse her grudge.

I was thus placed for some months between two
fires—I wished to act for the best and could do
nothing—I hesitated to choose between the two
persons equally dear to me; and when I could not
longer put off my decision, I sided with Khole,
whom, though in the wrong, I cherished most,
and who by degrees ruled me completely. Is there
anything we can deny those we fondly love? What
avails our faint inner voice—justice—when love
cries aloud? For their sake we abandon our views,
our principles, our most sacred convictions—as a
tree loses its withered leaves in autumn, without
its sound trunk being able to help it.

Madjid, a thoroughly noble-minded man, possessed the love of all his people. He was, however,
in weak health, unable to act always for himself,
and for this reason he had to leave a good deal to
his ministers. One of these, Slemān bin Ali, unfortunately had the knack of making himself indispensable to his master. He was a crafty, selfish
man, who gradually contrived to get all the power
into his hands, and to reduce the other ministers

to mere ciphers; he even carried his presumption so far as to act the master whenever a favourable opportunity presented itself. And yet with the dignity he arrogated, he was far from having attained those years which every Arab holds in respect and deference, or from possessing sufficient discretion to disguise his dandyism and libertinism. In his unbounded ambition, he sued for the hand of one of my stepmothers, a Circassian named Fatme, who was old enough to be his mother; she was foolish enough to accept him, but lived to regret this bitterly. Slemān's only object had of course been to get her large fortune into his hands.

This evil spirit gained a great influence over Madjid, and in secret he managed to incite all the brothers and sisters one against the other in order to increase his own power. He succeeded too well in his plots everywhere; quarrel upon quarrel took place in our family, many notables were insulted and neglected, and things grew gradually so bad that the people began to murmur and complain aloud.

Fortunately, there was one brave and honest man at least among the ministers, who did all he could to weaken the effects of Slemān's actions, and to redress them. This man was Mhammed bin Abd Allah il Shaksi, a very rich and also a very generous and noble-minded man, who would never have committed a mean or selfish deed himself. As a matter of course, he was by no means on good terms with his colleague.

My brother Bargash next endeavoured to turn the discord between the brothers and sisters, and the discontent of part of the people, to his profit. Madjid had only one daughter and no son; Bargasch was therefore the next successor to the throne, and had generally been regarded as the heir-presumptive since my father's death. That two elder brothers, Turki and Mhammed, were still living in Oman, was not taken into account at all, for Oman was such a long way off!

In the East, the heirs-presumptive to a throne are always in a hurry to possess themselves of it— they endeavour to forget the fact that others may have a better title, and speedily overcome all scruples about justice and honour.

This was the case with Bargash. He had failed in usurping the power at my father's death, but had never abandoned his plans. He began more seriously to think of carrying them into effect after having removed with his sister Meje from Bet il Mtoni to the town. They resided in a house opposite to the one in which Khole and myself lived, and which had once been used as a residence for the cavaliers of the Princess Shesade of Persia.

Now began a time of great excitement for all of us. I, as a sister, cannot well recount all that occurred, although there are certain acts which almost defy silence. But even the harshness with which he continues to treat me, cannot induce me to lift the veil, for I still remember our Arab saying, that "all the sea is not deep enough to wash away blood-relationship."

Hardly had the brother and sister taken up their residence near us, when a great friendship sprang up between Bargash and Khole, and the former soon began spending his days with us. Meje took this as a neglect shown to herself, and complaining about it to others, there came a soreness between the two sisters that prevented them looking at each other when they met. Things as-

sumed a more and more uncomfortable aspect,
till finally peace disappeared entirely from our
houses. I rejoiced at not being concerned in this
new quarrel, but being made the confidant of
both angry sisters, I was soon drawn into it
against my will.

Khole did not act rightly with regard to Meje—
indeed she was not quite herself all this time.
Bargash was her idol, to whom she sacrificed
everybody without hesitation, and I, to whom she
was all in all, followed her lead in everything.
Secretly, I felt a sincere pity for poor Meje, for, in
spite of her pride, I could not help admiring her
justice and common sense. She alone foresaw that
no good would come of this party conspiracy
against Madjid, and she never tired of warning
us.

The friendship which my two nieces, Schembūa
and Farshu, had for me was soon extended to
Bargash also. They lived just opposite our house,
theirs being only separated by a narrow lane from
that of Bargash. Our three houses formed thus a
dangerous centre for the conspiracy.

It became now Bargash's main object to gain
over a number of notables and chiefs. The Arabs
are divided into numberless larger and smaller
tribes, each of which has a chief, who is implicitly
obeyed. It is of moment, therefore, to each prince
to be on good terms, either openly or in secret,
with one or more such chiefs, to make sure of
their aid in case of need. They are, of course,
always promised some prospective post of importance or some other advantageous remuneration.
No tribe will ever desert its chief, for their attachment is proof against every temptation. Those
who can write never omit to sign the name of their

tribe; we, for instance, belong to the "The Bu-Saïdi," a small but brave tribe, and I have always to append this in signing my name in full.

Bargash gained over several of these chiefs, and by degrees they formed quite a small court round him, which caused a good deal of stir in the island; and by and by it transpired that the majority of his supporters were people of bad repute, men known to be turbulent and reckless, from whom he ought to have kept aloof altogether, but who were about his person night and day. And no wonder either—for what upright, honest man could have joined his conspiracy?

As the number of these bad and doubtful characters who gathered round him increased, and as soon as we clearly realized the true bent of his plans, all those withdrew from him who had more the interests of our family at heart than his wild projects. Their places were, however, soon filled again by a class of men that seem ever ready to grow out of the ground with the noble and self-imposed task of fighting the cause of the oppressed—whilst at the same time dealing a blow stemming from a long-cherished personal grievance. Dozens of these malcontents considered themselves already his future ministers or the happy possessors of other high appointments, or of fortunes that could in no otherwise have fallen to their lot, except by a baneful violation of the laws of merit. Characters of this sort arrived from all parts to join the conspirators, apparently with the desire to serve Bargash, in reality to serve themselves. The most desperate were not only received, but hailed with joy!

After having gathered together a sufficiently large number of such partizans, the details of the projected rising were more minutely considered.

The plan conceived was to seize Madjid unawares and to proclaim Bargash Sultan. Preparations for open fight had to be made, meetings were held upon meetings, always presided over by Bargasch himself, to gain over one or the other chief. They always took place at night, sometimes towards morning, when the moon had gone down. A state of feverish excitement and deep mistrust towards everybody had taken hold of us all; we were always in fear of being observed or espied, and frequently did domestic duties ourselves, only to keep our servants out of earshot of our dark designs, and visiting was long since at an end.

Bargash became more excited every day. Hitherto he had regularly attended, like the other princes, all the audiences presided over by Madjid; now, however, he began to neglect them, and to appear only once a week, until he finally remained away altogether. This with us is considered a sign of great discontent, and a subject keeping ostentatiously aloof lays himself open to punishment. There could be no longer any doubt now about his hostile projects, which many would not give credit to previously. His quick temper made him behave very imprudently, for he roused the suspicion of his adversaries, and in consequence the attempt at a sudden surprisal had to be abandoned.

In secret Madjid endeavoured once more to show me the error of my ways before it was too late. As he could not come to Bet il Tani himself under the circumstances, and as I had not been to his house for a long time, he sent one of my most favourite stepmothers to beg me in his name not to take part in the intrigues of his enemies, or to allow myself to be seduced by them; that I could never expect any thanks in that quarter, but

would be sure to repent my adherence to the bad
cause. I was also told that in that case I must take
upon myself all the consequences of my actions,
as he would be unable to make any exception on
my behalf or to protect me if a bombardment of
the house in our neighborhood was to take place
afterwards.

My noble brother's warning arrived too late. I
had already plighted my word to Khole and to
Bargash, and considered it my sacred duty to
keep and fulfil my promise. My stepmother left
me in deep sorrow, weeping bitterly; she had
meant well, and had at a later date the sad satisfaction of recalling to my memory the justice of
Madjid's prediction. To escape the risk of being
distrusted or called a mother of two faces* for
any supposed double dealing, I thought it best to
avoid all further intercourse with Madjid, and to
devote myself entirely to the cause of the conspiracy.

It would have been easy for Madjid at this time
to have had his badly-advised brother and his
adherents arrested, now that there were so much
stronger grounds for suspicion, and to imprison
them all in some fortress until they had repented
them of their ways. But it was not in his nature to
be severe, and he could not be brought to take
such a measure; he still hoped to see his brother
turn back, seeing that no other reason for enmity
existed between them, and fearing that a pre-
mature punishment might sever them for ever.
Above all, he was desirous to spare us four
women, mixed up in this affair, at all costs.

Thus for a long time Madjid shut his eyes; but
when whole crowds of men, muffled in their
"Barnus" besieged the doors of Bargash's house,

*A byword given in our country to false women.

the Government at last decided to have our
houses watched. By this measure however little
was gained, for the watchers were Bluches, soldiers enlisted in Beloochistan, who were greatly
attached to our dynasty and would rather have
run any risk themselves than compromise any of
its members. This the wily plotters knew perfectly, and made their arrangements accordingly.
We women undertook to carry out the more dangerous missions ourselves, without regard to existing custom. No one ventured to molest us, while
others were followed and searched. At times one
or the other imprudent person was arrested, but
this did no great harm to our proceedings. We
were all like so many busy ants, all working hard
for the success of our enterprise. Our spies informed us that the Government had at last decided to put an end to our doings by either
imprisoning all suspicious persons or evicting
them from the island. When this news reached us
our preparations were not yet completed, so we
redoubled our efforts. Quantities of hard cakes
were got ready and brought at night to Marseilles,
which was to be our head-quarters.

Although I was the youngest female member of
the conspiracy, they made me the secretary on
account of my ability in writing, and as such I had
to do all the correspondence with the chiefs. I was
indeed old enough already to have many pangs of
remorse, and the thought preyed heavily on my
mind that the ammunition and guns I was order-
ing were intended to cause the death of many
innocent people. But what could I do now? Was I
to break my word and forsake my dear sister at
the very moment when danger became imminent?
It was, indeed, not sympathy with the cause that
urged me on, but sheer idolatry of Khole.

Bargasch, the son of an Abyssinian woman, is a man of great talent, and he was much superior to us in intelligence and foresight. Proud and imperious in manner, he understood the art of impressing the masses; but the fact that of all our large family only four female members, and one single brother, Abdil Aziz, who was scarcely twelve years old at the time, and moreover Khole's foster child, sided with him, proves unmistakably how little he was generally liked. Since he had caused our father to be buried in secret, and without the customary ceremonies, he fell into universal odium—so that when he began to organize his conspiracy the true estimation in which he was held by his family came to the surface. I remember encountering upon one of my rare walks one night two of my sisters; they accompanied me to within five hundred paces of my house and then hurriedly retreated from fear of approaching the neighborhood of his dwelling.

We worked on unremittingly in spite of the searching watch set over us, and even the meetings were continued under real difficulties. Already the day was fixed for the open rebellion, when suddenly Bargash's house was surrounded by several hundred soldiers. The time had been chosen when he was sure to be indoors, with strict orders to cut off all communication until its occupants surrendered voluntarily. This change in the aspect of affairs was naturally a great blow, but we kept up our energies nevertheless.

Of course we expected the same fate to overtake us, and then indeed our cause would have been lost altogether. We afterwards learned that the ministers and the other members of the council had voted for the blockade of all the dangerous houses, but Madjid would not give his consent to this in his desire to spare us women.

A few minutes after the appearance of the soldiers we six conspirators stood at our windows, two in each house, to take council over the narrow street as to what should be done next. We were almost on the point of breaking down for good, but Bargash would not listen to anything like submission.

But a very distressing fact now rose to our minds. Hardly any of the houses in Zanzibar have pumps, so that people collect their water from public wells. Bargash's establishment had been provided, for precaution's sake, with a good supply some days before, but in the hot weather this water could not be used for drinking; at the best it would only do for washing and cooking purposes. Provisions were plenty, and the besieged had a sufficient stock to hold out for weeks; but water, the one thing most needed in the tropics, was wanting. Under such circumstances it would have been impossible to resist for more than two days at the utmost.

While the men were quite helpless, the inventive genius of a woman found a way out of this dilemma and saved them from sudden defeat. She proposed to make a canvas hose and to convey water through it to Bargash's house. The canvas was obtained, a few dozen hands got the hose ready within half an hour, and at dusk the captives could be refreshed with a deliciously cool drink. We had, of course, to use great caution to escape our watch's observation; fortunately, guards were placed only at the one door leading to the seashore—and they perhaps willingly shut an eye.

Hitherto our partizanship, I mean the women's, had been of great use; but now it devolved solely upon us to carry out the doubtful sequel. It was only through us that Bargash from his windows

was able to remain in communication with his
party. Several of the chiefs had been shut up with
him, and were placed in a very unpleasant position. As they could not move about the house
freely while my sister Meje stayed in it, they had
to confine themselves to the assembly-room on the
ground floor. The most influential and energetic
chief of the Hurt tribe was however at liberty and
able to go on enlisting soldiers.

Our whole plan had to be changed. It was
decided to collect all our followers at Marseilles,
the fine estate of my two nieces, and to fortify the
place. It was not a bad idea, for Marseilles was
already quite a little fortress and could easily
shelter several hundred men. All the arms and the
ammunition were carried there, the soldiers
levied were quartered in its neighbourhood,
whence they would exercise their instigations to
rebellion over the entire island. As we strained
every nerve the plan succeeded within a short
time. Common funds for our operations we had
none; we therefore drew upon our private purses,
from which every one of us also furnished a
number of well-armed slaves.

When everything had been secretly transported
to Marseilles, we took council to wield our final
stroke. This was nothing less than setting Bargash
free, to enable him, by restoring the head to the
conspiracy, to conduct matters personally from
Marseilles. We well knew that the undertaking
was one fraught with danger, but fear was far
from us: we were resolved to dare all risks.

Hitherto we had not attempted to pay a visit to
our captive brothers and sister, for we had no
wish to call any special attention to ourselves,
which would have endangered our enterprise,
and we were, moreover, afraid of being refused

admittance by the guards, a humiliation we were
not eager to experience. But nothing ventured
nothing won; all hesitation was now set aside, and
the evening was fixed upon to carry out the ab-
duction, as the only resource now left.

After dark one night Khole and myself left our
house, followed by a large and picked retinue, to
be joined by our nieces with theirs, who, as prear-
ranged, had left their home at the same time, and
together we proceeded to Bargash's house. Upon
arriving at the door our advance guard was
stopped, but the soldiers had no idea who was to
follow; we could only succeed by undaunted courage. "Khole," I said to my sister, "we will go
ourselves to the commanding officer and tell him
who we are—surely they will respect us!"

This proposal was in violation of all custom,
but the situation was too critical to allow of scruples; our undertaking was altogether out of the
common, so we might as well try and forget troublesome points of etiquette!

Khole and myself went up to the officers and in
impressive language made a thrilling appeal to
their manly feelings, which extraordinary and
quite unprecedented proceedings had the effect of
making their eyes stare wildly and their tongues
become speechless; but when at last the meaning
of our words began to filter through to their
brains they poured forth such humble excuses
and prayers for pardon, that, conscious as I was
of our guilty purpose, I almost betrayed my
shame. However, pluck once more came to our
rescue, and with countenances on which guileless
innocence of design was depicted we proceeded on
our dangerous way.

We reached our destination, and were allowed
to pay the prisoners a short visit, and having thus

effected so easy an entrance, we dared hope that our egress in company with our brother would be attended with equal success.

We found Bargash and Meje in a great state of excitement. They had witnessed the scene with the guard from above, and had begun to fear that we should be obliged to turn back after all, and leave them to their fate. But now Bargash raised another difficulty; he steadfastly declined to disguise himself in a woman's dress. For aught we knew our visit had already been reported and instructions been applied for. In his own dress he would never have been permitted to quit the house; strict orders had been given to shoot down at once every suspicious person. We felt convinced that no one had dreamt of our undertaking such an audacious deed, for if so, other measures would most decidedly have been taken beforehand. We were literally standing on a volcano, that might open and swallow us up at any moment.

Armed to his teeth, Bargash at last consented to be wrapped in a schele, which only left his eyes free and Abd il Aziz was disguised in the same way. We chose the tallest women of our retinue to walk by the side of Bargash, to render his height less conspicuous; and before starting we each said a silent prayer, which for all we knew might be our last.

To escape suspicion we moved on in the usual deliberate gait, while our hearts were throbbing and well-nigh bursting with suppressed anxiety. Moreover, we chatted as we went, though we must have made superhuman efforts to conceal the trembling of our voices. But now we reached the outposts, when—oh! rapture—the guard made way respectfully, and let us pass unmolested with our treasures. I need scarcely attempt a description of our relief after the horrible suspense we had endured, the breathless hovering between life and death when we approached the lion's jaws! That memorable night passed as all earthly things do—but its memory is ineffaceable.

We had written to inform several chiefs of our purpose, and they were to wait for us at a certain place outside the town with some of their followers. It was arranged that, unless we were there to keep our appointment at a given time, they were to consider our plan as aborted, and in that case they were to disperse and wait for further news. The meeting place was a long way off, hidden among trees.

We went through the inhabited part of the town at our ordinary pace, but once on the outskirts we took to our heels so as to be in time. We rushed over the fields like a hunted band, with our delicate feet in their gold and embroidered slippers, scrambled over hedges and ditches, on—on. Then our servants, who were ahead, cried out to us that we were making straight for a stubble field; but what cared we, so long as our obstacles were not human beings; but there was no fear of detection, we having put our lamps out on leaving the town. Soon, however, we had to slacken our pace, for we were getting near the appointed place, and we women had of course to observe some amount of reserve. Then slight coughs were given as signals, and a voice was heard to ask under its breath: "Is it you, Highness?" and an answer being given in the affirmative, a general, "Praised be the Lord," burst forth. We had reached our goal in safety.

Bargash, who had been terribly agitated on the road, but had hardly uttered a word all the time, threw off his disguise, bid us a hurried farewell, and taking his little brother Abd il Aziz by the hand, at once disappeared in the darkness, as he had to reach Marseilles this very night.

For a time we stood perfectly exhausted and speechless, looking after the retreating figures; but it had grown very late now, and we had to return home, which we did in silence, and not without some trepidation. We separated as we approached the town, and avoiding the principal streets, reached our homes, having first divided ourselves into small detachments.

But now in the quiet solitude of our chambers, the trials of the last few hours began to tell on us. It was, perhaps, not so much to the mental strain we felt ready to succumb; but certainly the violent and altogether unusual exertions were too great for our pampered bodies to pass over in silence. We all lay down and groaned and wept for the remainder of that night. Some of us fainted from sheer exhaustion. Sleep that would have put our shattered nerves right came not; so we could do nothing but live over again the horror of the last few hours, and repeating over and over again for our own consolation that our wildest hopes had been realized, and that our nearest and dearest were in perfect safety. Of course, the slightest sounds our ear detected, or those imagined by our fevered brain, during that endless night, our guilty consciences magnified into the tramp of horses and the clank of arms. Our distorted vision positively saw the approach of the enemy who had come to inflict the punishment for our deeds; and when those phantom shapes had vanished at last, our poor heads were once more distracted by fresh sounds proceeding from a new quarter.

We peeped from our windows and saw the

guards passing quietly up and down outside the
house in which Bargash had been confined up till
a few hours before. At dawn our servants summoned us to prayers as usual. Generally Khole
and I said our prayers in separate rooms: to-day,
however, not knowing what might be in store for
us at any moment, we met in the same room for
this purpose. Our fervent desire was that Bargash
might be safe at Marseilles by this time, about five
o'clock in the morning.

But soon enough bad news came in. Already at
seven o'clock, we heard that our enemies had
received full information of all that had passed
during the night. A Bluchi soldier had recognized
Bargash in spite of his disguise, but out of respect
to our departed father, in whose service he had
been for many years, he deferred giving the alarm, thinking that it was Bargash's intention to fly
the country after getting free, and seeing no reason for betraying us.

The market people, on reaching the town, reported having seen many Arabs hurry on to Marseilles, and a suspicion at once arose that this
might be in connection with the conspiracy,
though nothing certain was known. The Bluchi
now considered it his duty to reveal what he knew
of the case, and with that purpose apprised the
Government. Upon examination, he announced
in explanation of his delayed report, that he
would rather have sacrificed his life than have
compromised the women. I never heard what became of the generous fellow afterwards, whom
our deed had thrown into such conflict with his
conscience.

Nothing was now left for the Government to do
but to put an end at once to open rebellion.
Several thousand soldiers were despatched to

Marseilles. We conspirators had counted upon success by means of a sudden surprise or by skirmishes; but the open field had not been contemplated. The bombardment of Marseilles soon reduced that beautiful palace to ruins, and after an obstinate resistance and the loss of several hundred innocent lives, the rebels fell into the hands of the superior force.

The reader will naturally ask, what was the lot of us women for the active part we had taken in the rebellion, and what kind of punishment was adjudged to us? None. We should certainly not have come off so well had the decision rested with any one but noble and generous Madjid—for indeed we had deserved a heavy penalty.

The news of the fight and its result had not reached us when we learned one morning that Bargash, whom we still believed at Marseilles, had been totally defeated, and had returned a fugitive to his house. Meje was our informant. As for Bargash, he remained concealed, and would not even come to the window. But still he scorned the idea of surrender, and declared his intention of holding out to the bitter end.

Beside himself and little Abd il Aziz, who had shown the greatest bravery notwithstanding his youth, a number of notables and many servants had arrived in groups that completely filled the lower part of the house. With their assistance Bargash yet hoped to carry out his plans, though he had failed with a far greater force. We also, in spite of the heavy loss we had sustained in property, in soldiers, and in slaves, and though we had sacrificed the friendship of our other brothers and sisters and relations, had not yet come to our senses. In our blindness and obstinacy we would not believe in such a miserable failure.

The news of Bargash's return spread all over the town the same night. It was generally believed that he had come back to surrender to his brother, and Madjid himself desired to make his submission easy for him. Instead of soldiers, he sent his nephew, Sūd bin Hilāl, this time with a message to the effect that he would readily grant his pardon for all that had occurred, if Bargasch would promise to give up all rebellious plans for the future. Sūd, a very gentle and kindhearted man, was to deliver this message quite alone, in proof of his peaceful intentions.

At first Bargash would not even allow his nephew, who was considerably older than himself, to enter his house, and requested him to deliver his message from the street; but Sūd positively declined to do this. After he was kept a long time waiting, the gate was just opened sufficiently to allow him to pass in alone; after which he had to climb up the barricaded stairs. Preparations had everywhere been made to shoot down any one attempting to enter by force. The staircase could be closed at its upper landing by a massive trap-door, a contrivance which was only to be found in this house, and which dated from the times of our stepmother Shesade, and this door was covered with heavy boxes besides. In this rather humiliating manner Madjid's ambassador made his entrance; and the result of his mission was equally painful, for he had to leave without having succeeded, Bargash refusing in the most decided way to yield and to surrender.

Madjid had now no alternative left but force. In conferring with the British Consul, the latter convinced him at last of the necessity of putting a stop to these dangerous tumults, and offered his assistance to that end. An English gunboat happened to be in port, and owing to her small draft of water she was considered more suitable to anchor opposite Bargash's house, than our own larger men-of-war. The crew disembarked to blockade the house, and if this step still had no effect it was resolved to bombard the palace, and to shoot every soul in it.

I had one morning left my room, which looked out upon a narrow street, and from which there was no view of the sea, on my way to Khole to wish her good morning. I found her in great agitation, walking up and down her room, wringing her hands. "Oh, Salme, dearest, where have you been all this time?" she exclaimed, plaintively; and, showing me the English ship and the disembarked marines, she told me in broken sentences all that was happening.

On reminding her that it would never have come to this if she and Bargash had only yielded in time, I was again answered with the old reproach, that I showed too little ardour in their cause. But, in the name of heaven, I asked, what could I do more? Had I not compromised myself as much as they? Had I not staked my property without hesitation? Had I spared myself personally, whenever I could be of service to our party? All this appeared to be entirely forgotten now, when in the face of my cooled sense and justice, I could not longer lend any countenance to this irrational enterprise. But I think I could have borne the taunt from any one better than from her I loved with all my being.

The marines now began to fire upon Bargash's house, at first with their muskets only. The balls entered the windows, and one passed close to Bargash, and struck the wall behind him. When matters had become thus serious, he fled with

Meje, Abd il Aziz, and the other occupants of the room, to the back of the house, to escape the bullets which were now sent flying about right and left.

When the first shot was fired, Khole broke into convulsive crying, abusing Madjid, the Government, and the English all at one time, for the cruel measures they were adopting. The whole household, too, broke out in panic as the firing increased, for our house being immediately behind Bargash's palace, we were likewise exposed to great danger. Some rushed about wildly, taking a tender farewell from everybody, and asking forgiveness where they thought it was needed, whilst those who were more calm packed up their jewels to carry away in their flight; others again stood helplessly about, moaning and weeping, unable to collect their thoughts or come to a decision. Many prayed where they stood—in the passages, on the stairs, in the courtyard, or on the roof, which had been boarded in by palisades. Their example was soon followed by others, and instead of the general agitation we were soothed by the consciousness that not men's but the Lord's will is done, and that our fate is in His hands always. By and by we, one and all, were bent low with our foreheads on the ground in token of humble submission.

All these hundreds of people, who, after getting over their first terrors, put their faith in the Lord, might have fled easily. There was nothing to prevent us seeking a refuge at Bet il Sahel, but not one thought of doing this.

Unable to face such imminent danger any longer, Khole at last persuaded our obstinate brother to give in and tender his submission. Contrary to all rules of etiquette, she ran herself

to the British Consul to announce this, and to
demand a cessation of hostilities. It may be asked,
why she did not go to Madjid to settle with him
directly? This question was put by a good many
people in Zanzibar. They could not understand
that Khole's and Bargash's hatred of Madjid
should be so great as to prevent them meeting on
any consideration whatever. It must have been
that they were too much ashamed of themselves;
that they would rather humble themselves (for it
was a great humiliation in the eyes of every true
Arab) in asking the assistance and the mediation
of a foreign Power. At that time the English did
not possess the supremacy they have at present in
East Africa; they had as little to do with the inner
affairs of Zanzibar as the Turks or the Germans.
It is only since 1875—thanks to their slave policy—that their power has greatly increased, and
that circumstances are tending to the gradual
decline and ruin of our people.

Khole did not find the English Consul at home;
but as the people from Bargash's house called out
to the marines: "Aman, Aman" (Peace), they
stopped firing, and an end was put to further
ruin. If the gunboat had been in operation instead of the marines, there would be in all proba-
bility another sovereign seated on the throne of
Zanzibar to-day, and I should never have come to
Europe. But one thing is quite certain, that we
none of us would have got off so well if, in the
place of noble Madjid, any other person had
determined our fate.

To prevent the recurrence of such a rebellion, it
was decided to banish Bargash to British India.
This was done upon the advice of the British
Consul; the English, perhaps, wished to get him,
as the presumptive successor to Madjid, into their

power to train him for future plans of their own.
We met Bargasch and Meje once more that evening to bid our departing brothers good-bye, for
Abd il Aziz had declared of his free will to share
his brother's exile. They were ordered to embark
the next morning, and were conveyed to Bombay
in a British man-of-war. Bargash stayed there for
about two years, and then quietly returned to
Zanzibar, succeeding, in 1870, after Madjid's decease, to the throne he had so eagerly coveted.

Thus ended our enterprise, which had been
commenced with such sanguine hopes. It had cost
us dear enough, especially our nieces, whose
great wealth, however, soon recovered from the
heavy losses. Many of our best slaves had fallen,
and as many more were wounded and invalided,
reminding us continually of the mischief we had
been the means of causing, though this was the
smallest punishment we could expect to reap from
the evil seed we had sown. But one great grief was
still in store for us—the affection and regard of
our brothers and sisters, all of our relations, that
we had so wantonly forfeited, were lost to us for
ever, and the sting in our remorse lay in that we
felt their coldness to us to be in every way justi-
fied and the only attitude they could possibly
assume.

Madjid alone did not change from the large-
hearted magnanimous brother he had always
been. He was repeatedly advised not to let us go
without punishment, it being notorious that without our active cooperation Bargash must have
surrendered long before the sacrifice of life had
been resorted to as the last means of restoring
order. He replied that all this was quite true, but
that nevertheless it went against his principles to
publicly humiliate any woman—a generosity

which we were as far from deserving as he was from meriting the public opinion that his action was a sign of weakness on his part.

I cannot say that our life henceforth was a bed of roses in the town. Remaining friends we had very few indeed; whilst our foes thought fit to watch our every action. Even the crafty Banyans so far conformed to the general odium in which we were held, by keeping aloof from us, but only during the day, for at dusk their scruples seemed to have vanished, and they would creep in stealthily and press on us those wares which they had not been able to dispose of before. So, considering the scanty attractions the city could offer me for the present, I decided to withdraw for a time to one of my estates.

Chapter XXVII

KISIMBANI AND BUBUBU

A few days later I was hastening at sunrise, mounted on my little white donkey, to my plantation, Kisimbani. I intended to stay and take rest here for some time, until things had become a little more quiet and peaceable at home. Khole, Meje, and my two nieces soon followed my example, and retired likewise into the country.

Since my mother's death I had been but rarely, and then only for a day or two at a time, to my three plantations; and after all that had passed I now enjoyed the quiet and repose of country life all the more. My mother had always shown a preference for Kisimbani, and many things there reminded me of her, so I revisited all the spots where she had liked to walk and to rest. I was now going to take into my own hands the pleasures as well as the great drawbacks that rise in the path of unmarried Arabian ladies, our laws of seclusion precluding every possibility of applying for male assistance. Etiquette even forbids us to speak to those of our officials who are free men. Orders and accounts can only be given by, and settled through, the medium of slaves. Very few great ladies can write themselves, and fewer still single ladies have ever received a written account of any sort from their overseers, such as European landowners expect from their bailiffs once in the year. A mistress is generally satisfied if they provide the necessities of the household, and send in cash as many thousand dollars after the sale of the crops as they can. These sums are realized by the sale of cloves and cocoanuts; but it is thought mean to sell potatoes, yams, or any other vegetables raised on the estates; and the overseer is allowed to dispose on his own account of all the surplus. These people, who are mostly natives of Oman, soon acquire sufficient wealth with which they can return to their country and live and die in peace.

While I lived in town my overseer, Hassan, used to come once a week or fortnight from Kisimbani to hand in his report through my slaves and to ask for orders; but now that I purposed staying at Kisimbani for a time, honest Hassan was very much in my way. The poor fellow himself was made very uncomfortable at having to escape to all sorts of places lest he might even unintentionally happen to meet us. I therefore transferred him to another estate which he also managed, and replaced him by an Abyssian slave, called Murdjān (Coral), a superior man for his station, who could also read and write. He was full of energy, and well able to manage a few hundred country slaves. The Abyssians are very smart people as a rule, and we purchased them in preference to negroes.

I was now able to move and ride about as much as I liked without fear of confronting poor Hassan bin Alys at every turn of the road. I spent many happy hours daily in looking after my domestic animals, and visiting the old people in their huts, with dainties from my table for their toothless gums. The little slave children—who are considered as a sort of property by their masters—were sent to me every day to be washed at the well with Rassel (the leaves of a tree which, dried and powdered, make a lather like soap), and then fed. They remained in some part of the courtyard for the remainder of the day under the care of a trustworthy female slave, until their parents returned in the afternoon from the fields to take them home. They were much better off this way than tied all day to their mothers' backs, exposed to the heat and glare of the sun.

This free and untrammelled country life was exquisite enjoyment to me, and I rejoiced at having thus escaped all the troubles of the town. The wives and daughters of the notables on the adjoining estate called upon me, so I soon had my house full of guests for weeks and months together.

Many strangers also came in to refresh and rest themselves after a long march, in the room set apart for men. This is a custom always practised with us, and the number of these guests was very considerable, as Kisimbani stood near two much frequented cross roads.

Two sisters and one nephew had estates adjoining mine. The last was Fesal, the orphan son of Hilāl, of whom I have already spoken as a very kind, but greatly misjudged man. I was the first to know him really well; he attached himself to me with quite a childlike confidence, and came over to see me nearly every day.

I was also in constant communication with the town. Two sets of messengers started on alternate mornings and returned with the news in the evening. I was heartily glad to receive now only visits of a harmless nature, after the tangled net I had been drawn into in the capital.

The great excitement which had followed the miserable failure of the conspiracy had at last

given way to a feeling of greater quiet, but the
dissent between the brothers and sisters continued unabated. I was, therefore, in no hurry to
return or even to pay a short visit, though I could
have easily ridden there in two hours; but, instead, my friends came frequently to see me.

My happiness would have been complete had I
not missed one thing—the sea—which until now I
had had before me all my life. My three plantations were in the interior of the island, but as I
had decided to live in the country, and did not
know at that time what it was to have an un-
fulfilled wish, I made up my mind to purchase a
plantation at the seaside. To my regret this was
not an easy matter, as all estates possessing this
advantage were owned by people who cared more
for the situation than for their rental. The "Del-
lal" (broker) who had, through my slaves, received instructions to make inquiries, declared
that he would not rest until he had found such an
estate, but still he failed.

He had just arrived with this dismal news when
a lady friend called, who mentioned to me that a
cousin of hers had a small country seat close to
the sea, and that residing permanently in town,
he had no use for it, and might possibly be induced to sell or at least let it to me.

People in Europe are generally under the impression that the whole country is the private
property of the Sultan and of his family, and that
the subjects are quite defenceless in protecting
their property against them; indeed, that we have
merely to take what we covet, without asking the
owner's consent. But jurisdiction is not quite as
primitive as all that with the Arabs, and private
property there can no more be touched than anywhere else. The difficulties I had to content with,

notwithstanding the liberal offer I was prepared to make is, I think, a very good proof of my statement. I much regretted to learn during my last visit to Zanzibar, that a deteriorating change has recently taken place in this respect, for it appears that the property of the British Counsul was a present made to him by the Sultan, who had deprived the former owner of it without awarding any compensation.

On the following morning we rode over to the estate, which was called Bububu, to have a look at it. The house was shut up, and it took some time before we could gain admittance. The grounds looked as if they had been allowed to take care of themselves of late; but the house was spacious and well-built. Outside, in a courtyard, were the kitchens and servants' lodgings. A little river, reminding me greatly of my much-loved Mtoni, ran right through the court, and this was worth a great deal in itself in a hot clime like ours. The view from the upper story was perfectly charming, large and small palm trees rose on either hand, and the front was built so close to the shore, that its walls at times were washed by the waves.

I decided at once to buy or to rent Bububu, and sent my friend to her cousin next morning. She informed me that he could not make up his mind to dispose of it, but that it would give him great pleasure to offer it me for as long as I cared to reside in it. This, however, I politely declined, and succeeded at last in obtaining a lease at a certain annual rental.

About a week after signing the contract—for even that formality is gone through in Zanzibar— I removed to Bububu, where I once more delighted in the sight of the sea that I had known from my earliest youth. The only thing that saddened me was the parting from my nephew Fesal; he took our separation much to heart, as he had no companion beyond his old stepmother.

I took all my domestic animals with me; they seemed not a little surprised at finding themselves suddenly in a new place, but were evidently as satisfied with the change as myself. For hours together I would walk about here on the shore, watching the many ships and fishing boats that glided past on their way to the city.

I was now much nearer to the latter, and could reach it both by sea and by land. Almost every day my three brothers, Abd il Wehab, Hamdān, and Djemschīd, came out to see me, either on horseback or by boat. Many pleasant days and hours we spent together in this place, and in their company the time passed away very agreeably.

I saw much more society here than at Kisimbani. Not a single day passed without one or two, and frequently as many as ten, ladies coming to stay with me for some days. I always look back with pleasure and regret on this beautiful, unclouded period of my youth.

My stay at Bububu was not, however, to be of long duration. I was sweeping the sea one day with my glass, to see if any of my brothers were coming. A single boat soon came in sight, in which Abd il Wehab was alone this time, his looks betraying to me at once that he was the bearer of unwelcome news.

"What news do you bring, Abd il Wehab, my brother?" I asked, when he entered.

"I have been sent with a request to you to-day, sister Salme, which is far from pleasing to me," he replied. "Only guess from whom." At my pressing questions, he continued:

"You are aware that a new British Consul has lately arrived?"

"What do I care for him? Has he sent you, perhaps?"

"No!"

"Well, then, speak out and tell me all, without tormenting me any longer!"

"But won't you be angry with me, Salme?"

"No, no; but now out with it quick," I exclaimed.

"Well, I am commissioned by—Madjid, who entreats you, if you still have any love for him, to give up Bububu. The new British Consul sent yesterday to him to inquire if he could have Bububu as his country seat."

Madjid's request was a great blow to me. Any one else I should have refused point-blank, but could I again thwart Madjid, against whose government and life I had so wickedly conspired? I had so far made no attempt at meeting him, although I felt convinced that he had condoned the past and wiped it from his memory. Now that he, the injured and offended one, took the first step himself (this was his meaning, for otherwise he might easily have told the consul that Bububu was not his to dispose of), I thought I might repay a small portion of the debt I owed him, by granting his request; and I spoke to Abd il Wehab to this effect.

Madjid had sent me word that if I consented he would get Abd il Wehab to procure a proper town residence for me, as he was aware that I did not wish to return to Bet il Mtoni. But I had not yet made up my mind where to go, and I asked for time to consider his proposal.

I was, perhaps, for the first time in my life, really grieved at anything so material. But I had been so happy at Bububu, and could have had no desire for anything better. When Abd il Wehab left me after dinner, it was with the earnest request not to return to Kisimbani. Then I took a tearful leave of all my favourite spots.

I struggled long before making up my mind to return once more into the turmoils of the capital, for it seemed as if I could not shake off certain gloomy presentiments.

Next morning I wrote to Abd il Wehab that I should be ready to leave Bububu in a week's time, and would then place it at Madjid's disposal, and as I had decided to return to Kisimbani I made all necessary arrangements for this purpose. But in the afternoon my three dear brothers appeared, crying out simultaneously: "Salme, we will hear no more of Kisimbani! If you care for us in the least, you must return to live in town!" And Djemschid jestingly continued: "If you are going to hide yourself on your plantation, we shall come at night and set it on fire!" At the same time they begged me in their mothers' names (who were Circassian women all three) to come back to town. For the last time we all spent the day together at pleasant Bububu, and then they left me and rejoiced at having prevailed on me to live in the town again.

Chapter XXVIII

MY LAST RESIDENCE IN ZANZIBAR

I happened to be, a few days afterwards, one moonlight night, on the roof of my new town residence, procured for me by Abd il Wehab, talking to an old acquaintance, when Selim suddenly appeared to announce Khole.

"Oh, Salme, I never thought you were so bad as all that!" These were the first words she exclaimed on entering.

"Good evening, Khole; and what ill have I done to you?" I asked, quite taken by surprise, leading her to the seat of honour, the "Tekye."

"You really pretend you have done nothing to me? Is it nothing that you have given up Bububu to oblige Madjid and the godless Kafer (Englishman)?"

"But, my dear sister," I replied, a little hurt, "surely if I don't mind—and, besides, I explained the matter to you fully in my letter the other day."

"I suppose you wished to insinuate yourself again into the good graces of the damned?" (by whom she meant Madjid).

"No, you are altogether mistaken; it is no favour I want of any one, and that you know well enough yourself."

"Yes, I know that; but why did you grant his request?" she persisted, getting more and more excited. "And I understand it is he who induced you to live here instead of at Bet il Tani."

"No, it was not he who asked me to do so, but Abd il Wehab, Hamdān, and Djemschid wished me to live here," I said.

"Well, I see now that you have turned against us," she replied, rising and refusing the refreshments offered to her by the servant. "You may now choose between myself and Bargash on the one side, and the slave of the Englishman on the other! Good-bye!" And without listening to another word she turned and went.

I have never seen Khole since that day, though I lived for some years longer in the same town with her, and it was only after my departure that she relented. I often asked myself in what way I could have offended her, but could think of no intentional offence on my part; my only object in giving up Bububu had been to relieve my own conscience of some of its load. And now this absurd reproach that I had been moved by motives of ultimate gain! But on the evening when Khole had vented her displeasure on me I remembered she was very much excited, and might have said more than she meant.

Up to this time I had seen neither Madjid nor Khadudj; and in order to avoid giving fresh grounds for Khole's suspicions, I resolved to keep out of their way altogether. But it was to be otherwise, for hardly had I been a fortnight in my new place when Madjid himself came, followed by a great retinue.

"Good morning, Salme," he cried; "you see I am the first to come, though I am so much your senior, to thank you for getting me out of that dilemma with the Englishman."

"Oh, my brother, that was nothing, really

nothing worth speaking of," I stammered, for no one was taken more by surprise by this visit than myself. Nor did Madjid, in his kind and generous way, allude to aught that had occurred, but tried to put me at my ease at once by talking of all sorts of other things.

"You will, I hope, come and see Khadudj one of these days?"

"Yes, surely I will come," was the reply I naturally gave.

"And our aunt Asche, who loves you so dearly, now lives with us, and she will be so rejoiced to see you again."

Madjid stayed about an hour, and we parted perfectly reconciled. The news of his visit spread all over the town the same day, and it was of course also reported to Khole.

Now that Madjid had been the first to come to me, which I could never have looked for, the only course left open to me, even if I had remained unforgiving in my heart, was to return his call and also inquire for Khadudj and my aunt Asche. I could not then foresee how dear this simple act of courtesy was to cost me afterwards. This step is still considered the greatest crime on my part. Such excess of jealousy may appear incomprehensible, yet at the time it was unfortunately but too well in keeping with the rest of our family affairs, as I found out by and by. Indeed it had to be neck or nothing. Friendliness with both factions of our family was a thing utterly out of the question.

The two parties existed as before, and the intrigues continued unabated, only more secretly.

It is the nature of Eastern people to be very candid. They are unable to dissimulate in the masterly manner that answers so well here. An

Oriental rarely conceals his aversion to a person who has affronted him by look, word, or deed; he at once betrays his feelings as a child would. Dissimulation, if such a thing could be practised with any degree of success by our quick-tempered Southerners, would be simply put down to cowardice. They reason thus: "Why should I show myself otherwise than I am? Are not all my thoughts and feelings known to the Lord? Why then should I try to dissemble in the face of men or be afraid of them?"

The engagement and subsequent marriage of two of my sisters with two cousins happily caused a little diversion in our life; indeed, the continual quarrels and dissensions in our family were suspended for some months. As is frequently the case, these sisters married to two brothers had drawn a very different lot. The unhappy one had children and the happy one had to go without, however much she might long for them. Our circle was further increased by a good many of our Oman relations, who had come to our country on account of the precarious position of our brothers there, and for a time at least I could once more taste the pleasures of family life.

Above all, I shall never forget one of my friends. I may not mention her name or be more explicit here as to our relations or separation. All I can take on myself to state is that this true friend helped me to the last when I was about to leave my home under great perils. Being fully acquainted with all my domestic concerns, she could not fail to perceive what was going on; still she remained, until I was compelled to remove her by gentle force half an hour before I left. "Highness," she said, in taking leave, "may the Lord of the universe protect you! I am aware that I shall have to give up my life within twelve hours; but for your sake that is not too much!" Her parting words still ring in my ears, and I may well exclaim: A friend in need is a friend indeed!

If people wish to know what is really understood by perfect devotion and self-sacrificing friendship, they must go to the East. I do not mean to say that such friendship is not elsewhere to be met with; but certain it is that where an Arab once loves, his life is for evermore consecrated to the object of his heart.

Though the distinction of classes is nowhere more observable than in the East, it is not taken into account at all in a case of real friendship. A prince will be on the same friendly terms with the son of a poor stable-man, whom he is fond of, as with any of his more distinguished friends, and without making the least distinction between them; and a princess will treat the wives and daughters of a simple overseer as affectionately as the most exalted lady. My sister Meje, for instance, formed an intimate friendship with the daughter of an overseer. She invited her to her palace, and her attachment to the poor, shy, but highly-gifted girl remained a very close one until they were separated by death.

It is no rare occurrence either, that a lady of high rank makes a friend of one of her female slaves, not a negress of course, but some Abyssinian or Circassian; which ends in her being bought by her benefactress for five or six times her value, if purchase in her case be possible; her freedom being secured by a legal act for all times.

In case of imprisonment a friend will always spend several hours every day with the prisoner, and a banished person is everywhere accompanied by his friends. In misfortune and poverty the friends assist the luckless person with their fortune, nor is it ever required to appeal to the public for contributions on such occasions. All this is, as it were, instilled into us from early youth, and is thenceforward regarded as a matter of course.

Chapter XXIX

GREAT CHANGES

While all this bitterness prevailed in our family I was made happy by the affection of a young German, who lived in Zanzibar as the representative of a Hamburg mercantile firm. A good many untrue reports have been published with regard to these, to me, important events, and I feel it incumbent on me to briefly mention them here. During the reign of my brother Madjid the Europeans enjoyed a very respected position; they were often and gladly received as guests at his house and on his estates, and were always treated with marked attention on such occasions. My step-sister Khole and myself were on most friendly terms with all foreigners in Zanzibar, which led to various courtesies, such as the custom of the country admitted. The European ladies of Zanzibar for the most part called only upon Khole and myself.

Soon after my removal from Bububu I made the acquaintance of my future husband. My house was next to his; the flat roof of his house was a little lower than my own. He held his dinner parties in a room opposite to where I could watch them; for he knew that this display of a European festivity must be very interesting to me. Our friendship, from which in time sprang love, was soon known in the town, and my brother Madjid also was well aware of it, but he never showed any displeasure, much less made me suffer imprisonment on this account, as the gossips had it.

I was, of course, desirous of secretly leaving my home, where our union was out of the question. The first attempt failed, but a more favourable opportunity soon presented itself. Through the mediation of my friend Mrs. D., the wife of Dr. D., the British Vice-consul at the time, I was one night taken on board by Mr. P., Commander of the British man-of-war, *Highflyer*; and everything having been in waiting and preparation for me, we started at once and steered to the north. We reached Aden all safe, where I was received by a Spanish couple, whom I had known at Zanzibar; and there I was going to wait till my affianced husband could join me; for he was as yet detained at Zanzibar in winding up his affairs.

In the meantime I had been instructed in the Christian religion, and was baptized in the English Church at Aden with the name of Emily, and married immediately after according to the English rite. After our marriage we left for Hamburg, *via* Marseilles, where I was received in the kindest manner by the parents and relations of my husband.

I accustomed myself soon to my strange surroundings, and endeavoured to learn all that was necessary for me. My dear never-to-be-forgotten husband helped me on in all these stages, with the deepest interest. Especially fond he was of observing the first impressions that European life and the customs of the civilized world made on me. I have retained a most faithful memory of them, and may speak of some on a future occasion.

Our quiet, happy, and contented life was only to last a short while. Little more than three years after our removal to Hamburg, my dear husband had the misfortune of falling while jumping from a tram-car, and was run over. He expired three days later after great sufferings, leaving me quite alone in the world with three children, of which the youngest was only three months old. For a time I thought of returning to my native home, but fate decreed that two months after this unspeakable grief my dear brother Madjid was also to die, he who had always been so kind to me. He did nothing to harm my *fiancé* after my departure, but allowed him to settle his affairs in Zanzibar without hindrance, nor did he ever after manifest the slightest resentment at my secret flight. Like a true Moslem he believed in fate and predestination, and was convinced that it was this that took me to Germany. He gave me a touching proof of his brotherly love shortly before he died by despatching a steamer with a full cargo of all kinds of things to Hamburg for presents. The generous donor suddenly departed this life while the ship was yet on its way. I have never seen or received any of the goods intended for me, nor had I received any intelligence at the time of Madjid's generous intention. I only learned afterwards that his kind purpose was intercepted, and that the appearance of the ship at Hamburg at the time was reported to be for the purpose of repairs. Nine years later I heard from a friend, who had been on board the vessel at Gibraltar, and who had then seen the captain, that the cargo was intended for me. In spite of every effort to keep their arrival in port dark, the dusky crew had by some means found out my dwelling in Hamburg.

The poor fellows were wild with joy at having succeeded, and showed their attachment in the most touching manner.

Two years more I lived in Hamburg, but never free from misfortunes. I lost a considerable part of my property through the fault of others, and learnt now that the management of my affairs must be undertaken by myself. The deepest aversion to the place where I had formerly been so happy now completely overpowered me—in addition to which my life among the people of that city was not made as pleasant as I could have wished or expected.

I removed to Dresden, where I met the kindest advances from all sides. From that place I went to London, of which I am going to speak in the next chapter. Wishing to lead a quiet life for a time, I lived for some years in pretty Rudalstadt, and there also I made many dear friends, foremost among whom I must mention with gratitude their Royal Highnesses. I soon recovered my shattered health so far that I could think of removing to Berlin, for the better advancement of my children's education. There, also, my social life was of the happiest. I shall remain deeply grateful all my life for the interest evinced in me by the most exalted persons there.

Chapter XXX

SEJID BARGASH IN LONDON

I had always kept up a correspondence with my native country, and had never given up hoping to see it again, but the obduracy of my brother had rendered any reconciliation hitherto impossible. His implacability was not, however, on account of my desertion of the faith—it was what he chose to consider a personal affront to him—viz., my renewed friendship with his old adversary Madjid! But I continued to yearn for all my dear ones at home, and secretly I never relinquished the hope of being once more reconciled to them.

All at once a report was spread through the press—in the spring of 1875—a report that stirred my whole being, to the effect that my brother Bargash, the sovereign of Zanzibar since Madjid's death, was about to visit London.

I took no steps at first to verify this news, nor did I betray the uneasiness it caused me. I had experienced too many disappointments in my life to allow of sanguine hopes, and it required all the power of persuasion on the part of my friends to decide me to go to London myself. The Secretary of State, Herr von Bülow, held out hopes to me of the diplomatic aid of the ambassador, Count Münster, which I regret to say, however, proved of little assistance to me.

The short time previous to my departure I
employed in learning English, so as to render
myself a little less helpless. For nearly eight weeks
I was busily poring from morn till night over my
books, learning English words and reciting dia-
logues. The thought of having to leave my three
children behind dampened my ardour not a little
all the time.

After an exhausting, wearying journey, I arrived at last in the giant city, where rooms at a
hotel had been prepared for me by some friends
of mine, the only persons I knew in all London,
and those but slightly. I had only seen them once,
when they paid us, or rather my dear husband, a
short call on their wedding tour, yet they were
ever after kindness and devotion itself to me.

My brother's arrival was only expected a week
later, and in the intervening time I made myself
acquainted with all that was new and quite
strange to me. Count Münster, on whom I had
called at the earliest opportunity, kindly promised to assist me to the best of his ability.

Some few days after my arrival, while I was
sitting in the drawing-room of my hotel, buried in
sad thoughts, the card of Dr. P., M.P., the brother
of a dear friend of mine, was handed to me. I was
a perfect stranger to him and to his wife, since
deceased, but in both I subsequently found two of
the most kind-hearted persons, ever ready to
pluck the thorns from under my feet. They had
come to offer me their services, and to make at
the same time the welcome proposal of carrying
me off to their own home. I dined with them the
same day, and removed on the following to their
house, and as things had thus acquired a more
pleasant aspect, I took fresh courage, hoping that

the end of my mission would take a favourable turn.

My friends in Germany strongly advised me before starting to proceed as cautiously as possible, and in the first instance to try and procure the aid of the British Government in my behalf. I at last gave way to their earnest entries, though I had at first been resolved—after having often before realized to my cost how inexpedient it was of me, a stranger, to negotiate matters in Europe—to trust to God and myself alone. Pictures rose up in my mind of vague, empty shufflings, of diplomatic periphrases, of slight coughs given to gain a little time before speaking; these and many more such signs I was soon to be brought face to face with. I was to learn that my fate lay in the hands of those who study and practise, and finally excel in the art of prevarication.

It was not long after my removal to the residence of my kind friends, that the visit of Sir Bartle Frere, afterwards Governor-General of South Africa—a gentleman whom I had hitherto only known by name—was announced to me. If ever I received a proof of the truth of certain presentiments, it was on this day, on which the hopes most dear to me and the future of my children were buried for ever. A most unpleasant feeling took possession of me the very moment I beheld the great diplomat, who governed my native country as he chose, and who held my brother Bargash altogether in his power.

After an exchange of civilities, Sir Bartle began to make inquiries about my affairs, and appeared particularly anxious to learn the reason of my visit to London. I told him—although he seemed fully informed on these points already—all about my wishes. There was not much to tell after all, as I had only the one thought of being reconciled to my relations.

My surprise may be more easily guessed than described, when Sir Bartle, after I had done, put the plain question to me: "What did I consider of greater value to me—a reconciliation with my relations, or the securing of my children's future prospects?" Even now I am unable to say what I felt on hearing these words; I had been prepared for anything but for this question. I trust I shall not be accused of inconsistency or of want of courage, if I wavered and hesitated for a moment. What were my own personal hopes and wishes when the welfare of my children was at stake?

After recovering somewhat from the surprise and embarrassment into which this unexpected diplomatic move had thrown me, I requested an explanation as to the meaning of this question. Sir Bartle then declared, and in a very decided manner too, that the British Government was by no means disposed to mediate between myself and my brother; and that, as its guest, it would be highly unbecoming to cause him any annoyance.

It is to this day a matter of grave doubt which annoyance he would have considered the greater had he been at all consulted in either matter; signing the slave treaty, and therewith giving a formal countenance to the English protectorate, or holding out a reconciling hand to his sister.

On the other hand—and this was Sir Bartle's positive proposal—if I would promise not to approach my brother during his London stay, either personally or in writing, the British Government would undertake to secure the future of my children.

I was as sad and disappointed as a person can

be, who, pining for a refreshing drink from a cool
spring after a long and dreary march, finds the
longed-for well closed up by some magic power. I
had to choose between two alternatives: to act
either for myself, and without any help from the
British Government—and this with the certain
knowledge, that almost unsurmountable obstacles
would be raised in my way, which I was too weak
to overcome—or to accept the proffered aid of the
Government in the interest of my children. Mind-
ful of the promise I had given to my motherly
friend, Baroness D., at Dresden, not to go alone
and unprotected to my brother—though I never
doubted that he would respect English law everywhere, and in England especially, if I were to
confront him suddenly—I finally accepted the
proposal of the British Government.

A proposal, however, so vague, that a friend of
mine could not refrain from inquiring of Sir Bartle what inducement had actuated the Government to take so sudden an interest in my affairs;
whereupon the astute diplomat adduced three
reasons: (1) We do the Sultan a favour therewith;
(2) We keep the princess quiet for a time; and (3)
We deprive the chancellor, Prince Bismarck, of
all pretext of ever taking up the matter himself.
All these reasons seemed on the surface perfectly
plausible and reassuring.

In order to avoid even the appearance of a
premeditated meeting with my brother, either in
such public buildings to which everybody has
access, or in the park and in the streets, I studied
the programme of my brother's daily excursions
in the papers; I even requested my kind hostess
not to take me with her in her drives; but to this
she would not agree, saying that my health would
suffer, and proposed that we should take quite

opposite routes, and thus we went West when the Sultan had gone East, and *vice versa*. Such a precaution was indispensable as far as I was concerned, for I could not have trusted myself to remain mistress of my feelings if a meeting had taken place. On the other hand, there was but little danger of a recognition on his part—my own dear mother would not have known me again in my present attire, much less any one of my brothers, who had hardly ever had an opportunity of seeing me without a mask.

I should have preferred to leave London at once, where I had seen all my hopes destroyed, and to return home. But even this I was not allowed to do. I had to stay many weeks longer far away from my children, full of anxiety and care. Sir Bartle Frere had so willed it. Before taking my departure I was requested to send in a detailed memorial. Not only was I wholly inexperienced and unversed in this branch of business, but my sorrows had reduced my mental energies almost to those of an automaton. I, therefore, with what remaining hope I had of eventual success, accepted the offer of my kind friends to draw up the memorial for me, and after a protracted stay of seven weeks I was at last able to leave England and to return to my children; but with what a heavy heart I quitted its shores may be easily imagined!

Zanzibar was already considered at that time a future British colony, so my memorial was first to be submitted to the Indian Government. Several months had passed in nursing my hopes, when they were suddenly broken in upon one morning by the receipt of a letter from London, enclosing the copy of a document, forwarded to me by the British Government through Count Münster, declining to enter upon any of the terms of my petition that Sir Bartle had so warmly urged upon me. As a reason for this refusal was adduced: that, as I had married a German, and was residing in Germany, my case came within German jurisdiction. This flimsy prevarication was the more contemptible, as I had asked no alms of either of the two Governments, but, in the name of justice, the moral support of both. Sir Bartle Frere had himself incited the memorial—the same diplomat who had shortly before annihilated the object of my mission to London with the bribe of securing the future of my children! I had been given to understand that the memorial was intended to be a formal compliance on my part with the compact the English Government had entered into with me, and that the former would now carry out theirs as I had carried out mine. But oh! how dearly I was to pay for my credulity!

My husband had been a German, and I, therefore, would be regarded as a German subject also. Oh! now I perceive! I could lay, of course, no claims to English chivalry or generosity. And yet why, I ask myself, had the truth of my nationality never been realized till my concordance had been extorted?; why did I receive strict injunctions to conform to the compact as though it had been entered into with an English woman? I can only explain it thus: that until my brother had signed the treaty, and so long as he was within reach of any hints I might feel inclined to give him, and be *able* to give him, from my better knowledge of European tactics, I was bound over on my honour, as any ordinary English citizen, "to keep the peace," thereby acknowledging my power, as the Sultan's sister, of possibly "disturbing it." But no sooner had my brother regained his shores and I

mine, than the last card was played, and I suddenly became once more a pure German subject.
All this I concluded slowly and painfully, and
learnt subsequently that I had interpreted the
whole course of events rightly, that I was, in a
word, the victim of the "Humane Policy" adopted
by Zanzibar. Let me, however, here distinctly impress my readers with the fact that though I may
trace the source of all my miseries to the wily
machinations of the Government of England, I
feel in my heart not only gratitude, but the deepest affectionate remembrance of kindness and
sympathy received at the hands of English society.

Chapter XXXI

RE-VISITING MY HOME AFTER
NINETEEN YEARS

When I wrote the preceding chapter some years
ago, I did certainly not dream of the possibility of
ever seeing the most ardent wish realized that
filled my thoughts and my very being. The event-
ful years that had elapsed since I had last seen my
dear home, had been fraught with many storms
and hardships. I had meanwhile passed through
the most wonderful changes of life—I had out-
lived the most cruel trials. Thanks to my good
constitution, I was able to brave all the rugged
duties that devolve upon the dwellers of the
North, but only for the first few years. As they
went on I was made aware of my decreasing
powers of resistance.

About two years ago, I said one evening to my
two daughters: "Children, I cannot help thinking—and have been pursued by the thought for
some time—that this would be a favourable moment for returning to Zanzibar." I then explained
my views more fully. One of them reminded me of
the evil star that had frustrated so many of our
dearest hopes, and then drew a sad picture of the
renewed anguish and disappointment this enterprise might have in store for us. The other one,
however, replied eagerly: "No, mamma, nothing

must be left untried. You might reproach yourself afterwards with the thought that you had missed the right moment." And she thought as I did.

I took the necessary steps confidently, and was met in high official quarters with a kind encouragement, but the matter did not progress for a long time. After several disappointments, and when I had already given up all hope of ever satisfying my longing for home, I one day received a summons from the foreign office to hold myself in readiness to depart for Zanzibar shortly. The surprise caused by this news was so overwhelming as almost to deprive me for a time of all power of realizing my good fortune. Next to God I felt most thankful to the Government, and to our beloved emperor, for whom I as well as my children will always preserve the deepest gratitude.

I need not dwell on the preliminaries of our departure—they were those usually accompanying a long voyage. And as for the political features of the expedition, they were sufficiently explained by the daily papers at the time.

On the 12th of July, 1885, I was to be at Port Saīd. On the 1st of that month I left Berlin with my children, and went *via* Breslau and Vienna to Trieste, where we arrived on the 3rd. My children were charmed with all the beauty they saw. As for myself, I could not well help being more keen on the issue than on the incidents of our journey. The peace and quiet I had not known for weeks I found again on board the Lloyd steamer *Venus* after we had put out to sea, and here I tasted the first sweet enjoyments that offered on all sides. The weather was so beautiful that we could remain on deck nearly all day long.

On the 5th we touched at Corfu, visited the most beautiful spots in the island by a few hours drive, and rejoined our steamer in the afternoon, highly pleased with what we had seen. Past barren Ithaca on the south point of Greece, and lofty Candia, our vessel brought us, on the 8th, to Alexandria. A hushed and almost holy feeling of home overcame me as I entered this city with palm-trees and minarets, a feeling that can only be experienced but not described, and which only those understand who have, under similar circumstances, been long absent from their home. Of the real South I had seen nothing for nineteen years, and my winters had been passed in Germany by the fireside. Busily as I had always been engaged with the duties of housekeeping, my thoughts had ever wandered far away. To me the greatest pleasure and recreation had been to sit down quietly and alone with a book all about the South. Now that I was actually face to face again with Eastern life in the bustling port of Alexandria, I stood as one in a dream—afraid of waking to the fact that I had only been steeped into it by the perusal of some well-told, life-like description.

We were requested at the custom-house to show our passports, but I had decided to give my name only in case of absolute necessity, and I therefore asked my travelling companion if I might use one of her own cards, and, curiously enough, this was considered quite satisfactory, and we passed on. After this we had positively to fight our way, with the help of constables, through the clamouring crowd offering their various services; and finally, having reached a cab, we got in and asked to be driven to the hotel. But even here one of our persecutors managed to fasten himself on again, warning us, with much agitation, against proceeding any further without his assistance as interpreter, when, to his utter astonishment, I told him in Arabic that we were perfectly able to take care of ourselves.

The two days we spent in our expensive and dirty hotel passed quickly enough. I was most delighted with a visit to the Arab quarter, where I remained for hours watching the ever-varying scenes of its animated life. After being eyed rather suspiciously at first I began to talk to them in Arabic to their intense astonishment. "Mother *" they cried on all sides, "where didst thou learn to speak our language so beautifully? Surely thou must have been to Bagdad; how long didst thou live there?"

Mhammed, our Arab cabdriver, soon took such a fancy to us, that he beseeched me to take him with me as my servant. He assured me he would serve us faithfully all his life, and never touch a single bottle of our wine. He was quite downcast when he came next morning to drive us to the port, and I scarcely knew how to console the poor fellow.

Our short stay at Alexandria had been a most happy one. After a passage of eighteen hours we arrived at Port Saïd, where we went on board the *Adler*, one of the tugs of the East African squadron. Port Said is only a small harbour town, but everything is to be obtained there, and the shops contain everything one can possibly wish for.

Here the desert begins, through which runs the "canal" that connects the Mediterranean and the Red Sea. The channel is so narrow that two ships cannot pass each other; crossing stations have been established at various points, and their names put up, as "Gare Limite Sud," or "Gare

---

*"Mother" is a friendly term of address.

Limite Nord." Ships have to wait here sometimes
for hours, until a vessel coming the other way has
passed the station. At Port Saïd or at Suez a
channel-pilot, who understands the meaning of
the ball-signals, is taken on board every steamer,
indicating by their number and position whether
you may go on, or how many ships are expected to
pass by. No ship is allowed to go through the
channel under full steam, to prevent the undula-
tion damaging the sandy banks; at night all traffic
is stopped. Notwithstanding these several hin-
drances, the passage is quite an interesting one—
especially when some of the ships race through
the large salt lake to reach the canal first.

Near Suez the channel widens, and we entered
the Red Sea at last under "full steam." The heat,
which had been great before, became almost unbearable when we entered this branch of the sea
enclosed by high rocky walls. We could not keep a
dry thread on us night or day. I felt more at ease
in this, to me, familiar heat, than I had felt all the
long years I had been away; but my children were
quite prostrated with it. The port holes could not
be opened, as the sea was running very high; and
the air became so oppressive below that we preferred sleeping on deck at night on chairs instead
of retiring to our cabins.

Seven days it took us to get to Aden, and in that
port we had to remain five days before the *Adler*
received orders at last to proceed on the voyage;
and then who more rejoiced than myself? I was to
see my home again at last in eight days more.

We had not suffered from a rough sea as far as
Aden, but hardly had we got clear of that rocky
port, when that fearful south-west monsoon began to blow. We were now in those dangerous
regions, where H.M.S. *Augusta* had gone down

some weeks before. One morning at eight we were
just having breakfast on deck with the officers,
when the first tremendous sea came over and
speedily dispersed all the company. And now began three awful days and nights! We were in the
midst of an appalling hurricane. The foam of the
waves broke over the funnels, which, after the
storm was over, stood there perfectly white with
the brine. I must despair of giving an adequate
description of our dangerous situation; and our
bodily sufferings and discomforts, too, were very
great. The pitching and rolling the first day made
us, of course, very ill, but our miseries even increased. Our cabins were swamped, so that we
could not get into them. Indeed, in the face of our
great danger, we did not think of undressing for
three nights running. We all had to sit in the
gentlemen's saloon under umbrellas, for although
the ports and skylights were tightly screwed
down, and the latter covered with tarpaulins—the
state of our atmosphere may be better imagined
than described—the water oozed through the
decks. Toilet was dispensed with, for we had no
dry changes to replace the sopping garments we
were wearing.

After three days, at last the storm abated a
little, but though the sea still came over at times,
we could at least stay on deck, on a raised seat,
under an awning.

My anxiety had naturally been very great at
first, but I soon became quite calm and composed, remembering that we are at all times in
God's hands, and filled with gratitude that I had
my three children with me.

The island of Pemba came in sight on the 2nd of
August. The distance thence to Zanzibar is only
thirty miles, which can easily be travelled over in

three hours. As it grew dark we made for the northcape of Zanzibar, it being dangerous to enter the port at night on account of the many sandbanks.

It was a curious coincidence that I was to see my native home again in the same month in which I had left it nineteen years before, and exactly on the same day and at the same hour I had lost my husband fifteen years ago. I need scarcely speak of my heart's anguish on that day. Earlier than usual I retired to my berth, but never closed an eye all night. My whole soul shaped itself into a prayer, and God, in His mercy, heard it, and gave me comfort once more.

Our ship drifted slowly during the night towards the lighthouse, and when I came on deck early in the morning the palm-trees of my native home greeted me from afar. At sight of them I again broke down. I went back to my cabin and prayed. The conflict of my feelings was only an echo of the many conflicts my life had known. What indeed are we poor human beings but frail skiffs tossed on the ocean of life. I had left my native home an Arab and a true Mahometan; I returned an undeserving Christian, and half a German.

But at this moment it was given me to live all my youth over again. Everything stood vividly before me, and the merry pictures of the past rose one by one, and filled me with exultant joy. Even my happy, light-hearted children seemed silent and thoughtful in this hour. They clung to me all that day, and through their glistening eyes I could read the sympathy that their full hearts could not speak. Though my life has been robbed of some of its dearest possessions, God, in His mercy, has made me rich in giving me my loving children.

On nearing the town we learned, to our regret,
that the German squadron had not yet arrived.
As the *Adler* was to be of its number, there was
nothing for us to do but to steam back to the east
coast of the island, and wait about. In this manner we passed eleven days. On the 11th of August
at last the man on the bridge called out, "Ship in
sight!" which, however, did not raise great hopes
in us, as we thought it might be a passenger
steamer. But very soon we saw the vessel make
straight for us, so we got up steam, and hoisted
our flag. The vessel turned out to be the tender
Ehrenfels, which had been in search of us all the
morning, to bring us the commodore's order to
come into port, the squadron having already arrived there four days ago. We made for the port at
once, but could not run in that night.

Next morning at six o'clock we were all astir.
Far off in the distance we saw the forest of masts
in port; steaming close in shore we passed many
fine palm-groves and small negro villages. Come
to an anchor at last, we found four German men-
of-war present, H.M. ships *Stosch*, *Gneisenau*,
Elisabeth, and *Prince Adalbert*, two English men-
of-war, five steamers of the Sultan, and several
sailing ships.

Commodore Paschen thought it advisable to
treat me at first as "secret cargo," a name which
caused much merriment to all the officers of the
squadron. However, on the arrival of Admiral
Korr in H.M.S. *Bismarck*, matters were soon
smoothed for me. I was free to go on shore when I
liked. Apart from the feelings that moved me at
seeing my home again, it struck me as very
strange that I should be able to walk about those
streets in broad day, accompanied by gentlemen,
where I had formerly only been permitted to pass

at night, veiled. It may be thought that, after
nineteen years of European life, I might have got
over this, but Zanzibar brought it back to me with
far greater force than Egypt, where I had been
twice since, and did not realize my emancipation
nearly so much.

I fancied I could see the most undisguised surprise in the faces of all the people who crowded
round us when I visited the town for the first
time. They pressed round me on all sides, calling
out to me in Arabic and Swahili, "How do you do,
my mistress?" Large numbers collected in the
narrow streets before the shops we had gone into,
but made room respectfully when we emerged
again. Our escort increased day by day, and the
welcome on the part of the inhabitants grew daily
more cordial and more affectionate. All this, of
course, did not a little annoy the Sultan and his
counsellor, the British Consul-General; the former even thought fit to have a number of the
persons whipped, who had followed us. He, as
well as the Consul-General, made a complaint to
the commander of the squadron about this
friendly demonstration in my favour. When I
heard of this I thought it best to tell the people not
to accompany me anymore, but they replied that
no fear of punishment should prevent them from
showing their joy at seeing me again.

Frequently slaves came up to me cautiously, to
bring me their master's compliments. I was
begged not to have any doubt of their attachment
and fidelity; they placed their houses at my disposal, and expressed their earnest desire to pay
me visits on board. These slaves also brought me
letters secretly, which, in the absence of pockets,
they had concealed in their tiny caps. In passing
the houses I often saw a troop of ladies retire

behind a door when they saw me in the distance, and on my approach they would either address me or merely call down a blessing—such as: "God be with you and keep you in good health." My brothers and sisters, my relations and old friends, asked me frequently to come and see them, but I always declined their kindly invitations, not from any lurking resentment of former days, far from it, for my heart yearned for my own flesh and blood; but circumstances compelled me to act as I did.

Whenever we passed the palace in boats, or walked under the windows of the harem, we could see the wives of the Sultan waving their hands to us in a friendly manner. As I was accompanied on these excursions by several naval officers, I had to request these gentlemen, in the interest of the women, not to salute in return, not wishing to be the ruin of these imprudent fair ones. I avoided doing so myself, for I had been told that their lord and master was in the habit of concealing himself in some place from which he could easily watch and find out all that passed on the sea and in the streets unknown to them, and then follow up his discoveries with cruel punishments. This is not conjecture, but a fact well known; even to the Europeans in Zanzibar that happened scarcely a year ago. The Sultan from his hidden post had seen a Portuguese, gliding past on the water, bow to his favourite, a beautiful Circassian, and also saw her return the greeting; a custom she was by no means alone, or the first in observing, for thirty years ago, when I was quite a child, the English and French naval officers, who visited our island, and the foreign residents, always bowed to us, and we as invariably returned their courteous salutation; our gentlemen had never objected to it, and no one saw any harm in it. Bargash, however, was of a different opinion; he whipped his Circassian for the crime she had committed, with his own hands, and in so cruel a manner that she expired some days afterwards in consequence. He is said to have entreated, vainly however, her pardon on her death-bed, and even now has prayers said over her grave.

On our excursions into the interior we often encountered people mounted on donkeys. To show us their respect they always dismounted, led their beasts past, and then only remounted. Nor could any punishment inflicted by the Sultan make the inhabitants desist in showing their attachment, and it must have vexed him to hear the crowd crying beneath his palace windows: "Kuaheri Bibi! Kuaheri Bibi!" (Farewell, Mistress!) every time we got into our boat to return on board. I was told that whenever we neared the shore somebody would beat an old biscuit-tin like a drum to summon the people together.

Of course we were well set round with spies, mostly Hindoos, but to their great disgust we only conversed in German. Even on the night preceding our departure two of my friends (who had come on board to bid me good-bye under the shelter of darkness) called my attention to the dusky figure of a man, who had often honoured our ship with his presence in the guise of a hawker, and who in truth was a very active and clever tool employed by the now influential but former lamp-cleaner and court-barber, Madoldji Pera Daudji.

This Pera Daudji, a very wily and cunning Hindoo, has become the Sultan's jack-of-all-trades. The lamp-cleaner of old now devotes his services to the sovereign of Zanzibar in the high-

est and lowest positions. All diplomatic negotia-
tions pass through his hands, but the same hands
wait upon the guests of the Sultan's table. His
salary, thirty dollars a month, every one will admit to be a low one, but I was told that he made it
worth any one's while to increase it. This omnipo-
tent Pera Daudji is not above bartering his influence. Of course, his thirty dollars, that do not
even suffice to pay for his costly dresses, are
replenished from other sources of revenue. The
court jeweller, who refused to give a certain per-
centage on all orders to the ex-lamp-cleaner, lost
his custom in consequence. Pera Daudji honoured and entrusted a more accommodating com-
petitor with the execution of such orders.

My birthday happened to fall in this time, and
now I celebrated the same for the first time in my
native country, where it is not customary to do so.
The officers of the squadron did all they could to
make this day a real festive one to me, and they
succeeded well. I can hardly thank them sufficiently for all their kindness. One very remarkable thing happened on this occasion. In honour
of my birthday (a born Mahometan's!) a pig was
killed on board the *Adler*, and almost in sight of
Islam's most faithful worshippers. If this had
been predicted to me nineteen years ago by the
cleverest of our fortune-tellers, I should have
scorned the idea, in spite of all superstition.

Viewed from the sea, the town of Zanzibar
made upon me quite as favourable an impression
as it had done of old. Perhaps it looked even more
pleasant now, many new houses have been built,
the lighthouse in front of the palace, lighted by
electricity, looks really quite fine. By the officers
it was always called the Sultan's Christmas-tree,
on account of its many rows of lamps. I was much

less pleased with the appearance of the inner
town.

During my long residence in Europe I may
perhaps have become more fastidious than Oriental practice will allow of; I thought the inner town
in a sad condition of untidiness. Nearly every
house in the narrow and dirty streets was a heap
of ruins. Weeds grew everywhere, and even big
trees flourished amidst these ruins. No one
seemed to care; people in the most natural manner were picking their way over ash-heaps and
waterpools. The introduction of a good Board of
Works does not seem to be quite so easy, otherwise this state of affairs would have been re-
medied long since by the Sultan, who has had
sufficient opportunity during his stay in Bombay,
as well as in England and France, to become
acquainted with clean streets. But he has deemed
it necessary to introduce the manufacture of ice,
also electric light, a so-called railway and, I know
not what else in Zanzibar, not to mention French
cooks and French gastronomy.

The evident decay of the heart of the town
struck me painfully indeed. I had not then an
idea of the condition in which I was to see my old
Bet it Mtoni again, or Bet il Rās, that was only
just finished when I left. I was deeply moved when
we went to revisit the house in which I was born.
What a sight! In place of a palace there was
nothing but a fast decaying ruin; one of the stair-
cases had altogether disappeared, the other was
choked with weeds, and so tottering that it could
not be ascended without peril. More than half of
the house was a rubbish heap, just left as it had
tumbled down; the baths, once such a favourite
place of resort, and always filled with a merry
throng, had lost their roofs; ruins again indicat-

ing the place where some of them had been. There
I stood, gazing with burning eyes at the neglect
and desolation around with the recollection of
former and happier days filling my heart with a
painful mockery of all things earthly and human.

My companions little knew what anguish was
mine—they laughed or chatted, or played on
those heaps. Had I suspected what was awaiting
me in the old house of my birth, I should have
paid it a preliminary visit by myself. The figures
of former residents seemed to me to be hovering
around and gliding from under the dangerously-
leaning roofs, the half-hanging doors and falling
beams. More and more vividly did their faces and
shapes grow upon me. I was moving in their
midst, and could hear their own familiar voices.
How long this delusion lasted I know not, but I
was suddenly roused into the actual present again
by the kind officers and my children coming to
draw me away from the scenes that affected me so
deeply.

It is commonly thought, but without reason,
that the Arabs, in token of their love and respect
to their dead, allow the houses formerly inhabited
by them to fall into ruins. This is incorrect—it is
not this sentiment, but their innate indolence that
makes them look with indifference on decay. Arab
houses are but seldom repaired or renovated—
their lime and bricks are of a nature to be easily
decomposed by the climate—so that when a house
gets rather too much out of repair, a new one is
built instead, and the old one is left to crumble
away. The value of building ground is merely a
nominal one.

My nephew, Ali ben Sūd, the son of Zeyane,
had lived, up to his death, in one part of the
house, which still contained a few comparatively

well-preserved rooms. His attachment to the old ancestral seat of our family was so great that he could never live anywhere else, and so he died in this place two years ago.

In this wing we found two Arab soldiers, who had come from Oman but a few months previously. They had left their families at home, hoping to take back to them some of their earnings from the wealthy Zanzibar; but so far they had fared very badly, and were yearning to get back to Mesket as soon as they possibly could. Both complained of bodily afflictions, and begged me to cure them; one of them had sore eyes, and the other some internal disease.

When I inquired, somewhat surprised, why they lived in the ruins, I was told that they were not alone, but only formed part of the guard, which, incredible as it may appear, were set to watch over the ruins. This, I should think, could hardly have been a military measure, but probably one connected with the dread of the evil one. I may, however, be mistaken in this, as I have for too long a period lost sight of this kind of superstition and its adherents.

As a memento I took with me some grasses, a few leaves, and a stone I found in the niche where my dear father used to say his prayers.

On leaving the house a well-dressed, rather distinguished-looking Arab came up to us, introducing himself as the commanding officer of the guard. He remained some time with us, and finally escorted us to our boat. On approaching the Mtoni we observed a venerable old man standing in it, engaged in ablutions previous to saying his prayers; and when we came nearer we saw that he was stone-blind. Since my arrival in Zanzibar I had made it a point never to be the first in addressing any one, so as to get them into no trouble; but in this case, and with a blind man, I thought I might make an exception, so I went up to him, and wished him good evening in Arabic, not without some misgiving for disturbing him at his devotion, and I, a Christian too, was not calculated to draw forth a pleasant acknowledgment, especially as he could hear that we were a European party. I was not a little surprised however when he stretched forth both his hands, drew mine to his lips, and pressed them for a while to his face. I was really touched, and wished to remove the doubt of being mistaken for some other person. "But do you know who I am?" I asked. "Indeed, I do know you," he replied, "are you not my mistress Salme, whom I have often carried about as a child? Oh, we were so rejoiced when we heard you had come back. God help and protect you, you who are so dear to us all!" Such and other words like these the poor helpless blind man addressed to us on parting. The Arab officer, who had been a witness to this proof of faithful attachment, told me the old man acted as the Muedden (Muezzin) to the colony of Bet il Mtoni, and was at the same time appointed by the Sultan to say prayers over the tomb of Ali ben Sūd, whom the latter had so bitterly persecuted all his life.

The last remark struck me particularly, for I was quite well aware of the heartless and yet childish conduct of Bargash to Ali ben Sūd, and to my elder sister Raje. Raje, a real sister of Ali's mother, removed to Zanzibar from Mesket at a pretty advanced age some years ago, and was provided by the Sultan with a house and an annuity. It was but natural that his aunt Raje went to nurse him, when Ali ben Sūd, who, without any cause whatever, had incurred the bitter hatred of Bargash, was lying mortally ill at Bet il Mtoni, having no wife or children to look after him. But Bargash disapproved of the step she had taken— he was perfectly unable to understand or to appreciate any service of charity, or to show compassion. To make her feel his wrath, he not only withdrew her annuity, but actually, without any compensation, deprived his aged sister, who was old enough to be his mother, of her home. He did not appear at Ali's burial, a disregard hardly ever shown even to an enemy. And now he has prayers said over his grave! What unaccountable conduct!

As I am just talking about the head of our family in Zanzibar, I am tempted to lift the veil from another part of his life's history. I might feel a great reluctance to make known to the world the wickedness of people of my own blood—in spite of the many years I have been alienated from them, and notwithstanding the heartlessness and harshness shown to me by the same Bargash, in whose interest I have risked and imperilled my life and my fortune, for we cannot, do what we may, wipe out a certain compassion for the flesh of our flesh—were it not that Bargash's bowels of mercy are closed alike against subject and relation.

It is a fact well-known in Zanzibar that Bargash, on coming to the throne in 1870, suddenly, and without any cause, cast our second youngest brother Khalife into prison. The poor fellow there languished upwards of three years heavily chained, with irons on his legs. An explanation hereof could only be guessed—Bargash probably feared that Khalife, being next in succession, might behave to him in the same dastardly and treacherous manner as he had done himself to Madjid.

His conscience, however, suddenly smote him. When one of his sisters, whom he had likewise injured, was about to set out on a pilgrimage to Mecca, and dreading the efficacy of a curse pronounced in the holy city of the Prophet, he went to her to beg forgiveness. But his sister positively refused it until he had set Khalife free again.

In spite of this, he continued to have Khalife and his friends continually watched, and soon found out that the latter had a very faithful and wealthy friend. He well remembered the time when it had been a matter of great importance to himself to be allied to rich chiefs; nevertheless, he determined to deprive the successor to the throne, at any cost, of such valuable adhesion and assistance.

He sent for Khalife's friend, and thus briefly announced: "I understand you intend to sell your plantations; tell me the price you want for them, as I should like to buy them." "That must be a mistake," the man replied, "I never had the least intention to sell my property." "It will be to your own advantage, however, if you do sell them to me," he was answered. "Now go and consider the matter."

Some time after, the unfortunate man was again summoned before the Sultan, and received with the following words: "Tell me, now, what is the price for your plantations?" "I have never thought of selling any of them, your Highness." "It is quite indifferent to me what you think. I shall give you 50,000 dollars for them. Here is a cheque for the amount; go and make yourself paid."

The poor fellow departed perfectly heart-broken from the presence of the man who in this manner acts as the "father of his people." But even here the mortification did not stop. When about to cash his cheque, he was informed that the whole amount was payable only within twenty years, in annual installments of 2,500 dollars, the first of which was at his command now. The poor man was completely ruined, just what the Sultan wanted.

Another occurrence makes me blush with shame, and fills me with the deepest pity. One of my sisters had been most vilely calumniated—she was said to love some one whom Bargash objected to as brother-in-law. When he heard of this report he went to her himself, and taxed her with it. In vain she protested her innocence and utter igno-rance of the whole matter—the conscientious brother carried duty so far as personally to ad-minister fifty lashes to his own sister! In con-sequence of this brutal treatment the poor girl was ill in bed for more than a month, and suffered from the effects long after. I have no doubt that he will have prayers said over her grave after her death as he does over those of his wife and of Ali ben Sud.

Europeans may frequently be heard to praise the engaging manners of the sovereign of Zanzibar. From the above it may easily be judged how much of this praise is deserved. One thing, however, is certain, that from the bottom of his heart Bargash has never hated anything so much as the mere name of Europeans.

It may be presumed that I did not expect much from him as to my private claims. The press made a gratuitous statement that I had returned to Europe in full possession of my inheritance, con-

sisting of the proceeds from the sale of no less
than twenty-eight houses. This is absolutely untrue; I have not received a penny, and my
claims—admitted as just ones even by the British
Consul-General, and that is saying a great deal—
remain unsettled to this day. My generous brother
offered to pay me the large sum of 6,000 rupees in
full settlement of all my claims, which kind offer I
declined with thanks, this sum being only the
merest fraction of what I am entitled to. Five of
my brothers, five sisters, my aunt Asche, three
nephews, one niece, and a very rich stepmother
of mine, have died since he has held the reins of
government; and I am entitled to part of the
inheritance from all these. The Sultan waived,
under some futile pretext, our reconciliation
urged by the German Government; and no doubt
his delight was great when their interest in my
cause was finally submerged by political ones.

Everything was tried from official quarters to
set the people against me. Some of our officers
had asked me to select for them some articles of
jewellery they wished to take home to their
friends. To get these we went several times to a
jeweller, who worked also for the Sultan, without
our being aware of it.

The Sultan no sooner heard of our purchases
from his faithful Pera Daudji, who had to report
all news to him, then he sent for the jeweller, upon
whom he poured out the full measure of wrath
and abuse for daring to sell us his wares. But the
tradesman, generally so pliant, quietly replied he
could not presume to turn his master's sister out
of his shop. This answer displeased the Sultan still
more, so he threatened to withdraw his custom
altogether. But the jeweller, with great com-
posure, announced the fact that he had for some

time contemplated taking his departure from Zanzibar, and that he would embrace this opportunity for shutting up his shop, and thereby avoid giving me offence.

In the same way an attempt to annoy me was made by prohibiting the owners of donkeys to let out their beasts to me, while some of my former slaves, who had ventured to pay me a visit, were imprisoned.

Such and other absurd measures were taken, but had just the opposite effect. The people gave their opinion of such proceedings in words like these: "Piga kana kasi ya watoto, Bibi!" (They behave like children, O Mistress!)

When I arrived at Zanzibar I was doubtful of the reception I should meet with there, but confident, too, that my brother would not delay in carrying out the expressed wishes of Germany, and I was not mistaken. He would, at all events, out of respect for Germany, *tolerate* me. But the bad treatment that my other brothers and sisters had experienced at his hands could hardly lead me to expect any friendly advances on his part; and, as for the rest of the inhabitants, it gives me the greatest pleasure to state that they gave me tokens of their kindly feelings only. Arabs, Hindoos, Banyans, and natives repeatedly entreated me to remain in Zanzibar for good, which could only strengthen my belief that there was no religious aversion felt to me. One day I met two Arabs, with whom I entered into conversation. Hearing from a third person that they were relations of mine—I had not recognized them—I told them afterwards I should not have addressed them had I been aware of this, as I knew my relations were not all inclined to be friends with me. But they both replied at once that, whatever happened, they could never forget that I was the daughter of my father. And when I touched upon the religious question, one of them said "this fate had been destined to me from the beginning of the world." "The God who has served you and us from our home is the same God whom all men adore and revere. His mighty will has brought you back to us, and we all rejoice at it. And now you and your children will stay with us henceforth, will you not?"

Proofs of affection and love like these, and the deep and indescribable joy of beholding my native land once more, will always associate that voyage with some of the sweetest hours of my life.

But the hour for parting came at last and found me oh! so loath to say a long farewell once more to the few but very dear friends I had still. They fully shared my grief, and perhaps I could convey its expression best to my readers, and thereby put a fitting close to my book, by giving the English rendering of a letter that they jointly sent to me after I had reached Germany again. But its sweet tenderness and originality I cannot reproduce:—

You went from us without a word at parting;
This has torn my heart, and filled my soul with sorrow.
O! that I had clung to your neck when you departed
    hence,
You might have sat on my head, and walked on my eyes!

You live in my heart, and when you went
You poured grief into my soul such as I ne'er felt
    before;
My body is wasted, and my tears fall fast
One after one down my cheek like the waves of the sea.

O Lord of the universe, let us meet again ere we die!
Be it only one single day before death.
If we live, we meet again;
When we are dead, the Immortal One remains!

O! that I were a bird to soar to thee on wings of love;
But how can the bird soar whose wings are clipped?

In the foregoing pages I have endeavoured to draw a picture of Oriental life and its customs, especially with regard to life at Court, and the position of woman in the East. Some of the subjects contained in this book may be thought to possess less general interest, but, as part of the whole, my description would have been incomplete without them. It must be remembered that I have not been writing a novel or a tale of fiction, but the faithful recollections connected with the life of my native land in all its phases.

If I have naturally felt tempted to exalt such of our customs and institutions which, in my opinion, are deserving of commendation, I have, on the other hand, never endeavoured to excuse or disguise others which, in the eyes of more highly-cultured nations at least, may justly be ridiculed or thought objectionable; and if, in drawing comparisons between foreign and Eastern customs, I have not shrunk from speaking my mind openly and candidly, and have sometimes sent home a shaft, I may aver, in justice to myself, that I have by no means spared myself, but have readily and frankly admitted the errors into which I fell.

Even in this century of railroads and rapid communication, so much ignorance still exists among European nations of the customs and institutions of their own immediate neighbours, that one can hardly wonder how little is actually known about those of races far removed. The ablest and most conscientious writer must always, to some degree, fall short of giving a perfectly precise and faithful picture of a foreign nation;

and, in the case of an Eastern nation, he will, of course, find himself heavily handicapped out of all proportion when family and domestic life generally is so jealousy guarded from the gaze of the outer world.

Having been born and bred in the East, I am in a position to set down the unvarnished reflection of my Oriental experiences—of its high life and its low life—to speak of many pecularities, and lift the veil from things that are always hidden from profane eyes. This, I hope, will constitute the main value of my book, and my object will have been fully gained if I have been able to contribute my share, and, above all, if I have succeeded in removing many misconceptions and distortions current about the East.

My task is done—and, in conclusion, it only remains for me to say farewell to my kind readers, who have followed me through these pages, and who, I trust, will always bear a friendly memory for one whose life has already gathered so rich a store of changes and vicissitudes.